IMPROVING TEACHING

1986 ASCD
Yearbook

Edited by
Karen K. Zumwalt

Association for Supervision
and Curriculum Development
125 North West Street
Alexandria, VA 22314

ASCD publications present a variety of viewpoints. The views expressed or implied in this publication should not be interpreted as official positions of the Association.

ASCD stock number: 610-86001
ISBN: 0-87120-134-8
Library of Congress
   Card Catalog No.: 85-73379

Price: $13.00

Contents

Foreword

A YEARBOOK FOCUSING ON TEACHING IS ESPECIALLY APPROPRIATE FOLLOWING ASCD's major efforts gaining national attention to 1985 as The Year of the Teacher. The United States Senate passed S. J. Resolution 48 declaring 1985 as The Year of the Teacher, and more than 40 governors signed proclamations recognizing the importance of teaching. ASCD produced and distributed nationwide television public service announcements and a documentary on the theme, "Teachers Make a Difference." All of these efforts were motivated by recognition of the critical importance of teaching and of the need to respect and reward teaching in order to attract intellectually capable young people to enter the profession.

During the past year, opportunities to interact closely with leaders of the National Education Association and the American Federation of Teachers have revealed exciting evidence of growing professionalism in these two great teacher associations. Each of them is devoting increasing attention to promoting new ways of helping students learn more effectively.

Redefining teaching is one of the six priority areas in ASCD's five-year plan. These priorities are designed to help realize our mission of "developing leadership for quality in education for *all* students." The 1986 yearbook presents one element of redefinition—avenues for the growing professionalism of teachers.

Self-directed growth based on analysis of one's work is a mark of professionalism in fields as varied as medicine and athletics. The doctor and the professional athlete each study their results and use the insights gained to plan ways to improve future efforts. Improved performance gains direction through analysis and discussion with colleagues and coaches. Importance of opportunities for continuing growth is recognized in budgeting and in the scheduling of professional duties. Work to improve performance, far from being a sign of weakness in the athlete or doctor, is a sign of continuing growth toward professional excellence.

All too seldom have teachers been afforded the benefits of time and collegial coaching that can facilitate professional improvement. Giving the profession the respect it deserves includes finding new ways to support teachers' self-direction of their professional growth. Teachers, administrators, and boards of education need to work together to help the possibilities become realities.

This yearbook presents a variety of models for educators to work together for mutual growth. As more and more of these models are implemented, we will discover that leadership has, indeed, developed to produce quality in education for *all* students.

CAROLYN SUE HUGHES
ASCD President, 1985-86

Introduction

TEACHERS AND TEACHER EDUCATORS HAVE RECEIVED THE BRUNT OF MUCH CRITI-
cism recently. Teachers have been charged with mediocrity, illiteracy, and in-
competence. Good teachers are said to be leaving the profession more rapidly than their less able peers. Prospective teachers are said to be "poor
students drawn from the bottom quarter"; their caliber is "low and continues to decline significantly."[1] Teacher education programs have been de-
clared inadequate, ineffective, and, in some cases, totally irrelevant and detrimental to the entry of quality people into the profession. A rather dismal
picture predicting an even more dismal future.

Yet amid this depressing scene is a bright light; the public has rediscov-
ered something most educators have always known—the importance of the
teacher. There can be no excellence in education without first-rate teachers.
One can change the curriculum, buy more materials, refurbish the physical
environment, lengthen the school day, but without good teachers, change
will not produce the desired effect.

Much attention is now focused on recruiting able students into teaching,
improving teacher education programs, and retaining good, experienced
teachers. Enhancing the professional aspect of teaching will, it is hoped,
have a positive impact on these goals. To gain the respect they deserve,
teachers need the freedom to act like professionals in their classrooms and
school communities. Along with such increased autonomy comes the teacher's responsibility to continue growing professionally.

Opportunities for growth need to be appropriate to the kind of educators we want teaching our children. With this in mind, I have become increasingly distressed with the rush to apply "effective" teaching research
findings to improve teaching and teachers. Besides the fact that there are and
should be a diversity of views about what constitutes good teaching, it is de-
meaning for a competent professional to submit to instruction that is often
remedial in nature and tone. Experts and their research can be useful to
teachers. Unfortunately, in too many cases research is being used to control
teachers, a measure of remediation for perceived deficiencies that may be
suitable for a few, but is certainly not appropriate for the large majority of
professional educators.

---

[1]David G. Imig, "Education Students: Dubbing Deserved?" *AACTE Briefs* 4, 8
(October 1983): 2.

The problem seems to stem less from a lack of confidence in teachers' acceptance of responsibility for professional growth and more from the erroneous view that the *application* of research findings will improve education. The linear model in which school people apply findings provided by researchers has limited value for improving education. Unfortunately, research on teaching in particular seems a logical candidate for direct application. The potential of research to improve education does not come by generating rules of practice but rather from informing the deliberations of teachers and from encouraging similar inquiry from them.[2]

Given these concerns, clarifying the value of research on teaching seemed like an appropriate focus for the 1986 ASCD yearbook. A few weeks before I was to meet with the ASCD Publications Committee, the 1984 yearbook, *Using What We Know About Teaching,* arrived in the mail. After my initial dismay that the book I was proposing had already been written, I realized that I had the unique opportunity to build upon a prior publication. The 1984 yearbook has influenced both the substance and format of the 1986 publication.

The 1984 book attempted to deal with the "chasm" between researchers and practitioners and between teaching as a science and as an art. No matter how admirable an effort, it is clear that no single book can close that chasm. In fact, in the process of trying to do so, a new duality appeared—the "bridge builders" versus the "fearful ones"—and an old one resurfaced: the separation of curriculum and teaching. The editor and many of the writers clearly favored the bridge builders, who see teaching as an applied science, albeit an artistic one. The dichotomy between curriculum and teaching was underscored by Madeline Hunter, who wrote, "While highly related, teaching is distinct from determining curriculum."[3] Unfortunately, both dualities add little to our efforts to improve education.

There are many ways to build bridges—and much to be gained from eliminating distinctions between teaching as science and as art and between curriculum and teaching. In practice, I think, such distinctions are blurred. As professional teachers make decisions, they call upon other sources of knowledge besides science and intuition and make decisions that are both curricular and instructional.

To paint a realistic picture of what knowledge is useful to teachers and how they use it, I decided to give authors a simulation exercise based on actual observations of teachers. By forcing the authors to base their responses on such observations, perhaps the usual generalities could be avoided. And

---

[2]Karen Kepler Zumwalt, "Research on Teaching: Policy Implications for Teacher Education" in *Policy Making in Education,* Eighty-first Yearbook of the National Society for the Study of Education, Part I, ed. Ann Lieberman and Milbrey Wallin McLaughlin (Chicago: University of Chicago Press, 1982).

[3]Madeline Hunter, "Knowing, Teaching, and Supervising" in *Using What We Know About Teaching,* 1984 ASCD Yearbook, ed. Philip L. Hosford (Alexandria, Va.: Association for Supervision and Curriculum Development, 1984), 170.

by forcing them all to respond to the same simulation exercise, not only would similarities and differences be more apparent, but a show-and-tell nature would be avoided. Eleven authors, writing from different vantage points and offering different kinds of expertise, were asked to respond to a teacher-initiated professional development activity. Researchers were chosen who hold very diverse views and have conducted very different kinds of studies. Since researchers have no monopoly on the expertise useful to teachers, other professionals were also invited to respond. They include a classroom teacher, a teacher center specialist, a staff developer, a curriculum developer, and a principal.

In the chapters that follow, all authors respond to the following hypothetical situation:

Several teachers, who have been working together on their own self-initiated staff development effort, have been awarded a small development grant. They have decided to use some of the money to invite an outside resource to work with them.[4]

Before selecting someone to work with them during the next year, the teachers have decided to invite several individuals to observe them and share their reactions. They prefer not to guide the observations because they want to get a clear sense of how each individual looks at teaching and how each envisions working with the teachers on their teaching.

Based on observations of at least two teachers, the authors were asked to respond to the following questions:

1. In observing teaching, what are you looking at and for? What did you see?

2. What kind of initial feedback would you give the teachers? Why?

3. What kind of discussion/reaction would you hope would ensue?

4. If you were chosen to continue working with the teachers, in what ways do you envision you and they would be working?

Despite the common task, the resulting chapters offer a rich array of alternatives designed to facilitate the professional development of teachers. As described in the concluding chapter, they also expand the concept of knowledge sources and how that knowledge can be used to improve teaching. Although the authors approached the task from different roles and different views of research and teaching, their approaches blur the separations be-

---

[4]In real life, the teachers might decide not to allocate any of their professional development grant to engage an outside resource. In preparing the book, I realized that this option would merit a book in itself. Hence, for comparison purposes, to keep the book manageable, and to expose variations on the use of outside expertise, I stipulated in the simulation that the teachers had decided to use *some* of their money to work with an outside resource. This choice does *not* imply that outside resources are more desirable—the expertise represented by a group of teachers working together may, indeed, entail the most powerful form of professional development.

tween teaching as art and teaching as science, between developers and users of knowledge about teaching, and between curriculum and teaching.

Differences, however, do exist among the authors—differences that would undoubtedly be significant to any group of teachers trying to decide which author they would like to continue working with. These differences, and the similarities, are explored in the final chapter.

I hope that this collection of papers demonstrates that bridge building in education is a complex enterprise that must recognize the diversity we value—diversity in teaching and among teachers, in sources and uses of knowledge, in educational goals and strategies. The teachers in the simulation were to choose with whom they wanted to work—and as professionals the choice should be theirs. Helping teachers to clarify and articulate which approach and which focus would be most useful to them is the primary purpose of this book. Helping those who work with teachers to question their own orientation and approaches is another purpose. To these ends, readers may wish to play out the simulation, either by choosing the author with whom they would like to work or by answering the questions posed to each author. The ensuing dialogue is what bridge building in education is all about.

KAREN KEPLER ZUMWALT
Editor
1986 ASCD Yearbook

1. Developing Teachers, Not Just Techniques

Douglas H. Heath

In observing teaching, what are you looking at and for? What do you see?

Because I believe that it is schools and not just classrooms that have the more enduring formative effects on children, I seek to understand a particular school from the first moment I am asked to visit it. Who initiates the contact? Why invite me? To whose expectations and hopes am I to respond? How enthusiastic are faculty members about working with me? How committed is the administration to working for improvement? How conscientiously does a school prepare for my visit? How cooperative are faculty members and students in providing information about themselves? How openly do faculty members and the principal talk about their school? How excited am I about visiting the school?

When I arrive, I ask myself many questions: Is this school so big I'd feel lost in it? How proud are faculty and students about the school? What are the boys' bathrooms like? Do the corridors remind me of state mental hospitals? Are students I see in the hall aloof, sullen, cheerful, effervescent? Do any spontaneously greet me? Does the principal call students by name; do any stop us to ask him or her a question? Do faculty greet me warmly in the teachers' room, or do they ignore me? Would the noise in the cafeteria give me indigestion? Where are the "warm" areas of the school—where faculty and students go when they're down? Where do I feel chilled? How flexibly,

Douglas H. Heath is a consultant and Emeritus Professor, Haverford College, Haverford, Pennsylvania.

imaginatively, even colorfully, have teachers created their work spaces? Would I want to teach in this school?

How do I feel when I walk into the classroom I am to observe? Is this teacher's space any different from that of other teachers? What do the arrangement of desks, the presence of plants, the orderliness of the room, the comments on the blackboard tell me about this teacher's assumptions about how students are to behave and learn in this classroom? What does the room tell me about the teacher?

In short, I observe everything that tells me what the people are like in this school. Those who have visited hundreds of schools and classrooms know it does not take long to sense the effect of a school's tone and spirit on how adventurous, enthusiastic, and devoted a teacher becomes over the years. I need to learn very quickly just how much freedom and independence teachers feel they have, if they feel they can change, dare to risk. That is why I am there: to encourage them to risk growing in new and untried ways.

I have learned from my work with many faculties that we teachers share four handicaps that can critically limit if not bar our growth as well as efforts to improve our classrooms and schools. So I look for signs of those handicaps. If they are present, then I know that to work with faculty on technique or specific curricular issues is not likely to result in sustained improvement. I must find ways to help faculty members understand and cope with these handicaps if they are to continue to grow after I have gone.

Handicap 1. At nine o'clock one Tuesday morning I visited a new teacher's 4th grade English lesson. Children were sprawled on a rug around Ruth, who was sitting on a chair reading a book about a man who had recently lost his wife. Some children were playing tic-tac-toe in a corner; several had their eyes closed; two girls kept interrupting to ask questions, which Ruth patiently answered. Eventually she firmly asked the two to stop playing tic-tac-toe. But she read continuously, pausing only to ask a few questions. "How would you feel if you had just lost your mother?" "What do you think she died of?" Thirty-five minutes later I still could not figure out what her goals were for the day and how her students should have changed by the end of the class.

During the next 1½-hour social studies unit, each child fashioned a log cabin out of a half-pint milk carton and then brought the edifice to a large table where Ruth was constructing a Puritan village. Again, I had to ask, "Why? Why spend 1½ hours building a cabin which could have been done in the evening as homework and brought to school the next day?" Again, I could not figure out what was being learned. What were Ruth's goals? Just to make a Puritan village?

Ruth eagerly sought me out during the lunch hour to ask for my views. I tried to ask gently, "What were your priority goals? What were you trying to accomplish?" Ruth responded like most teachers, "We are studying the Puritans and learning about the history of our country." Other teachers have told me, "The students are learning about exponents," or "French irregular verbs," or "how a root grows." From what I observe about how children are most frequently taught, I doubt few would recall much about Puritan villages two years later, be able to work a problem with exponents if they had not used them since, or give the third-person singular of the verb "etre." I seldom hear teachers offer such goals as, "To help students learn to attend, to keep a complex idea in mind and to reflect about it," or "To learn how to think in logical sequences," or "To learn the skills of *how* to learn a language later in life, like Japanese."

The head of Ruth's school said she could not get her teachers to be analytic about the whats and whys of their teaching. That is a universal lament. By not having an articulated educational philosophy about what student outcomes are most important for their future, our actual goals become what the textbook dictates we should complete before the end of the term. So information that is most ephemeral, that is seldom used, even as content which one learns to attend to, reflect on, logically analyze, or learn how to learn about, becomes the focus of our effort, rather than general adaptive skills which will endure.

Handicap 2. Two years ago, the faculty of Westmont, a K-12 suburban school, unanimously accepted the recommendation of a long-range planning committee that, as its priority goal, the school should enable its students to become autonomous learners. The school recently had been evaluated by a visiting team. The team's report began, "We commend you for your explicit priority goal. We visited every classroom. We did not see one example of teaching that might achieve that goal."

At Westmont I visited the three 8th grade algebra classes, then asked the department head the question any observer would ask, "Why were all of the students in each class working on the same chapter at the same time?" It seemed clear from observing their homework and listening to their questions that they varied greatly in readiness for the topic the teachers were lecturing about. She agreed, but replied, "It really would be nice if the teachers could have smaller classes so they could individualize their instruction. They can't with 28 students in each class." "Is there anything they can do to teach to such variability?" I asked. "Other than sectioning, which we do, no," she said.

Our second handicap is not knowing how to design systematic sequential strategies by which to achieve our goals. One reason is that we frequently fail to define our goals in ways that can be implemented. Margaret Mead once said, "A clear understanding of a problem prefigures its lines of solution." To rephrase this insight for teachers, I like to remind them that, "A clear definition of your priority goal prefigures how you could begin to implement it." Not until the Westmont faculty could clearly articulate what it meant by "autonomous learner" could it proceed to implement that goal. Not until the mathematics head redefined "teaching" to mean creating an effective learning environment rather than didactically lecturing about algebra did she realize that each class had several highly capable students who could assist less able ones.

Handicap 3. Mr. Schmidt, as he preferred to be called, was a scholarly German immigrant who had found his way to a small, isolated, rural school where he taught 10th graders modern European history. He was talking pedantically about the Nazi invasion of Poland when I entered. He seemed to be so inwardly focused on his lecture that he never "saw" his drowsy and obviously bored students when he infrequently glanced at them. He never once varied the rate of his speech, stopped to ask a question, or showed in any way he was aware that these children of farmers may never have heard of the Nazis, or may not know where Poland, let alone Europe, is, or the meanings of about every fifth word that he uttered. He was the only teacher in this school who did not seek me out later to learn what I might suggest about his teaching.

While seemingly singular, this actually is a typical example of our tendency not to be reflective about the effects that our own teaching, the dynamics of our own classrooms, and the climate of our schools have on the educability of our youth. Few of us take a genuinely diagnostic view about our own teaching to ask questions like, "I know I talk 85 percent of the time in class; just what skills and traits do my students need to profit from my talking so much?" "My students can't sustain a meaningful discussion. They don't listen; they are so self-centered. What am I and the other teachers doing that makes them that way?"

Handicap 4. Before I visit a school, I frequently ask the faculty and students to describe the school, a typical student, and occasionally a typical faculty member by checking appropriate words on a 150-word list. They also circle every word they wish they could have checked. Generally, we and our students see ourselves as conservative, traditional, conscientious, and hardworking; only 15 to 35 percent of faculties ever describe their school, typical student, or faculty as imaginative, adventurous, intellectually exciting, curious, initiating, playful—or even joyful! New teachers describe us similarly. However, both beginning and experienced teachers wish we were more adventurous and intellectually exciting. When asked to select the ten attributes most facilitative and supportive of one's own growth, teachers always include adventurous and intellectually exciting.

To grow is to risk, to try the untried and uncertain. Teachers who are comfortable and set in what they are doing, or are fearful of making mistakes, or are unwilling to share with others their puzzlements and apprehensions may not only be uneducable but also passively resistant to whatever I have to offer.

Kathy was a teacher who had risked constantly in her class, where more than half of her 30 1st and 2nd graders were from low-middle-income families. She risked trusting her students, as I discovered one morning when I arrived at 8:30, having forgotten that school did not begin until 9. Five children were already there: one was making a pyramid for the Egyptian unit;

another was reading; a third was practicing numbers on the blackboard; two were making a common drawing while talking quietly with each other. Twenty minutes later all 30 were there, each working individually or with another on some project. Not once did I have to quiet the group or break up an argument.

When Kathy arrived, we talked about her goals and methods for another 20 minutes, after which she said it was time for the class to plan its work for the next day. She expected her children to learn and work on their own, to discipline themselves, and to work with others when they needed to. She had created some rich resources, with many homemade, sequential, self-educating projects, like several on Egypt that a child could complete on his own. She had also developed a workable scheme by which each child could record and monitor his own work for the week. Kathy had taken many disciplined and obviously well-considered risks over the years in order to create such a classroom in an otherwise conventional and traditional public school. Kathy was so maturely autonomous she did not need my assistance.

What do I observe when I visit a classroom? I look for signs that a teacher is educable: does the teacher have a desire to learn and change, the self-confidence to risk making mistakes, the interpersonal openness to really listen and work with another, and the skills to articulate the goals of a worked-out educational philosophy? Finally, can the teacher implement reflectively and imaginatively steps to achieve such goals, and monitor reflectively and diagnose perceptively how well such strategies are working?

What kind of initial information would you give the teachers? Why? What kind of discussion/reaction would you hope would ensue?

The critical query is "Why?" Our own values about what is important affect what we have learned to observe and interpret. Given the type of future that students and faculty will encounter, I believe the most appropriate educational goal is to empower a person to become a self-initiator and a master of the processes that contribute to his or her continued growth. The techniques I suggest will most likely fail with next year's class. Why? Next year's class has three angry, negativistic boys who egg on the other children to resist us. Or it is just less "smart" than our typical class. Or we have become so accomplished with our technique that we have unknowingly become less excited when using it. Or the Egyptian unit that asked the children to build a model of the Aswan dam in the sand box and list three reasons for its benefits will have to be modified as we learn about the dam's negative effects on the Nile delta. Or our cherished curriculum and the innumerable ways we have enriched it over the years—the pictures of Egypt we have cut out of the *National Geographic,* the artifacts we have lovingly collected, even the jokes and stories we garnered from a trip to Egypt ten years ago—become obsolescent when the new principal tells us that his recent graduate course on Piaget has convinced him that our egocentric children are too cognitively immature to really understand Egypt, where it is, and how its people differ from ourselves.

Any meaningful education that is to have enduring effects must be character transforming, whether educating students or teachers. So I ask myself, "How can I work with a Ruth or a Mr. Schmidt or a faculty not clear about its goals in a way that will increase their curiosity and desire to grow, their self-confidence and willingness to risk, their interpersonal vulnerability in order to learn from their colleagues and students? How can I help them clearly articulate their goals, imagine more creatively, and reflect more self-consciously about *how* their teaching affects the growth of their students?"

My initial response to a Ruth or a Mr. Schmidt would be, "How did you feel about the way the class was going?" or, "I don't know your students or what has been happening these past weeks. I'm really coming in quite cold, and I don't feel I understand what you have been trying to accomplish and the problems you feel you have been facing. So before we talk about today's class, which might have been atypical, would you tell me how the class has been evolving and the concerns you have that you feel I might be of some help with?"

Why this initial response? Because I really do not know what has gone before that might have affected Ruth's decision to read to her children at 9 in the morning (maybe she had asked them to watch a PBS program the previous evening) or why the students in Mr. Schmidt's class seemed so listless and tuned out (maybe there was a severe drug problem in this class). I need to enter as deeply as Ruth and Mr. Schmidt will allow me into their view of themselves and their class. I need to create an empathic rapport which is genuinely felt by both. Otherwise, I risk creating resistance or passive negativism. Ruth responds, "Why didn't I think of that clever idea? Thank you." But the next day Ruth continues to read for 45 minutes at 9 a.m. Or if I had been more perceptive, I might have casually said to Mr. Schmidt—if I really believed it—"I was impressed by how much control you had over your material and how unappreciative some of the kids seemed to be with the work you had done to prepare for today."

If Ruth is genuinely curious about what I had observed and is open to a searching discussion of the class, I would ask a series of open-ended questions, asking first what she felt the students should learn from being read to, what outcomes she hoped would occur, what the children might secure from the book she had chosen, what happened during the class that pleased her, how she would describe the students' behavior as she read, how she felt about some children's seeming lack of interest, what she might do tomorrow to involve the students in ways that would achieve her goals more efficiently. Only after I felt I understood her view of her class and how responsive she might be to my observations would I then begin to help her analyze in detail the events in her classroom and construct alternative approaches by which to achieve her goals.

Mr. Schmidt poses a different and more complex problem that demands an entire chapter to describe. Essentially, I would search for clues to answer the key questions: Are his unempathic relations with his students and didactic teaching style carry-overs of a Germanic idea of teaching that has been solidified with the rigidity and pretentiousness of a highly intelligent but overly intellectualized person? If so, then I would *not* initiate any discussion about his teaching that might trigger defensiveness. I would be more indirect. Ideally, I would hope he could participate in an experientially oriented educational conference for several days at some remote center with teachers other than his own faculty. The conference "style" would involve him playfully in a variety of teaching modes that indirectly required trust, empathy, and spontaneous emotional involvement—small-group tasks, group dramatic productions, late-evening group singing and folk dancing, volleyball games, and rich discussions over the dinner table. The conference would not directly provoke intellectual discussions about teaching but near its end would ask small groups to reflect about what they had learned and the implications for their own teaching. Why this type of formative experience for a Mr. Schmidt? He needs to experience directly in a trusting setting some potentials of which he may not be aware and explore how they might enhance his own teaching and personal growth.

Less ideally, I would invite him to visit classrooms with me that modeled a variety of teaching styles and afterwards ask him questions like, "What were your impressions? How do you feel the students felt in that class? What was it they did that gave you that feeling? What did you think of the teacher's response when Henry kept closing his eyes or Susie kept passing notes to Betty—you know, the kinds of things kids do in all of our classes, like what Jim and Helen did in your class yesterday?" Just as we learn the importance of proofreading our papers by proofreading another's, so we may understand our own behavior by seeing it externalized in another. And at some point during our informal day together I would inquire about how he was taught, what differences he noted between the German and American character and the ways children were taught, his thoughts about what he had observed, and his feelings about being in an isolated rural area where the "scholarly" ideal was not obvious in the values of the natives. Why these queries? To provoke a reflective dialogue that might open him to a different perspective about his purposes and strategies for the culture in which he taught.

In summary, how would I initiate a consultative relationship with a teacher whom I have observed? I would find out how educable the teacher was for what I might have to contribute. For a curious and reasonably self-confident, nondefensive teacher like Ruth, I could work immediately on improving her skills, such as analyzing and articulating her goals. For a Mr. Schmidt, my focus might have to be more "characterological." He was not going to change a culturally reinforced personality style, but I would hope that exposure to a richer variety of teaching styles and questions might waken emotional potential and provide a different view of what education could be about.

If you were chosen to continue working with the teachers, with what kinds of ways (processes and content) do you envision you and they would be working?

The work of a very competent and imaginative teacher like Kathy can be unwittingly undone, even silently sabotaged, by colleagues not emotionally supportive of her efforts. The 3rd grade teacher to whom Kathy's children go may believe that children should sit quietly, listen, and do just what she tells them. Unless we teach in a one-room school and teach the same students for several years, I doubt that we in our individual classrooms will have much of an enduring effect on most students' characters. Growth in our classrooms must be nurtured and supported by the climate of the school, by a widely and emotionally shared communion of values about how we want our students to grow and how we are to relate to them as persons and as students. So if asked to work with an individual teacher, I respond, "Well, I'm uncertain this is the most economical and effective way for me to help your school at this time. Research and my own experience suggest that perhaps we should first begin with the entire professional staff to deepen its collective understanding of its goals, encourage its corporate ability to create appropriate teaching strategies, create a shared expectation that it is safe to risk, and empower the faculty to monitor more reflectively its own collective effort to enhance its effectiveness. In other words, it may be more economical of scarce time and energy, and even scarcer funds, to work at the system level, rather than with an individual, given how pervasively the character of our school affects how we can grow as a faculty."

If I am to work with the administrators, faculty, and staff that first day, what attitudes influence how I would like to respond? First, I must seek to empower the faculty in ways that will enable them to continue growing after I have gone. Second, I assume 99 percent of teachers care deeply about their students' growth, wish to be as effective as they can, and, in fact, can change and become more educable, as I have defined the term. Third, faculty must live with the consequences of any change that is introduced, so they must "own" any decisions about change. Fourth, the consultant-faculty relationship must begin with the concerns and values of the faculty, not those of the consultant. Fifth, morale and growth of faculty, as well as of students, are, as I have suggested, influenced by the character or climate of the school, just as the latter will be altered by the professional growth of the faculty. Sixth, teachers' insights and experiences must be interwoven and integrated with existing knowledge of maturation and the educational principles known to most efficiently enhance such maturing.

Although the focus of my work with faculties depends upon their goals and hopes, my approach is guided by my 25 years of research-based understanding of healthy adult growth. I have studied the meaning of psychological maturation (Heath, 1965, 1977, 1980), how students grow in powerfully liberal educational settings (Heath, 1968), and how adults, like teachers, continue to grow during their thirties and forties (Heath, 1979, 1981, 1983). The cumulative research suggests that maturing in our cognitive skills, values, interpersonal skills, and in our attitudes about ourselves proceeds in five interrelated ways: increased capacity to symbolize or become aware of our experience, to become more other-centered, integrated, stable, and autonomous. Furthermore, the evidence has now become quite compelling that the maturing of our intellectual and interpersonal skills, values, and self-concept is the most powerful contributor to our subsequent happiness and vocational, marital, and familial adaptation. This model of healthy growth has provided me with a research-based rationale by which to order the goals of a liberal education and suggest ways to implement them.

Growth is initiated by the necessity to adapt to problems that produce pain, frustration, and conflict that are not resolvable by earlier learned ways of coping. We humans have the remarkable potential for becoming *aware* of ourselves, for being able to put problems into words, numbers, drama, art. When faced by a problem, we reflect, we become more aware, we search for hints or clues, we explore the consequences of our hunches. We reflect more about our feelings, values, our interpersonal styles. We try to understand why students or colleagues react as they do. Research clearly shows that the more mature person is a more reflective, self-insightful, understanding person.

How does this initial phase of the growth process apply to organizing a day-long series of workshops? Faculty must be disrupted initially, but in a supportive way, by a meaningful problem and helped to become more aware of how to understand it. What commonly shared but meaningful problem frustrates today's teachers? NEA and my own studies show that many of us find today's students more difficult to work with than yesterday's. Since an important intrinsic satisfaction is to feel competent in achieving one's goals, I ask faculties in groups of three to induce from their own experience the principal strengths and limitations of their students that facilitate or undercut the achievement of their goals. When the groups reconvene, I ask teachers to call out the strengths and limitations they identified. I respond with what researchers have discovered, anecdotes and impressions I have garnered from many other faculties here and in other countries. To date few faculties have failed to mention that today's students have shorter attention spans, are more passive and dependent upon teacher direction, are less imaginative and seemingly more bored than earlier students. As we search to understand why today's students may be more dependent on external structure for the organization of their learning, the discussion provokes reflection on how we make students more passively dependent on us in the classroom.

Faculty now know me as a colleague struggling with the same issues. They have become involved in an important issue. They have discovered that their problems are those of their colleagues, and some now have a different view about possible classroom goals, such as how to create more active participation. They have become more reflectively aware.

The second phase of the growth process is to expand one's understanding of a problem by sharing, in Dewey's words, "multiple perspectives." We now know that a mature person is less self-centered and more *other-centered*, empathically able to understand how another feels and thinks about an issue. The consequence is that a mature person has more altruistic and social values, more analytic ability to examine issues from different viewpoints, and is more interpersonally caring and accepting. Just as I seek to enter into the interior world of the teacher with whom I am working, so I try to create a process with a faculty that aids them to be more open to the insights of others through cooperative problem-solving tasks. Integrating faculty comments within a larger context of research and other information about characterological changes in students here and abroad helps some to understand their own students from a much broader, even reassuring, perspective.

I earlier suggested that faculty are typically unable to articulate an educational philosophy that has clear priority goals. So the goal of the next 1½ hour workshop is, given our appraisal of today's students, to define the goals we should have for our work with them. I again turn to the insight and experience of teachers by asking them in small groups to agree upon the six to eight qualities they believe are most critical for students to learn in order to adapt to the problems they face in the 21st century. I poll the groups for their priorities, compare their lists with those of many other faculties, and then introduce them to research results about effective adults and the early predictors of such competence. If a faculty has completed some information about its own vocational adaptation before my visit, I will use those data to illustrate what we now know contributes to a satisfying job. And if comparable data have been secured from the students, the faculty develop an expanded awareness of what contributes to being an effective student.

By the end of this workshop, some begin to question the adequacy of responding to my query about their goals with an answer like Ruth's, "To learn about a Puritan village." For the first time, some teachers recognize the wisdom of the liberal-education tradition that insists that our goals should be to enable students to become mature persons capable of adapting effectively to the problems they will confront. Finally, I cite the evidence that the most powerful contributor to students' success will be their psychological maturity, not their grade average or intelligence test scores.

By lunch time the faculty has induced from its own experience in several learning groups insights that provoke some to reflect more thoughtfully about why they teach and for what they should be educating.

The third phase of maturing is to *integrate* what has been learned into a working hypothesis or plan of action, to perceive relationships between seemingly disparate ideas, to begin to act in ways consistent with one's values, to learn how to develop cooperative relationships. Again, the research evidence is clear: The more mature person is more *well-integrated*, able to think relationally and logically, has a more consistent set of values upon which he acts with integrity, and can work with others more cooperatively.

Because most of us are not very reflective about the dynamics of our schools and classrooms and fail to understand how the school as a systemic context of values affects us and our students, I introduce the third 1½-hour workshop by giving examples of how a school's climate can either support or seriously impede a faculty's classroom efforts. My goal is to help faculty think about their efforts, to discover inconsistencies between the dynamics of the school and their goals, to learn how to assess the emotional commitment, and not just intellectual assent, of the faculty to the school's goals. Again, I rely on information from teachers and students completed earlier to illustrate how the faculty may not see students the way students see themselves; or how the assumptions of their curriculum do not match their own perceptions about the readiness of their students for that curriculum; or how the faculty, board, and administration may be living in three different schools, particularly if each group describes the school differently.

To involve the faculty more directly in understanding their own data, I usually ask them to form small groups with others from the lower, middle, and upper schools to interpret the data about their own division to the other two. Faculty quickly discover, even if they have one, two, or three schools called by the same name, that they may not be working in the same or similar schools; they learn where they may be miscommunicating with each other; they may discover just how well they agree or how much they disagree about how they want their school to be different; they may even discover that despite agreement on goals for the school, the majority of teachers have no emotional commitment to achieving such goals.

This exercise upsets some faculties, particularly more complacent ones. They must wrestle meaning from their own collective perceptions and in the process they risk discovering that they may not be as well-integrated a school as they thought. Not infrequently faculties become collectively upset about similar issues and begin to develop some priority goals.

The fourth and fifth trends that describe the developmental process are the initiation and testing of a plan of action, its revision, and eventually its autonomization. Again, research is clear that a mature person is more *stable* and *autonomous*. Such people have a more confident sense of self, more stable values to which they are commited, and can form more enduring relationships with others. But such stability also means that these growths are now embedded in one's character, which is no longer a garment of roles to put on and off to meet new demands. There has been a permanent personality transformation, as we see in the elementary school child who now has so stabilized his reading skills that he can transfer them to any other written material regardless of how much stress he is under. Because we teachers think of imparting information rather than of transforming character, we don't teach in ways to make that content an integral part of students' personalities and so enable them to now use it in widely different situations or courses.

Because faculties like that at Westmont don't know how to implement their priority goals effectively, I like to take the faculty in the last 1½-hour workshop into some of my own classes. I describe how I have tried to consciously use some 20 principles that define for me how to teach more effectively. By this time the teachers understand why I teach in a way that encourages my students to be self-educating. They also have experienced during the day some of the principles that define effective teaching. And I hope that some have begun to understand that we are aided to grow, not just by learning a technique, but by developing and owning a point of view, an integrated philosophy of what and why we do what we do. More important than acquiring a bag of teaching tricks is becoming a more mature and educable teacher aware of and master of the values, attitudes, and skills that contribute to continued growth (Heath, 1971, 1979).

To illustrate more concretely some of the educational principles that contribute to the maturing of students and faculty, I describe a few techniques that could be used to implement those principles. When I finish demonstrating the principles in my own teaching, I challenge the teachers to identify a priority goal for themselves, for example, increasing student desire to learn or fostering empathy or logical thought. I next ask them to use such principles when creating some sample teaching strategies to encourage curiosity or empathy or logical thought. Occasionally, groups of six to eight teachers each plan a dramatic skit that illustrates how they might teach in ways to enable students to become more autonomous learners, for example. If I am due to return to work with the faculty again, I assign them homework: risk teaching differently the next month to achieve a priority goal.

When I visit a classroom, create a workshop, or focus on teaching, I rely on the following principles to guide my observations or plans, for they define effective teaching. I highlight some of the principles by citing examples or techniques to show how they could further teacher maturation.

Selected Principles of Effective Teaching

To increase awareness:

1. *Clarify expectations about how a person is to grow.* Ruth could list on the board each day, as Kathy did, not just the assignments but more generic skills, values, and attitudes, such as "Learn to hold in mind a complex paragraph."

2. *Provide models of goals.* Because Kathy taught a combined 1st and 2nd grade, the 2nd graders were models to the 1st graders of the skills and

knowledge they too would have by the end of the year as well as models of how to be self-educating.

3. *Teach a person how to reflect about the processes of personal growth.* The workshops were designed to enhance the faculty members' awareness of their own growth and its relation to the ethos of their school.

To increase empathic other-centeredness:

4. *Create a climate of trust that encourages nondefensiveness and openness.* The first faculty workshop sought to reduce verbal inhibition and to encourage greater sharing among the faculty about issues many had never discussed before for fear they would appear inept.

5. *Expect each person to be responsible for the growth of others.* Mr. Schmidt could apply this principle by having students work in pairs to draw a map of Europe.

6. *Provide opportunity for each person to assume alternative roles.* The head of Westmont's math department could implement this principle by offering academic credit to better students who provide individual and small-group tutorial work to those in need.

To increase integration:

7. *Consistently encourage active involvement in learning.* Both Ruth and Mr. Schmidt were violating this well-established principle of good teaching. Each workshop for the faculty was designed to provide some active involvement; most faculty report they are exhausted by the end of the day!

8. *Provide experiential types of learning about which a person learns how to reflect.* Note my ideal growth experience for Mr. Schmidt.

To stablilize the growth process:

9. *Require* constant *externalization and correction by action.* A natural and educational way to do this is not by increasing the number of quizzes or recitations but by encouraging students to review and explain the homework or an issue in class to each other, if only for a few minutes.

10. *Allow a person to experience the consequences of individual decisions and acts.* Kathy learned early that she could not give as much freedom to her children as she first thought. The consequence had been noisy chaos. She learned how to take small steps as she developed progressively more demanding, structured projects.

11. *Appreciate and affirm strengths.* Appreciating Mr. Schmidt's strengths might have encouraged him to seek me out.

To develop more autonomy:

12. *Express* realistic *faith in a person's capacity to be responsible.* Kathy expected her children to be responsible and had learned to help them become so.

13. *Progressively reduce structure and expectations to provide a test of*

individual autonomy. Kathy's 2nd graders were given more free time in which to plan and carry out projects they generated themselves with less direct guidance from her.

14. *Encourage individuals to be self-affirming and self-rewarding.* Encourage the Ruths and Mr. Schmidts to describe their teaching strengths.

The purpose of education is, as Dewey claimed, to further a person's healthy growth or, as Whitehead (1929) said, to develop the self or, as Esther Raushenbush (1965) has insisted, "to make maturity the more it might become." To educate liberally is to empower a student to mature. We have lost that historic insight by thinking of education as 20 Carnegie units, by providing funds for teachers to take yet another summer course when they need the challenge of white-water canoeing or working in an industrial lab or hiking in Austria—activities that would draw out their potential to become richer, more cultured and mature human beings. Certainly, teacher "development" is not designed to provide just another technique. Instead, it facilitates the development of a more liberally educated and mature person—the model of what we hope our students will become.

References

Heath, Douglas. "Academic Predictors of Adult Maturity and Competence." *Journal of Higher Education* 48 (1977): 613-632.

Heath, Douglas. "Adolescent and Adult Predictors of Vocational Adaptation." *Journal of Vocational Behavior* 9 (1976): 1-19.

Heath, Douglas. *Explorations of Maturity.* New York: Appleton-Century-Crofts, 1965.

Heath, Douglas. *Faculty Burnout, Morale, and Vocational Adaptation.* Boston: National Association of Independent Schools, 1981.

Heath, Douglas. *Growing Up in College: Liberal Education and Maturity.* San Francisco: Jossey-Bass, 1968.

Heath, Douglas. *Humanizing Schools: New Directors, New Decisions.* New York: Hayden Book Co., 1971.

Heath, Douglas. *Maturity and Competence. A Transcultural View.* New York: Gardner (Halstead-Wiley), 1977.

Heath, Douglas. "Teaching for Adult Effectiveness." *Journal of Experiential Education* 1 (1978): 6-11.

Heath, Douglas. "The Maturing Person." In *Beyond Health and Normality,* edited by G. Walsh and D. Shapiro. New York: Van Nostrand, Rinehart, 1983.

Heath, Douglas. "Toward Teaching as a Self-Renewing Calling." In *Exploring Issues in Teacher Education: Questions for Future Research,* edited by G.E. Hall and S.M. Nord. Austin, Texas: Research and Development Center for Teacher Education, 1979.

Heath, Douglas. "Wanted: A Comprehensive Model of Healthy Development." *Personnel and Guidance Journal* 58 (1980): 391-399.

Raushenbush, Esther. Talk to Quaker educators, 1965.

Whitehead, A.N. "The Aims of Education." In *The Aims of Education and Other Essays.* New York: Macmillan, 1929, p. 13.

2. Using Time Effectively: A Self-Analytic Approach

Jane A. Stallings

THE BELIEF THAT DRIVES THE SELF-ANALYTIC APPROACH TO STAFF DEVELOPMENT and observation is that people learn through an analysis of their own behavior and the thoughtful application of ideas to their own situation. Although the observation system we use provides quantitative results, it also offers a qualitative description of classroom activities. By understanding their classroom behavior, teachers make decisions about what to change or not change. In essence, the observation and staff development program helps teachers become more aware of their own behavior. Through an interactive small-group process where good ideas are shared, teachers help each other gain a sense of professionalism. They can and do solve their own problems. In the best sense, teachers in this system experience themselves as researchers in their own classrooms.

The two English teachers selected for observation teach low-achieving junior high school students. English in this case includes reading, writing, speaking, and spelling. Each of the teachers volunteered to be involved in our Effective Use of Time program. This is a self-analytic program that helps teachers and students use available time to their best advantage.

Jane A. Stallings is Director, Peabody Center for Effective Teaching, Vanderbilt University, Nashville, Tennessee.

The Observer's Lens

Given our Effective Use of Time framework, my classroom observation was necessarily comprehensive. It focused upon the type and duration of the activities provided, who took part, the nature of interaction between teachers and students, students' on-task rate, intrusions from outside the classroom, and the classroom climate. Research we conducted in 1978-1979 indicated that low-achieving students engage in their tasks for longer periods and register greater gains on reading achievement tests when teachers were well-organized and provided both interactive instruction activities requiring students to use several modalities (Stallings et al., 1978; Stallings et al., 1979). One part of our observation system operates like a camera taking snapshots of the classroom participants. The snapshots reveal what the teacher and each student are doing, such as reading silently, doing written assignments, discussing or reviewing, socializing. The snapshot also reveals the materials being used and who the teacher is working with. Five snapshots are taken in each class on three sequential days, providing a total of 15 snapshots. This information allows us to approximate how much time was spent on each activity.

In addition to the snapshot, our observation provides approximately 900 interaction frames for each teacher. This record includes the number and kinds of questions the teacher asked, the frequency and types of student responses, and the types of feedback the teachers gave. The record also indicates the behavior control methods used by the teacher.

The Teachers

The two teachers I observed taught in quite different schools. When studied with our three-dimensional lens, characteristics and skills of the teachers were sharply different.

Teacher A

Alice Jones teaches in a large, urban junior high school serving middle to low-income families. Thirty-five percent of the students are black, most of the others are white. The teaching staff includes black and white teachers in approximately the same ratio as the students. Eight teachers attend the staff development program we offer in the school. Esprit de corps is apparent among the staff members. Teachers seem to know each other well enough to banter lightly and kid each other. There is quite a lot of laughter when they meet as well as an air of professionalism. They are rarely heard making excuses for problems, such as the homes from which the children come. They tend to speculate about solutions to problems. They seem to have a healthy respect for the administration and feel ownership of the school. When stu-

16

dents pass in the hall, there is a feeling of high energy but not hostility.

In this setting we find Alice Jones' students starting the period solving a riddle written on the chalkboard. They were all in their seats when the bell rang. While they wrote all of the answers they could think of, Alice took the roll and passed papers. These organizing details required five minutes. Alice then monitored the students, often complimenting them by saying, "You really have a lot of ideas." She read some of the answers and asked from time to time, "What made you think of that?" There was considerable laughter and pleasure in this activity.

Alice next introduced the reading assignment, an Ernest Hemingway story about a father and his son. The son was quite ill and had a fever. She introduced new vocabulary and then asked the students to read one section silently. Following this, several students read passages aloud. For low achievers, they read quite well. The meaning of each passage was discussed in a lively manner. How did the father feel about his son? Why do you think the boy didn't want the father to come into his room? Skillfully, she included all 16 of the students in this discussion.

She next had students read aloud the words of the father and son. One student read the words of the narrator. This section revealed the son's belief that he was going to die and his misunderstanding of degrees of temperature. The final discussion centered on Celsius and Farenheit scales. What are the differences? What key mistake did the son make? What was the pressure the son felt? Why did he think he was going to die? Alice asked about types of pressure they felt. The students kidded about her pressure on them when giving tests. Alice told a story about her lost ring and a fib she had told her 3rd grade teacher. It was a warm and friendly exchange. The silent reading, oral instructions, and discussion required 35 minutes.

At the conclusion of the discussion, students were told to answer the questions at the end of the chapter. They were encouraged to finish before the end of the period. Alice walked up and down the aisle complimenting correct responses and guiding where they were incorrect. As students finished their work, they went to the back of the room and sat around a table. They chatted rather loudly while the others tried to finish their work. As more students went to the table, the noise became louder. Alice reprimanded Buddy, who responded loudly, "I wasn't talking!" She ignored him and continued to help one student. The last six minutes of class were totally lost for most of the class.

Feedback to Teacher A. In our Effective Use of Time Program (EUOT) teachers receive profiles of behavior in a meeting with six or seven colleagues. The profiles are explained, and then the teachers examine their own profile. I go over the log and profile with each teacher and answer questions. Then as a group we share ideas on how to become more efficient managers and provide more effective interactional instruction. Most of the best ideas come from teachers sharing what works for them. Basically, the model develops analytic and problem-solving skills. The five cornerstones of the model are:

1. Learn by doing.
2. Link prior knowledge to new information.
3. Learn to recognize and solve problems.
4. Provide a supportive environment, be risk takers, it's okay to fail if we learn from it.
5. The best teacher is a good learner—a researcher—one who can ask questions and find answers.

Given the comprehensive observations in Alice's room, we would start by showing her a table of how the class time was spent, what activities occurred, and the percentage of time students were off-task. As indicated in Figure 2.1, a good balance of activities occurred during the class period. Alice would be encouraged to continue serving this healthy, balanced diet to her students. She would be commended for the variety of questions she asked and for her ability to get all of the students involved in the discussion. She would be asked to describe to the other teachers how she monitors seatwork, guides students, and checks for student understanding.

Figure 2.1. Teacher A and Student Time Spent on Activities and Off-Task Rate

Student Activities	Time (minutes)	Percent	Teacher Activities	Time (minutes)	Percent
Organizing Sponge	5	9	Organizing Roll	5	9
Silent Reading	5	9	Monitoring Silent		
Oral Reading	10	18	Reading	5	9
Instruction	10	18	Oral Reading	10	18
Discussion	10	18	Instruction	10	18
Seatwork	15	28	Discussion	10	18
			Monitor Seatwork	15	28
TOTAL	55	100%		55	100%

Average Student Time Off-Task 11%

Alice's analysis of the snapshot and log would reveal the students' high off-task rate at the end of the period. Rather than telling her what was wrong and how to fix it, I would ask her, "Why might that be?" Her analysis would lead to improving the last part of her lesson plan. Alice and other teachers in the group would be asked to generate ideas for keeping students involved all period. These might include structured cooperative group activity—games relating to the objectives. All teachers would be encouraged to develop clear, firm, consistent expectations for what to do when the assignments are finished. Each teacher would be asked to make a commitment to something they would try in their classrooms the next day. The following week would include discussion of their efforts to effect changes in the classrooms.

Teacher B

Bill Smith's school serves a suburban, primarily white junior high population of 2,200 students. For the most part, the parents are semiskilled or professional workers. Ninety percent of the students are bused to school.

Eight teachers are taking part in our Effective Use of Time Staff Development Program. They are from one department and know each other very well. The newest teacher has been there five years. While they understand and support each other, they all seem to resent and fear the principal. They feel powerless to affect school policy. A primary complaint is that, in addition to homework and the six periods they teach, teachers are required to have bus duty, hall duty, restroom duty, and lunch duty. All of these extra responsibilities mean time is not available to prepare and copy materials, plan with colleagues, or meet with parents or students. Teachers feel that schedules for classes and lunches could be organized to synchronize lunch period and homeroom. A different schedule would allow teachers to have a free lunch time. Efforts to think creatively about the scheduling problems have been rebuffed by the administrator. They feel he comes down hard on anyone who suggests change. The administrator rarely observes teachers and yet evaluates them. The teachers have a feeling of helplessness and seem to be only carrying out a necessary job. They lack the shared vision and feeling of professionalism that was evident in Alice Jone's school.

When the bell rang, Bill Smith was still in the hall. He had hall and bathroom duty. The 26 children sat quietly waiting. Some students were finishing their assignments; others simply sat and waited. A few talked quietly for nearly five minutes. When Bill entered the room, two students waited at the desk for him to fill out an absence form. Bill then took the roll, noting three absences. Ten of the 55 minutes of this class had now passed. Bill asked to see everyone's homework and checked it in his grade book as he walked up and down the rows. He announced, "Today is the day for students to make their one-minute speeches." There was an audible groan. He gave the rules and expectations for the speeches. They are to speak about the careers they wish to pursue and tell why this career attracts them. They should mention some of their heroes or people they look up to. Speeches should be exactly one minute long. He assured students it is important to be able to speak before a group. Their next speech will be two minutes long. They are warned of five-minute speeches required in high school.

When Bill called for volunteers, no hands were raised. He called on a girl who spoke about wanting to be beautician. They make a lot of money; they make people look pretty; they can work in a lot of places; some get to fix movie stars' hair; it only takes one year of training. Her hero is her mother who helps her with homework. Bill complimented her for the content and the timing. All of the other students were attentive during this speech. Several other students took their turns speaking. Each was critiqued by Bill. Some were chastized for being too short. "John, you should have timed yourself at home. That was only 45 seconds." During one student's speech, a neighboring teacher came in to borrow a book. Bill spoke to her about some missing materials. The student continued with his speech. When the student sat down, Bill said, "Fine," although he had not heard all of the speech due to the distraction. The other students were now getting restless. They whispered a bit to each other, sometimes grimacing when someone spoke. This activity continued for ten more minutes. Two boys entered the room needing a signature and homework assignments. The student continued to speak while Bill stopped to interact with the two intruders. When this student finished speaking, he sat down. Bill again said, "Fine." The other students were paying less and less attention. Bill demanded that everyone listen politely when someone was speaking. The students continued until the bell rang for dismissal. Twenty-six students had spoken.

Making speeches is a special activity and not typical of Bill. Thus, I observed him on the following day to record a more normal day. This lesson was focused on how to use a dictionary.

When the bell rang, Bill entered the room (no hall duty today). Students were asked to alphabetize their spelling words while he took the roll. They all worked quietly. He finished the roll and signed some absence cards, then asked, "Did anyone get as far as the M words?" Two hands went up. "Good for you!" "Did anyone get further than that?" One hand went up. "David, that's wonderful!" "How far did you get?" "To picture," replied David. "Did everyone get to the H words?" All heads nodded. "Great, you got right down to work today."

He next asked students to correct the words on their homework sheets. He read answers and they marked their own sheets. These two activities required 20 minutes. All of the students were involved.

Next, Bill explained how to use the dictionary using the second letter to find the word. Each child had a worksheet. He asked them whether the word *bear* will come before or after *barn*. *Big*—will it come before or after *bun*? He checked for understanding by having them call out before or after when he said two words. Most of the students took part in this activity; however, a few did.not respond vocally. They seemed to be off in space.

Bill then switched procedures and asked, "Given *dance,* would you go to the back or front of the dictionary to find *dead*?" This switch from "before or after" seemed very confusing to the students. I don't think he knew he had switched from "before or after" to "front or back." Now he asked, "Is dog in *front* or *back* of duck?" The students looked puzzled. In the midst of this, two students entered the room to collect forms and money from candy sales. The students in the class waited and chatted. After this interruption, Bill continued explaining and asked students to use the guide at the top of the dictionary pages. He told them to work independently. The explanation and question-and-answer period required 20 minutes.

As the students did their written work, many hands went up to request help. Bill moved to those with hands up. Several students were uninvolved in the work. A boy in the right front corner did not do any work and he went unnoticed for the entire period. He was never called upon. As Bill approached his desk, he picked up a pencil. As Bill passed by, he put the pencil down. A boy in the front of the second row combed his hair. Was he finished? Perhaps. Two girls whispered when Bill was on the other side of the room. After 10 minutes, Bill asked a few more questions about "front and back." Is *pill* in front or back of *pail*? A few students responded, but many did not. Papers were collected and the last few minutes of the class were spent by having individual students spell the days of the week. School announcements were made at the end of the period over the loud speaker.

Feedback to Teacher B. In an Effective Use of Time Staff Development meeting with other teachers in his department, Bill would be given a profile of how class time was spent. He would be helped to analyze his data to see the relationship between the length of the activity, interruptions, and the students' attention span (Figure 2.2). The interaction profile would indicate how many questions he asked, praise or compliments he gave, and guidelines for improvement or reprimands for behavior he offered. It would also reveal the number of interactions with people from outside the classroom.

Figure 2.2 Day One of Teacher B and Student Time Spent on Activities and Off Task-Rate

Student Activities	Time (minutes)	Percent	Teacher Activities	Time (minutes)	Percent
Waiting	5	9	Late—Hall Duty	5	9
Organizing	5	9	Roll	5	9
Discussion/Reports	45	82	Discussion/Reports	40	73
			Interruptions	5	9
TOTAL	55	100%		55	100%

Average Students Time Off-Task 18%

During the workshop, findings from research and classroom experience would be shared. Research suggests that low-achieving junior high school students have difficulty keeping their attention on one activity for an entire period. They give better attention when the activities provided in the daily lesson are varied. Bill would be encouraged to think about the impact of having all the speeches in one day. If other teachers or Bill did not come up with an idea, I would suggest that he consider planning 20 minutes for three class periods for making the speeches. To keep students' attention, he might require them to listen to each other and keep notes, making one compliment and one recommendation for each student speech. Students might receive a grade for these critiques.

Bill's second observation would include positive comments about the several different kinds of activities that were planned and carried out (Figure 2.3). The class was well-organized and students were involved at the beginning of the class. He was supportive of their efforts to alphabetize spelling words. He gave a good explanation of how to use dictionary guides. I would mention that when he gave examples of how to find words using second letters the children became confused. I would suggest Bill stay with one set of descriptors—either "before and after" or "front and back." Low-achieving children need a clear structure and help to develop hooks upon which they can hang new information.

Figure 2.3. Day Two of Teacher B and Student Time Spent on Activities and Off-Task Rate

Student Activities	Time (minutes)	Percent	Teacher Activities	Time (minutes)	Percent
Organizing Sponge	5	9	Organizing Roll	5	9
Review Homework	5	9	Review Homework	5	9
Explaining	20	37	Explaining	20	37
Seatwork	15	27	Monitoring		
Oral Drill & Practice	5	9	Seatwork	10	18
Intercom			Drill & Practice	5	9
Announcement	5	9	Intercom		
			Announcement	5	9
			Interruptions	5	9
TOTAL	55	100%		55	100%

Average Students Time Off-Task 22%

If others do not come up with specific ideas for additional practice and checking for the students' understanding, I would suggest that Bill have the students use flash cards with Before and After printed on them. When he asks, "Does pony come *before* or *after* picture?" the students can all hold up a card. This procedure allows Bill to see whether all of the students are grasping this concept. It allows him to continue with more examples or proceed with the lesson.

During seatwork teachers would be encouraged to monitor all students, not just those with their hands up. To Bill, I would mention the students who seemed to be frequently off-task and ask if this was typical behavior. We would discuss possible solutions for helping them become more involved. The teachers would be encouraged to collectively share information with the principal about the effect of disruptions and intrusions on their efforts to keep students involved and their need to use classroom time to teach. While we acknowledge their school problem, we would not allow the teachers to make it an excuse for not trying to do their best.

Continuing the Process

If teachers reviewing the various observation systems and staff development programs chose to continue with our Effective Use of Time Program, I would ask them to become officially involved in it.

Our program is delivered through a series of six 2½-hour workshops spaced over one semester. Each workshop focuses on a specific set of skills. Before the workshops start, each teacher is observed for three consecutive days in one class period. From these observations, individual profiles of teacher and student behavior are prepared. Recommendations for teacher change are based on criteria of effective instruction collected over four years of classroom study.

For example, the profile of Betty Brown, indicating the percent of her and her students' time spent in different activities, is shown in Figure 2.4. The criteria for using time were established by the studies previously mentioned in which students were able to gain an average of one year, eight months in reading ability within one school year. The profile in Figure 2.4 suggests that Betty Brown should increase discussion and instruction while decreasing the amount of time students spend on seatwork. Also, the time she spent doing organizational tasks during class should be decreased. The students are socializing or uninvolved 29 percent of the time. Past studies indicate that low-achieving students are off-task most during lengthy seatwork assignments. They are more likely to stay involved when classtime includes some reading, writing, explanation, and discussion so that students aren't required to spend an entire period on one activity.

The interaction profile of Betty Brown is shown on Figure 2.5. This suggests Betty should increase her interaction with students by asking more questions (Variables 7, 8, and 9). More feedback should be provided (Variables 17, 19, and 20). Her method of controlling behavior is to correct through negative or threatening remarks. We would recommend a more positive approach by increasing Variable 18, Praise for Behavior. In addition to the snapshot and the interactions, an observer's log is kept. The log is like an anecdotal record, which describes specifically what was being taught and the emotional climate during each snapshot and interaction period. Using these three observation tools, we can provide a comprehensive report on the teacher and the classroom.

Initially developed and certified by the National Joint Dissemination Review Panel for use with secondary reading teachers, the Effective Use of Time Program was subsequently modified for use with teachers at all grade levels and in most subject areas. The critieria for using time in typing or physical education classes, for example, would be different, but criteria may be set for any subject area and grade level. Although the focus of each workshop remains the same, the reading materials and specific goals might differ for each teacher. The following section describes the workshops that are provided.

Figure 2.4. Observation Profile of Betty Brown's Classroom

Observation Variables	Criterion	% of Time Spent — Criterion	% of Time Spent — Betty's Class	Goal
Teacher Involved In				
Monitoring Silent Reading		15.00	.00	Monitoring 35% or Less
Monitoring Written Work		20.00	36.00	
Reading Aloud		6.00	.00	Interactive Instruction 50% or More
Instruction/Explanation		25.00	10.00	
Discussion/Review Assignments		10.00	13.00	
Practice Drill		4.00	.00	
Taking Test/Quiz		5.00	.00	
Classroom Management with Students		2.50	.00	Organizing 15% or Less
Making Assignments		10.00	20.00	
Organizing - Teacher Alone		2.50	18.00	
Social Interacting With Students		.00	.00	
Student Uninvolved		.00	.00	
Providing Discipline		.00	3.00	
Students Involved In				
Reading Silently		15.00	2.00	Seatwork 35% or Less
Written Assignments		20.00	55.00	
Reading Aloud		6.00	.00	Interactive Instruction 50% or More
Receiving Instruction/Explanations		25.00	26.00	
Discussion/Review		10.00	12.00	
Practice Drill		4.00	7.00	
Taking Test/Quiz		5.00	6.00	
Social Interaction		.00	14.00	Off Task 6% or Less
Student Uninvolved		.00	12.00	
Being Disciplined		.00	3.00	
Classroom Management		5.00	.00	Organizing 15% or Less
Receiving Assignments		10.00	10.00	

Figure 2.5. Interaction Profile of Betty Brown

Variables	Criterion Percent	Betty's Class Percent	Recommended
001 All academic statements	80.00	65.28	Increase
002 All organizing or managing statements	15.00	30.76	Decrease
003 All behavior statements	3.00	3.83	OK
004 All social statements	2.00	.00	OK
005 Total for discrete variables	100.00	100.00	
006 Teacher instructs/explains	12.00	15.45	OK
007 Teacher asks direct questions or commands	10.00	4.00	Increase
008 Teacher asks clarifying questions	3.00	.13	Increase
009 Teacher asks open-ended questions	3.00	.79	Increase
010 Student asks academic questions	2.00	1.32	OK
011 Teacher calls upon new students (academic)	6.00	5.02	OK
012 Students respond academically	15.00	5.00	Increase
013 Student shout-outs/initiates remarks	.00	7.39	Decrease
014 Student doesn't know answer	1.00	.13	OK
015 Student refuses to answer	.00	.00	OK
016 All praise	8.00	2.00	Increase
017 Teacher praises or supports academic responses	6.00	2.00	Increase
018 Teacher praises behavior	2.00	.00	Increase
019 Teacher corrects academic responses	6.00	4.35	Increase
020 Teacher corrects with guidance	4.00	.00	Increase
021 Teacher corrects behavior	2.00	3.03	Decrease
022 Teacher monitoring academic work	6.00	10.96	Decrease
023 All written work	.00	.00	OK
024 Students read aloud	10.00	4.62	OK
025 Teacher reads aloud	1.00	2.24	OK
026 Teacher working alone	3.00	6.00	Decrease
027 Intrusions	.00	3.14	Decrease
028 Teacher involved with visitor	.00	2.20	Decrease
029 Positive interactions	4.00	.52	Increase
030 Negative interations	.00	1.50	Decrease
031 Teacher touching	5.00	.00	Increase
032 Teacher movement	3.00	1.12	Increase
033 All activity-related comments or actions	16.00	9.77	OK
034 Student organizing comments	1.00	.13	OK
035 Student academic comments	3.00	.13	OK
036 Teacher organizing comments	5.00	1.98	OK
037 Students academic discussion	7.00	7.66	Increase
038 Students cooperative group academic discussion	5.00	.00	Increase
Total Number of Interactions for Teacher 905			

Workshop #1. Learn About Research on Effective Use of Time. The teachers receive individual observation profiles covering how both teacher and students spend class time. Teachers make a commitment to try some time-saving activities. All teachers are asked to name something they liked about the workshop session (this is a Plus) and something they would like to be different (this is a Wish) for the next session.

Workshop #2. Organization and Management. Teachers discuss what succeeded and what failed in their classrooms. Good ideas are shared. Observation profiles are assessed for students' behavior. Peer observations of Student On-Task Rates are arranged, and reading is assigned. Teachers make a commitment to try some new ideas in classrooms the next day. (Plusses and Wishes)

Workshop #3. Student Behavior and Motivation. Teachers share ideas about motivating specific students. They discuss control systems, not just how to stop misbehavior, but how to understand and deal with the cause of problems. Reading is assigned. Teachers make commitments to try some new ideas in their classrooms. (Plusses and Wishes)

Workshop #4. Lesson Design and Implementation. The group critiques each teacher's prepared unit and lesson plan. The teachers train to observe their peers' interactions and levels of questions. Reading is assigned. Teachers make a commitment to try some new ideas in the classrooms the next day. (Plusses and Wishes)

Workshop #5. Interactive Instruction and Higher-Order Questions. Teachers discuss their peer observations. They review homework exercises and practice questions and feedback strategies. New information is related to prior knowledge. Teachers make a commitment for the remainder of the semester. (Plusses and Wishes)

Workshop #6. Feedback From End-of-Semester Observations. To let teachers see how they have changed, we compare their first observation profile with the profile made after the five initial workshops. Teachers make a commitment for continued change. A suggestion is made that teachers continue to meet formally and informally to exchange ideas, problems, and solutions. (Plusses and Wishes)

Working In Schools. We would suggest that the school administrator be aware of and support the teachers' efforts to use time effectively. Whenever possible we would meet with the teachers and principals to discuss how the faculty could work together to make the best use of the available school time. We would be available for consultation and encouragement as needed.

A Final Word

Essentially, this is a pyramid program where teachers train teachers. Trainers are certified at the Peabody Center for Effective Teaching in Nashville, or a Certified Trainer may travel to school locations. This program is presently funded by the National Diffusion Network.

The intention of our program is always to develop teachers who can analyze student behavior and their own teaching methods. If a new idea makes teaching easier and more fun, then it works for that teacher. We want teachers to feel safe enough to try something new, risk failure, and try again. It's okay to fail; we can learn from the failure. We want teachers to feel powerful and professional, not powerless. We want teachers to analyze change in themselves and their students in one semester. We enjoy the glow of their pride. We want them to find the excellence inside themselves and to trust it.

References

Stallings, J. A., R. Cory, J. Fairweather, and M. Needels. *A Study of Basic Reading Skills Taught in Secondary Schools*. Menlo Park, Calif.: SRI International, 1978.

Stallings, J., M. Needels, and N. Stayrook. *How to Change the Process of Teaching Basic Reading Skills in Secondary Schools*. Final Report to the National Institute of Education. Menlo Park, Calif.: SRI International, 1979.

3. Trusting Teachers to Know What's Good for Them

Betty Dillon-Peterson

As a long-time observer of education in the United States, I am constantly surprised at its variety—and its sameness. This notion was reinforced for me as I made the first of the two school visits in preparation for this chapter. A short distance from my home in Lincoln, Nebraska, is Interstate 80. An almost constant procession of cars and monstrous chromed vehicles roars across the prairie day and night, bound for more populous parts of the country. In many ways this highway is an example of what we sometimes call progress. In sharp contrast, within a few hundred feet of a towering interstate overpass sits a one-room school little changed from the time when the only roads in the area were rutted dirt tracks used by horses and wagons. On the day I visited, the teacher summoned her seven students with an antique school bell. The class included a kindergartner, a 1st grader, a 3rd grader, two 5th graders, and two 6th graders. A friendly dog followed on the heels of the children but was summarily dispatched to the school yard.

Inside, modernization had been limited to an indoor bathroom and central heat. The well-worn, well-maintained wooden floor revealed where the potbellied stove had sat. It was easy to imagine the students wearing

Betty Dillon-Peterson is Director of Curriculum/Staff Development, Lincoln Public Schools, Lincoln, Nebraska.

ankle-length gingham skirts and knickers—until the teacher noted that the VCR and television set had recently been stolen.

The children moved readily and easily into the day's activities. There was an obvious good feeling to the classroom and clear respect between the teacher, whose career spanned more than 30 years, and the students. Although there was no sense of tight control, the children were extremely well-behaved. The opening exercise, after the Pledge of Allegiance, involved unscrambling words listed on the blackboard. Although some of the words were too difficult for the younger children, all of the students were attentive and actively involved in trying to figure them out. Several times the 1st grader said confidently to himself, "This isn't hard. I can do this!"

My second visit was to a teacher in a 3rd-4th grade team in an individually guided education (IGE) school. This school has a rich ethnic mix with students from Afghanistan, Botswana, Cambodia, China, Czechoslovakia, El Salvador, India, Japan, Korea, Nigeria, Taiwan, Thailand, and Viet Nam. In the foyer an emorous chain covers an entire wall, each link bearing the picture of a child. The message over the chain reads, "We need each other to be strong."

The class was one in which the teacher was piloting a new objectives-based math curriculum and its management plan. The 27 children were learning place value. There was a lot of student activity in the room, all cheerful and most of it directed toward the learning objective. The teacher, whose fresh collegiate look belied her years of teaching, mixed teacher input, checking for understanding, student participation, and unruffled classroom management in appropriate proportions.

The two learning environments I observed were both different and similar. IGE schools were developed and introduced in part to provide an ungraded, continuous-progress environment tailored to individual student needs. One-room schools are also, by nature, less graded and more oriented to continuous progress and individual attention than are traditional schools. In these two schools, student-teacher ratios were very different, but there was little difference in availability of equipment and materials. The teachers appeared to be equally competent and effective with the students. It was obvious that the children and teachers liked each other.

Too infrequently do educators reflect on what they consider to be the basic and vitally important aspects of our profession. The simple question, "When you observe teaching, what do you see?" is very thought-provoking. The following somewhat stream-of-consciousness impressions were reflected in the copious notes I took as I observed the two classrooms.

In both cases I was very aware of the environment—the sizes of chairs for students of varying ages, the posters and plants that made the classroom an inviting place to be. I saw the children first as a group and later as separate individuals. I noted the unusual perceptiveness of one young child, the sensitivity and caring behavior exhibited by another toward a classmate, the quiet ones, and the nearly hyperactive students.

Next, I focused on the teacher. I found myself reliving my own very similar teaching experiences, anticipating what the teacher would do next and surmising the reasons behind her behavior. In both cases I particularly noticed the teachers' enthusiasm, the way they responded to the children, the way students responded to them, and the way the teachers responded to individual student needs while keeping the activity moving along.

Finally, I thought about what was being taught, whether it was at the right level of difficulty, whether the children appeared to understand, whether they were interested, whether they understood the purpose of the lesson. I noted the kind and variety of materials being used. In a general way my observations were guided by the method of teaching analysis developed by Madeline Hunter.

Some questions I asked myself: What is the teacher's objective for this lesson? How are the teacher's actions directed toward that activity? What prior learning have the students had that relates to today's lesson? How has the teacher determined that this learning in appropriate for these children today?

Professional Development—Based on Introspection

What kind of feedback would I give teachers similar to these who were planning for their own professional development? I would first ask them to focus specifically on their teaching and on themselves as teachers. There is a tacit assumption that teachers generally are not capable of assessing their own effectiveness or of learning to apply appropriate techniques based on that assessment. The responsibility for assessing effectiveness, recommending improvement, and enforcing those recommendations is assigned to the supervisor—often in a paternalistic way that does not result in autonomous, competent learners responsible not only for their own education but also for that of their colleagues. To help teachers become fully autonomous learners, I would begin by asking the two teachers to talk about the lesson they had just taught, describing how they had analyzed the situation, what they perceived student learning needs to be, and how they had planned to deliver the lesson. I would also ask how they felt the lesson had gone and how they might change it if they were to teach it again. At this stage, I would focus entirely on the positive things that were happening in order for the teacher to understand what had been effective and why.

Next I would tell the teachers as specifically as possible what I had observed, reporting directly from the anecdotal notes I had taken. Once again, the focus would be on positive behaviors that illustrate principles of teaching and learning. For example, I would tell the first teacher that students actively participated in the warm-up activity 29 times, pointing out that no one student had dominated. I would remind her that active participation increased the likelihood of student learning. I would call to the second teacher's attention the fact that students were extremely interested in her modeled example—so much so, in fact, that their usually wiggly and socially interactive selves were temporarily still. I would also note that she had successfully employed a principle of motivation through the use of her highly effective example.

After discussing this particular lesson, I would encourage them to videotape and analyze their own teaching and offer to arrange exchange visits between colleagues to enable them to look at teaching from a different perspective. I would see my role as helping these teachers to select or organize a format for observation and feedback to provide us all with a common frame of reference. If it appeared appropriate, I would suggest that these two teachers exchange visits to broaden their perspectives.

Professional Development—A Self-Directed Process

Throughout its history, staff development has too often been perceived as something one person prescribes for someone else. I have found that teachers seldom have been afforded the dignity or time to reflect on their teaching. I also know from experience that, given the encouragement, teachers are entirely capable of identifying directions for self-improvement and carrying out plans to improve their effectiveness.

For example, recently a group of junior high teachers and a supportive principal became concerned about the substantial number of 8th graders who were not succeeding. These students were not classified as needing special education and fit only the nebulous category sometimes called "strugglers" or "gray-area students." The teachers were encouraged to develop a program to reach these students and were paid to do so over their summer break. With assistance from other teachers in the school, they carefully selected 27 students and created a highly structured, caring, teamed environment. The degree of success experienced by these formerly doubtful students was remarkable. They now complete their work and *are* succeeding. Their parents are now lobbying the school for a 9th grade program and making comments such as, "My child has never liked school until now." "I think if he has another year like this, he may be able to make it through high school." One student, who would not agree to complete his homework before leaving the building (a condition of the program), was dropped from the program. He is now petitioning to get back in. Clearly, this was not an other-directed activity. These teachers drew upon their own considerable expertise to plan and carry out a program as effective as any that could have been designed by an outsider.

Obviously, not all teachers are so self-directed. Many have had their decisions made for them for so long that their self-confidence has atrophied. Unfortunately, teacher independence is seldom encouraged by heavily bureaucratic systems that reward centralization and conformity rather than individualization and differentiation.

For these reasons, my work with any individual or group focused on self-improvement would be aimed at nurturing leadership capacity and responsibility for successful change. There are definite advantages to having two or more people working together on professional development, even if they take different directions. Such collaboration builds a feeling of support, ownership, and competence as well as commitment to professional development for themselves and others. Properly done, collaboration can provide a very high order of Maslowian satisfaction. Hence, I would try to arrange for the teacher in the one-room school to join a group of teachers from another school or meet with other teachers in a similar setting on a regular basis.

If, after my initial visitation and feedback session, I were asked to continue working with the teachers, I would suggest that we determine our direction collaboratively. If there were no obvious concerns, I might suggest that we use a consensus-building process to explore our basic educational philosophies. There is great intellectual stimulation (largely lacking in typical educational discussions) in articulating, even debating, what is essential in education. And it is a boon to effective communication within a team, school, or district.

As an example, one of the great advantages of team teaching is that it provides an arena where great energy and dynamic interplay go into the hammering out of a philosophy with which its creators can live comfortably and draw support for their collective efforts. Teaching has too often been called a lonely profession, and this may be true because what is done is so mechanical and superficial. Even the discomfort that is often present when thoughtful professionals meet is occasion for celebration and growth. This is particularly so if collaboration occurs within a framework of mutual acceptance and with a facilitator who knows and respects the participants and is, in turn, known and respected.

Once a set of educational principles had been agreed on, we could focus our efforts by comparing how well we are doing with how well we feel we could do in a particular dimension and selecting the area where we find the greatest discrepancy. This could determine the direction for work as a total group, by groups of two or three teachers having similar priorities, or even by individuals. Next, we might set objectives describing as specifically as possible what changes we would like to effect through our staff development efforts on the principles identified as highest priority. I would encourage teachers to think in terms of the impact on students, but the primary focus would be on what the teachers needed to know or do differently in order to improve their instructional delivery, personal satisfaction, and, ultimately, their students' learning.

Once objectives had been established, I would assist the teachers, if asked, in describing appropriate activities, identifying human resources, scheduling and assisting with the management of the process, assessing the effectiveness of the efforts, and planning for next steps. I would suggest that teachers keep logs on their self-improvement efforts and that they share these impressions with each other by meeting regularly and supporting each other's efforts.

My major role would be that of facilitator, broker, or provider of resources, reminding of the purposes of the effort, encouraging and commending, questioning, coaching, cheerleading. I would not be *the* expert unless one of the development areas targeted happened to be one in which I have special expertise, such as classroom climate, student problem solving, or planning, or unless I were *asked* to provide leadership for it. I would see myself as a member of the group with management responsibilities rather than its "leader."

I would even encourage participants to assume management responsibilities. To the greatest extent possible, I would like them to feel that they genuinely *owned* the plan and its execution. If I were to assume too much responsibility for organization and management, the program could be perceived as *my* program and something the teachers were involved in because they were expected to be or to please me or some other authority. None of these motivations has been proven to be strongly effective in bringing about change. In fact, the highest level of professional development is probably achieved when professionals accept the responsibility for assessing their own needs and carrying them out. A short time ago, I accidentally discovered a delightful example of this. An excellent "mature" teacher casually mentioned how much she had learned from her young colleague across the hall. The younger teacher had come to the district from another where she had become skilled in a particular teaching method. The local teacher suggested that the newcomer act as a "mentor" in teaching her the process. How stimulating for a younger teacher to have such validation from a respected older educator. And how refreshing for a highly experienced teacher to pick up new and better strategies to keep her psychological batteries charged!

Values Undergirding this Approach to Professional Development

Each of us has a deeply rooted value system that guides all aspects of our behavior. In responding to the questions posed here, I hope that I have given evidence of my commitment to the following beliefs, which have successfully guided my own work for the last 30 years.

● Almost all teachers and administrators care about students and genuinely want to prepare them to be capable adults who will live satisfying lives.

● Given encouragement and appropriate opportunity, almost all educators want to continue learning how to do their work more effectively and will work enthusiastically toward that end.

● Because teachers tend to teach as they were taught, significant change is difficult, but it can be facilitated through their own personal analysis, determination of direction, and commitment to specific efforts that are supported over time with adequate resources.

● Teachers have much undifferentiated knowledge about how to accomplish improvement goals. They need the opportunity to reflect, focus, and plan with adequate human, financial, and time-resource support in order to draw on this knowledge.

● Significant behavior change is most likely to occur when it is introduced, practiced, and self-critiqued in the context of the work situation and applied to real problems with appropriate outside support as needed.

● Effective, long-term change results most often in relation to an effective planning process rather than in relation to isolated, miscellaneous, short-term activities, however interesting and pertinent they may be.

● There are within any school district, however small, staff development resources, primarily within the individuals themselves, to solve almost any instructional problem.

● Adults learn better when they are treated as autonomous decision makers.

● A self-developed or self-selected structure for identifying direction and assessing needs usually provides a better basis for substantive improvement than one that is imposed from outside.

It is interesting to note that a common outgrowth of the recent studies of educational excellence is strong support for more checking-off of student progress, more academic learning time, more content, and higher expectations. None of these are inappropriate. What is inappropriate is the assumption that some kind of "prescription"—often written by someone in a hierarchical position—is the way to accomplish excellence in these ways.

Rather, I believe, like Goodlad, that real improvement is more likely to occur in relation to collaborative decision making within a school norm of growth and high standards. The power lies in having those who must actually work to *solve* the problem describe and *own* both the problem and its solution and to rejoice in that solution. Basically, it comes down to a philosophical question: Do we trust each other to be true professionals, or don't we?

4. Consulting with Technical Instructors in a Business Environment

Lyn Corno

"WHAT WILL SHE BE ABLE TO TELL ME ABOUT HOW TO TEACH COMPUTER SOFTWARE? I've been doing it for 15 years!" "She's got a Ph.D. in educational psychology, but what does she know about operating systems for mainframe computers?" Questions such as these are among the real challenges I have faced as an educational consultant to a high-technology corporation I shall call "Compuco." This environment will serve as context for the hypothetical staff development project I describe in this chapter. My observations and many of the responses I provide are derived from actual consulting projects. The role of staff development "expert" at an international computer company is one I have assumed several times in the past five years.

The Target Environment: Compuco

Compuco offers a variety of product-related short courses, typically two to ten days long, to their own customers as well as users of compatible computer equipment. The division of Compuco targeted for this hypothetical consulting assignment offers courses in large-scale computer operating sys-

Lyn Corno is Associate Professor of Education, Teachers College, Columbia University, New York City.

tems (software), both introductory and more advanced. Since software education is a revenue-generating operation at Compuco, the education division has a keen interest in quality control and reputation-enhancing activities. As an outside consultant, the work I was asked to do related to both.

Compuco courses are taught at several geographically dispersed "education centers," including some in Europe. They are located in urban areas for easy access. The education centers maintain sophisticated teaching equipment, including ergonomically designed classrooms, multiple-media presentation facilities, a production department that assists in materials acquisition, development, and packaging, and multiple computer terminals in each classroom for laboratory work. All these facilities are used routinely.

Compuco's students are all adult professionals in the data processing field who attend courses to keep up on industry advances and maintain the data processing operations of the companies that employ them. Course instructors are also data processing professionals, many of whom have excelled in particular areas of software design during the course of their typically extensive careers. They are "subject matter specialists," most with limited teaching experience and no formal backgrounds in education or psychology. While these professionals desire assistance in learning more about teaching, depth of subject matter knowledge is considered the key ingredient to effective teaching in this environment. Many instructors are skeptical of the potential utility offered by standard pedagogical or curricular assistance, yet it is they who requested the implementation of a staff development program.

There is a sense in which these instructors, perhaps more than anything else, approach their task with naive theories about effective teaching—views of how to teach that are grounded in their own idiosyncratically collected empirical data. Just as naive theories of subject matter can interfere with effective learning in school children (Resnick, 1983), so these naive views can interfere with the development of more substantially grounded, sophisticated views of teaching in adult instructors. This chapter is in part about how such naiveté might be productively confronted and overcome in the work environment.

The Project Goals. One management requirement was that a volunteer team of software education instructors work with me to identify the following project goals: to design and implement an Instructor Development Program that would (a) introduce new instructors to divisional education procedures, (b) provide the means for special training as indicated by performance reviews, and (c) offer incentives for conducting inquiry on their own teaching and devising creative improvements.

The Preliminary Analysis

Many more observations and discussions with instructors were made than can be illustrated here. The following pages summarize my interpretations and the kinds of recommendations made to the instructional team. The observation method used was a classroom narrative, semi-structured to target three categories of information. The observations were of one introductory and one advanced course covering the same subject matter: the operating system used on IBM and IBM-compatible mainframe computers, known as Multiple Virtual Storage (MVS).

MVS is a highly dense operating system with "multiple" layers of software, each of which serves different complementary functions, but without which none of these computers could operate. The operating system forms the basis for all data storage and manipulation on the machine, and allows various forms of computer hardware to intercommunicate. Courses in the workings of MVS and related system architectures (e.g., MVS-XA) are the bread and butter of Compuco's software offerings. I purposely selected instructors to observe who were known to have quite different teaching styles and methods. The advanced "MVS Measurement and Tuning" (MVS M&T) course observed was co-taught.

For ease of interpretation, I structured my observations to obtain three categories of descriptive information. These categories reflect the features on which instruction at Compuco is typically evaluated and so "fit" the vision of teaching held in that environment. The categories are not exhaustive or presumed to be mutually exclusive:

• *Instructional activity.* Concerns information on the mode(s) of delivery used; the types of activities engaged in; the pacing and difficulty level of instruction.

• *Instructor performance.* Concerns instructors' demonstrations of subject matter competence, broadly defined, as well as presentation styles and responsiveness to students.

• *Student learning/satisfaction.* At Compuco a standard Course Evaluation Form is completed by each student at the end of each course. These forms were obtained and reviewed for each class observed. Evaluation forms provided information on student perceptions of course content and instructor as well as their subjective assessments of knowledge acquired. Examinations are not given in these courses, so no objective assessments of student learning were available. Observations noted evidence of apparent student confusion and comprehension at appropriate points.

The observation summary and interpretation that follows is similarly organized according to these three categories of information. In business consulting situations, it is common for such a summary to be presented to instructors and management as a preliminary report. The report would later serve as the basis for more specific recommendations concerning the proposed Instructor Development Program and detailed intervention with individual instructors. Readers should be able to discern in this section what I looked for and saw in software education at Compuco, as well as the kind of initial feedback given to instructors and management.

Executive Summary of Classroom Observations

Instructional Activity. All observations were of instructor-directed sessions. No labs or student-directed sessions were observed, partly because few such sessions were run, and partly because my interest was in instructors and "typical" instruction.

The typical mode of delivery across all courses was what might be called the "participatory lecture." While there were variations in the extent to which instructors encouraged student participation, no class used a one-way lecture. The consistent method of delivering lecture information was the overhead projector with sequenced foils. Copies of foils were given to students as handouts, and foils were either projected directly on greaseboards (where instructors wrote on the boards to extend or highlight foils), or on a screen (where instructors wrote on the foil as it sat on the projector). Notepaper, marker pens, and reference manuals were always provided for each student. Instructors stood in front of the class when presenting information; students were seated at desks in rows (except if asked to come to the front to present something). Standard procedure was to hold class for approximately 50 minutes and break for ten. Students were free to get up and get coffee or leave briefly during class sessions if necessary. Routine activities included an "administrivia" discussion at the start of a course, statements of topic objectives or class activities at the beginning of a new topic, previews of "coming attractions," reviews of material covered during a class session, immediate positive responses by instructors to student questions and comments, and presentation of course completion certificates and evaluation forms at the end. In general, instructors used the participatory lecture delivery mode because it was considered standard procedure at Compuco and was accepted well by students. These comments reflect unquestioned assumptions about teaching that serve to maintain the status quo here.

With subject matter that is highly symbolic and dense (as is the content of computer operating systems), however, variations in delivery can be important. They can, for example, reduce the information processing burden and stave off boredom during classroom instruction. A self-paced unit at a terminal, integrated with a short video presentation, or a topic on which students work in small groups to solve a problem are examples of variations in delivery that might be interjected effectively into software education classes here. While students were invariably attentive (as evidenced by notetaking, visual tracking of the instructor, paging through handouts, and interjected questions/comments), they all spent most of the class time doing basically the same thing—namely, listening to the instructor, taking notes, and occasionally asking questions. (The one exception was the use of student "case study" presentations in MVS M&T.) This situation could be altered even slightly with potential improvements to the quality of education offered at Compuco.

The typical sequence of instruction—irrespective of course area or level—was a three-phase "episode" consisting of (a) presentation of information by instructor, (b) questioning students and permitting them to ask questions and comment, and (c) instructor feedback/response. This sequence occurred in general topic discussions as well as in discussions of subtopics within a topic. So there appeared recurring "*presentation-questioning-feedback*" (PQF) loops throughout the sessions in all classes observed.

Variations in this PQF instructional sequence occurred mostly at the *questioning* phase. There were always questions asked, but some instructors waited for students to ask them (and this was sometimes rare). Other instructors asked many questions of students, forcing them to demonstrate what they had learned. This phase of instruction can be considered an opportunity for the instructor to "check" on student learning—to see if students are understanding, and so forth. But to do this, the instructor must ask some questions, as well as wait for student answers. Even a quick and clumsy check is nearly always preferable to a lack of information on whether or not students understand, since the point of instruction is, after all, student learning.

Instructors also differed at the *response* phase, i.e., in how they handled student questions. Some instructors would give detailed, to the point, explanations, or detailed explanations that diverged somewhat from the point; others would give shorter, often analogical, explanations. The quality of an explanation as an aid to student understanding is often related to appropriate choice of an analogy or example that serves to clarify otherwise obscure meanings.

One aspect of good teaching, then, is to know and use effective analogies and examples. To subject matter experts, examples that might illuminate a point for a novice learner are not always apparent. There is a difference between knowing the structure of a subject and knowing how that subject is efficiently learned. The latter has been called "pedagogical knowledge of a subject" (Shulman, 1985) and is an important component of the knowledge base for an effective instructor.

Some instructors automatically made reinforcing comments when students answered questions correctly—"Good," or "That's right, yes!" Others more typically provided less explicit positive responses such as "Uh, huh," or a nod and a smile. Neither of these responses is better or worse in an absolute sense. The relative effects of any response to a correct or incorrect student answer depend on the student.

In the *presentation* phase, the variation that most often occurred concerned the use of foils. Foils were used either as instructional "tools," or as a kind of "course outline." As an example of the former, most instructors described parts of foils—usually the highlighted parts—and talked about items that related to but did not duplicate what was on the foil. This is a way of using the foil as an instructional tool, for it lets the students "fill-in" gaps.

In contrast, some instructors described all points on their foils, and elaborated the points as well. This king of foil was usually lengthy and dense, and served as a course map or outline for the student to follow.

In general, using foils as an instructional tool requires more of the instructor's discussion to be handled extemporaneously (or with only the support of lecture notes). This tends to make for a more polished presentation. It also means (a) that their points may be made too quickly for students to take notes, and (b) that instructors really need to "have their topics down cold." Such "smooth" presentation skills can be learned, however, through appropriate development activities.

Presentations also varied in the area of foil transitions. Some instructors explicitly marked transitions between foils by stating, for example, "Let's go on to the next foil. . . ." Others tended to avoid marking a transition and moved through the foil sequence without comment. Marking transitions seems to aid learning most when the transition is actually a move from one subtopic to another, rather than simply to the next foil in a sequence for one subtopic. This demarcates topic areas explicitly, encouraging students to keep related material together and apart from less-related material.

Research shows that excellent instructors make an explicit effort to structure and separate the critical subject matter from the less critical. An effective instructor knows, for example, the most frequently encountered M&T problems and the two or three "best fixes." These are aspects of subject matter that students have difficulty identifying on their own. So efforts to sequence information logically, to use key examples and analogies, to emphasize or summarize important points, and to clarify common sources of difficulty are all important under this principle and can be made to occur more automatically in class with practice.

The instructional sequence of Presentation-Questioning-Feedback is *the* most common form of instruction used in classroom teaching (Bellack et al., 1966; Gage, 1978). There is research supporting its effectiveness in aiding learners to acquire large bodies of information quickly (such as "lower-level" learning objectives) with assistance from an experienced instructor. As mentioned, the presentation phase uses reviews, rephrasing, analogies, "war stories," and the identification of key issues or problems to give a body of information a structure that is meaningful to students and easily learned. The questioning phase encourages learners to consolidate information through limited practice, and the feedback phase supports and extends what has been learned. The basic sequence is used in much self-paced written instruction, such as so-called "programmed instruction." It has many advantages over written instruction that does not contain the questioning-feedback portion of the loop (e.g., textbooks) because of the learning principles—reinforcement and practice—it encourages.

When students are expected to go beyond information given, however, this instructional sequence tends to be less effective. To apply what is learned to situations different from those discussed in class, to adapt what is learned when new variables enter a task, or to critically evaluate the usefulness of what is learned is "higher-level" learning activity. The accomplishment of such goals is aided by instructional activity that encourages students to compare what they learn to other situations, to apply information themselves, and to use a reasoning process to extract key points or add new points as needed. Relevant activities here include case studies, student presentations, labs, and small-group or study group interactions, which again benefit from the direction of an experienced instructor. Thus, the use of case studies and student presentations in MVS M&T (where learning objectives are higher level because the course is advanced) is a highly appropriate and effective form of instruction.

Other variations in the instructional activity observed seemed to revolve around the level of the course (basic or more advanced). These included pacing, degree of student participation encouraged, and type of instructional activity. Generally, the more advanced courses appeared faster paced, encouraged more student participation, and used instructional activities—such as case studies and student profile presentations—as in MVS M&T. The exception was MVS Concept and Facilities (MVS C&F) in which students knew very little about computer architecture yet had considerable ground to cover in a short time. In this course, the instructor *pulled* knowledge from students regularly by questioning them and worked at a relatively fast clip. It was appropriate to involve students here since students who have little background in a subject have fewer "hooks" on which to hang details. These students had little background in computer software, which made it difficult to learn the components of the MVS system. The instructor used constant questioning to shape a general structure of software architecture on which he hoped details about MVS could be hung. He also took one MVS job and traced its path through the system with supporting foils, diagrams, and graphics. This effective strategy might serve as a useful model for other instructors teaching short, basic level courses.

Instructor performance. The software instructors appeared uniformly knowledgeable in their subject areas, as reflected by their ability to field most student questions immediately or at least bring back answers later. This knowledge was also reflected in the observation that many instructors designed sessions around critical examples or stories about solutions to core problems. These examples generally involved problems commonly recurring in the software under discussion. They also tended to be problems the instructors found interesting. Knowledge of the seminal problems in a field often separates the experts from the novices. Experts will continue to fine-tune the knowledge and skills they have acquired as part of their own professional development, and this fine-tuning should be encouraged and reinforced by the organization.

Instructors varied considerably in their presentation styles. The range was from a semiformal, almost British university manner with careful, polished demeanor and elegant, logical sequencing, to a quite informal teach-

43

ing style typical of American elementary classrooms. In the latter the instructor moved rapidly among the rows of students, calling on students by name, and illustrating key ideas with personal experiences in addition to his slant on the subject. Between these extremes was a relaxed but professional style often seen in American colleges that reward effective teaching. These instructors were organized, prepared, and attentive to students' verbal and physical cues. Material was presented at a practical level, with an emphasis on students being able to use what they learn quickly. The instructors' enjoyment of the teaching experience was generally evident.

Such variety in presentation styles should be seen here as a positive aspect of the software education. Variety inhibits boredom. Students should encounter a range of personal styles; they themselves display different styles. At no time were *negative* style characteristics observed—no disorganization or nervousness; no aggressive unawareness or unpleasant behavior toward students, or ignorance about key areas. These negative style characteristics do not aid teaching, just as they would not enhance any type of interpersonal encounter. In sum, the instructors performed in accord with accepted canons of effective teaching, yet displayed an interesting variety of personal teaching styles. The development and refinement of unique instructional styles should be encouraged by the organization, and instructors should be helped to understand the most effective means for offering students a variety of instructional styles during team-taught courses.

The common wisdom on effective instruction also supports the importance of a certain responsiveness to student comments and concerns—a consideration of students as individuals. The software instructors responded with immediacy to students and in a positive way. There were some variations in style of response, again reflecting personal style differences. Here responses ranged from careful, polite, and respectful, to a more teasing or challenging response that came rapidly and assertively. Between the extremes was a good-natured, friendly response that encouraged students yet also dealt seriously with their questions. Again, no one response can be said to be best overall. It is generally considered wise to avoid unconstructive criticism, aggressive probing for more information, and ignoring students altogether. Again, nothing like this was seen in these classes. It is the case that some types of responses are better received by some students than by others. Research has been unable to show which students benefit most from what kinds of responses, however. Effective instructors become adept at varying their responses to students in accord with their judgments of student preferences, and this, too, can be fostered with effective teacher training.

Student learning/satisfaction. A summary of statistics for each key category of the Compuco Course Evaluation Form (pooled across classes) follows:

	Mean	Standard Deviation
Course Design and Content	1.43	.37
Instructors	1.36	.40
Overall	1.34	.48

The numerical ratings showed all courses rated by students as falling between excellent (1) and good (2) on the 5-point scale. The highest rating was 1.3; the lowest was 2.08. The average of all courses for each of the three subareas shown above indicate most students strongly agreed or agreed that both course content/design and instructors were excellent. The range for instructor ratings was 1.36 (high) to 1.64 (low). T-tests computed on the difference between highest and lowest ratings in each of the three evaluation categories (design and content, instructor, and overall) showed significant differences in the existing sample. (A difference > approximately .3 points between any two means was statistically significant in this sample.) These data suggest that the evaluation form did allow students to reliably discriminate their education preferences in the classes observed.

Another measure of the reliability of these scales is the reliability statistic, which was computed for the two categories, design/content and instructor (both categories contained more than one item on which students responded). These were .68 and .87, respectively. The figures are evaluated on a scale of 0 to 1.0, where 1.0 indicates perfect reliability (or precise and accurate measurement of the category). Coefficients of .65 or above are considered acceptable for subjective measures such as this. The higher statistic for the instructor category is somewhat inflated due to students' tendency to mark the same rating on all six items in the category. In general, when students liked an instructor, they liked the person and were not terribly discriminating about the different features of "instructor performance" measured. This is also a common result when people are rated subjectively on general characteristics by others.

I hasten to point out that, while the rating differences did appear statistically significant, they may not be *practically* significant, especially in the case where two instructors team-taught the same class (in MVS M&T). A more meaningful way to think about these numbers is from the standpoint of the difficulty level of the course. Students tended to rate higher the more "basic" level courses *and* their instructors. The more intensive, more demanding courses received slightly lower ratings from students. Again, there was a statistically significant difference between ratings pooled for the two basic courses and ratings pooled for the three more advanced courses, with considerable overlap between two of these.

Some educational research has shown that students report more satisfaction with courses in which they work relatively less hard than in courses where they have to work harder to learn. More of this research has been conducted with children than with college students, so caution is warranted in applying the results. But it is the case that Compuco's software education courses become considerably more demanding mentally, with increases in subject matter depth. While there is typically some corresponding increase in time spent during instruction (e.g., MVS C&F is 1½ days; MVS M&T is 4 days), there still may not be enough time for an average student to feel he or she has time to assimilate all the information presented in the more advanced courses.

Written comments of students in the more advanced courses seem to support this possibility. There were more comments requesting additional instruction in the advanced than in the basic courses. Data for the item "I acquired valuable skills and information" show 47 and 50 percent of the students responded "strongly agree" in the basic courses. The comparable statistics in the advanced courses were 16, 33, and 50 percent, respectively. These results suggest that more students felt they got the gist of what was presented and that it was useful to them in the lower-level courses. Since this probably occurred as a result of the increase in information and detail in the higher-level courses, it suggests that simply extending the number of days of instruction may not compensate.

In conclusion, the Course Evaluation Form appears to give accurate data on students' perceptions of software courses, and these data can be used both to judge the course and consider instructional changes in a number of areas. The numerical data should also be useful as a basis for bottom-line acceptable student ratings. The trend here suggests a base standard of 3.0, such that courses should only be offered which receive overall ratings of ≥ 3.0. However, this trend should be examined across other courses as well before any cutoff score becomes policy.

Finally, the evaluation data from students reflect a way of measuring the extent to which key guidelines for course design and instruction are regularly incorporated into course offerings, and a way of documenting the consistently high ratings of software education offerings by students. *These numbers would not be well used as performance evaluations for instructors since they appear so heavily tied to the level of the courses taught, and since students have difficulty discriminating among instructors in team-taught courses.* The written comments students make, obviously, will be useful in confirming hunches derived from the numerical data as well as in providing targets for changes within courses, such as additions of new topics and alterations in existing topics. Software instructors should be given instruction in the systematic use of student learning/satisfaction data for making course evaluation decisions in these areas.

Action Recommendations

The foregoing summary and interpretation of observation data would typically conclude with a set of "action recommendations"—proposals for instructor-development activities that would assist software instructors to implement instructional changes in the context in which they work. Environmental assumptions would need explication, and a list of potential issues and areas for instructor development would be created. Again, the list would be organized into three categories: instructional activity, instructor performance, and student learning/satisfaction. The following are examples of recommendations made from each area:

• *Instructional activity.* Instructors should be familiarized with the basics of the instructional sequence, PQF. Not all instructors capitalize on the utility of this sequence. Instructor training or consultation should emphasize the Q-phase and how questions can serve as efficient, informal indices of student understanding, as well as prompt students to integrate and rehearse what they learn. It should also include consideration of the kinds of teaching situations in which the questioning of students is particularly important (for example, in basic level courses with beginners).

• *Instructor performance.* A program should be developed to assist instructors in defining and refining their own teaching styles. This will be particularly important for instructors who have not taught before. It is recommended that a videotape be made to portray the variety of acceptable styles at Compuco in the context of actual course teaching. The voice overlay should allow each instructor to comment on his or her teaching and explain the various events that take place. New instructors should view this tape, and videotape-feedback of their own teaching should be included in a later phase of their development. This later phase should include identifying areas in which instructors feel they would like assistance or advice.

Style differences could be considered by instructional teams when they schedule classes and assign topics. By devising class schedules that reflect a balance of instructor styles, those styles could be evaluated for their effects on student learning/satisfaction. For example, there may be some optimal mix of instructor styles that yields "rave" course reviews (and perhaps increases business in the long run).

Determining the combinations of instructor styles to constitute team-taught courses should be based on what is known about the course, the target students, the instructors involved, and the psychology of instruction. In areas where instructors develop personal objectives for advice and consultation, support should be provided to aid their accomplishment.

• *Student learning/satisfaction.* A procedure should be devised for routinely summarizing Course Evaluation Form data in a readable, concise format that can be efficiently used by instructors to gauge their course effectiveness (from the students' point of view) and to make future instructional decisions. It is recommended that the data be collected on a computer-readable form and fed into the computer after each course. A data-based management program could then be used to reduce and track data across courses and instructors. Summary reports should be generated for each instructor

47

after each course and for management biannually.

The months of instructor development work that follow proposals such as this inevitably prove both challenging and enlightening to the staff developer as well as the participants. Given the considerable talents and professionalism of the software instructors at Compuco, any instructor development program had to be driven by the needs, interests, and time constraints of the instructors themselves (see, e.g., Dillon-Peterson, 1981). It was particularly appropriate to build the program around the significant subject matter expertise of the instructors, while attempting to illuminate the various ways of making these subjects more "teachable." While subject matter depth is in place here, pedagogical knowledge of the subject appears less than adequate for some instructors, whose teaching also reflected less than ideal perceptiveness and creative inquiry. One's naive view of teaching is often modeled after the teachers one has had. Overcoming such naiveté and replacing it with more sophisticated views is a difficult task in staff development.

In the business world, as with efforts at teacher change (see, e.g., Cazden, 1985), there is one staff development activity that seems to result in less defensiveness and denial than some other approaches. That approach uses observation and student evaluation data with instructors on a one-on-one basis to convey student reactions to various activities. When concrete examples of student puzzlement and misunderstanding are made apparent, the kinds of changes that might help are often generated by the instructors themselves with little or no assistance. They are then urged to try a change and to reflect upon the results. Some vehicle is used (e.g., videotapes and peer observers) to record student responses, and results are again discussed with staff development experts. While a development procedure such as this does require a motivated instructor, it must be recalled that positive student response is literally the bottom line for these instructors. In a revenue-generating business environment, education is a product and students are discerning consumers.

While such a program benefits from a staff development expert, it ought not to be "conducted" by consultants but rather by the instructors and managers themselves. Compuco's management has worked with me to develop a program that provides the support necessary to help instructors accomplish the above-exemplified recommendations in timely fashion with minimal disruption of their schedules.

The software instructors at Compuco determine the kinds of activities they wish to engage in and with whom (consultants, other instructors); they then complete the activities on a schedule agreed upon by management. Progress reviews are built in, the form of which is determined by instructors and managers according to preference and type of activity. As development activities are completed, management recognition is given—attendance at conference and social activities within their fields are offered as perquisites.

Accomplishments are noted on performance reviews.

An Instructor Development Task Force has also been formed to assist in the implementation process. The task force consists of the division general manager, a mid-line manager charged with implementation responsibilities, and two instructors (recognized as "master" instructors). The instructors rotate annually so that newly identified "masters" earn the chance to assist in instructional development activities. And finally, each component of the instructor development program at Compuco has been shared with all technical instructors in the company in hopes that similar efforts might also be undertaken in other divisions.

References

Bellack, A. A.; H. M. Kliebard; R. T. Hyman; and F. L. Smith. *The Language of the Classroom.* New York: Teachers College Press, 1961.

Cazden, C. "Classroom Discourse." In *Third Handbook of Research on Teaching,* edited by M. C. Wittrock. New York: Macmillan & Co., 1985.

Corno, L., and R. E. Snow. "Adapting Teaching to Individual Differences Among Learners." In *Third Handbook of Research on Teaching,* edited by M. C. Wittrock. New York: Macmillan & Co., 1985.

Dillon-Peterson, B., ed. *Staff Development/Organization Development.* Alexandria, Va.: Association for Supervision and Curriculum Development, 1981.

Gage, N. L. *The Scientific Basis of the Art of Teaching.* New York: Teachers College Press, 1978.

Resnick L. B. "Mathematics and Science Learning: A New Conception." *Science* 220 (1983): 477-478.

Shulman, L. S. "Research Programs for the Study of Teaching." In *Third Handbook of Research on Teaching*, edited by M.C. Wittrock. New York: Macmillan & Co., 1985.

5. The View from Next Door: A Look at Peer "Supervision"

Valerie Bang-Jensen

MANY EXPERTS IN THE FIELD HAVE QUESTIONED THE VALIDITY OF THE TERM "PEER supervision" because supervision implies "a superordinate-subordinate relationship" (Alfonso and Goldsberry, 1982). Semantics aside, if instructional improvement and teacher growth are the principal goals of supervision, peer collaboration can be a more effective, efficient, and rewarding way to meet these goals than traditional hierarchical supervision.

My view of instruction is from next door. In addition to teaching a full-day kindergarten, I use daily release time to work as a writing facilitator in my colleagues' classrooms. As part of a pilot project to reinforce an ongoing inservice program on the teaching of writing, teachers may request my help over several weeks to develop their writing programs. Our focus is to improve both the quality of student writing and the teaching of writing.

Along with many other districts, Ithaca has endorsed the New York State Department of Education recommendations for using the process approach to teaching writing. This approach emphasizes a child's control over and responsibility for his or her own writing and relies heavily on conferences rather than written correction to encourage children to use brainstorming, drafting, revising, and editing.

Valerie Bang-Jensen is a teacher and consultant for the Ithaca City School District, Ithaca, New York.

The Ithaca Writing Project was formed to help assess student writing and to develop inservice workshops for teachers. Because the process approach to the teaching of writing often requires structural and attitudinal changes in teaching styles, the writing facilitator program was implemented to provide intensive daily help to colleagues.

What Do I Look For When I Look at Teaching?

While I bring experience in the teaching of writing to my work with teachers, I also bring beliefs about teaching, learning, classroom environment, supervision, and instructional improvement.

What I bring to my role as writing facilitator is not "super" vision, as mocked by Elliot Eisner (1982), or a preconceived, idealized notion of how a subject should be taught. Rather, I bring to my observations a synthesis of variables and a generalized conception of the elements that go into effective teaching. Fundamental to effective teaching are a knowledge of the subject area; an appreciation of children's social, emotional, and cognitive development; a concern for both the planned and "hidden" curriculum; a repertoire of instructional techniques and classroom management skills; and an awareness of one's own strengths and the needs of each particular class. A coordinated approach that considers and synthesizes all these elements into an effective program to meet one's goals is, in my view, the essence of good teaching.

I observed two teachers early in the school year. Both had invited me into their rooms to observe their initial attempts at introducing writing to their classes.

Kate

Kate, a teacher with 15 years of experience, was excited about teaching writing in her 1st grade classroom. She had the room across the hall from me last year, and had observed kindergartners at work writing. Impressed by their success, she was motivated to experiment with her own class during the last months of school and attended a teacher workshop over the summer. When we met for lunch during August to bind blank books for the school year, Kate confessed that she was eager for school to start.

My visit to Kate's room took place early in the school year. As I entered, the last round of a 1st grade trivia game was under way. "Who can name the days of the week?" asked Kate. Thora did and earned points for the class. Months of the year were harder and, after a collaborative effort, the game was over. The children applauded and looked at Kate expectantly. "Please push in your chairs and go to the meeting area for writing time." Soon, six children were jostling around as Karim leafed through the pile of carpet squares. "Please take the one on top, and find your own space. I see that Nadia is ready; so are David and Sean." Continuing to reinforce those who were ready, Kate put a piece of paper on the blackboard. When all of the children were seated quietly, she began.

"Yesterday when we had writing, I noticed that some people had trouble thinking of what to say. Writers can help each other. Today I want to write about when I broke my arm, but I'm stuck and need you to help me by asking me questions about it."

"Arjun? I'm glad to see that you remembered to raise your hand."

"How did it happen?" Kate described playing King of the Mountain with children in her neighborhood and being pushed off the hill. Then she wrote on the paper, "How did it happen?" and said, "That will help me remember what to write."

"Cyrone?"

Cyrone asked whether it had hurt. Kate wrote, "Did it hurt?" on the board, and said, "Yes, and the woman whose house I went to didn't believe me."

"Sarah?"

"Which hand was it? Are you right-handed?"

As Kate answered, she wrote the question on the board.

"No, it was my left arm, but that makes me think that I can tell about how my family waited on me while I had the cast on."

After several more questions, Kate took down the paper. "I'll be using these questions to help me decide what to put in my story. Tomorrow we can help someone else. If you get stuck at your desk, what could you do?"

Two children raised their hands.

"Sam?"

"We can ask the teacher."

"What could you do that we just did, Sam?" reminded Kate.

"Oh, we could ask questions."

"Yes, that would help someone else. What if *you* get stuck?"

"Catherine?"

"We can ask somebody to ask *us* questions."

"Good. I hope you will try it. Now it's time to start writing. When I call your name, you may get your folder and go to your desk to start working."

Kate read the names from each folder, giving them to the appropriate student. The children walked slowly to their desks, many of them opening their folders as they went. Chris returned to the meeting area.

"I need more paper."

"It's on the writing shelf," said Kate.

Karim began sharpening a pencil. "Please use the sharpened pencils on the writing shelf."

When all of the folders were distributed, Kate sat at a desk, unfolded her list of questions, and began to write. A moment later, she went to Sean's desk where he was working in his math book. As she spoke with him, he put the book away and opened his writing folder. Kate returned to her desk and began to write. The room was quiet.

Linda

Linda's 2nd grade class of 25 was learning along with her. A first-year teacher facing insurance forms, teacher association demands, parent conferences, and a new basal reading series, Linda was nevertheless eager to have me work with her. She was convinced that the process approach to teaching writing was compatible with her philosophy of teaching and would favorably influence other areas of her teaching. In preparation, Linda ceased assigning ditto "story starters" to her students, read *Writing: Teachers and Children at Work* (Graves, 1983), requested folders from the office, and observed Kate's class during their writing time. And she told me that she was excited but nervous about having another teacher in the room.

A week later, I arrived at the beginning of the writing period. Joe was sitting in the "writer's chair" at the front of a large U-shaped arrangement of desks. He quietly read his story to the others, the paper covering his face. The others had listened patiently when he started, but their attention soon wandered and they rolled pencils and tapped their fingers. Linda asked him to read in a louder voice so we could hear him. Joe read his story again, telling us that he would soon be returning to his country on an airplane. When he stopped and looked up, several children had their hands in the air.

"I heard that you are going to your country. What is your country?"

"Taiwan," Joe replied, smiling, and called on another classmate.

"I heard that you're going on a plane ride—a long one." Joe smiled, confirming the remark.

Next, Diallo shared his story about five dogs he knows. He told about how he made five chapters, one for each dog. His story had been bound into a book, and he now read the revised, edited version. He finished quickly and looked up expectantly. Again, several classmates were eager to tell Diallo what they heard him describe in his story, what parts they particularly liked.

Linda thanked Diallo for sharing. "Now it's time for writing. Remember to use these blue pencils. They don't have erasers, and that will help you remember that erasing isn't important when you first write your ideas. Mrs. Bang-Jensen and I will be writing our own stories at the beginning of writing time, so we will come around and talk to you in a little while. Get started, everyone, and save your questions for later."

Immediately, two children raised their hands; one walked over to Linda's desk.

"I just have to ask you one thing."

"I'm writing," Linda replied, "I will see you when I am finished. You need to write."

Another asked, "If the teachers are writing, when will they have time to publish? It's my turn today."

Linda, continuing to write, said, "I want to see you writing."

Everyone settled down at desks. Several children began to draw lines on blank paper with rulers; most children were writing. Five minutes passed. Linda put aside her writing and began to circulate around the room, stopping occasionally to work with individuals in a quiet tone. Occasionally we heard, "Nice work . . . nice story. . . ."

Designing a Program: A Focus on Writing

It was clear that both Kate and Linda had made an effort to become familiar with resources for the teaching of writing: state guidelines, trends and research, what they could glean from their observations of students, and, in Kate's case, an inservice workshop. In addition, they referred to the following guidelines we had developed as a faculty:

● Help children write with authority about what they know.

● Write for an audience to develop a sense of reader.

● Write multiple drafts; work through a process of drafting, revising, editing, and sharing.

● Learn about the qualities of good writing: revising for a variety of reasons—clarity, interesting leads and endings, vocabulary.

● Develop appropriate mechanical skills.

● Develop fluency and a willingness to write frequently.

Steps toward these goals were evident in both classrooms. Linda, in her insistence that the children use pencils without erasers, is striving to help them see that writing can be changed, that it is an ongoing process with appropriate times to draft, revise, and edit. She has resolved to discard the story starters that she relied upon during the first hectic weeks of the semester; she wants to give her students the message that they are quite knowledgeable about many topics, as Diallo wrote about dogs, and Joe about his country.

As recommended by Ralph Tyler (1949) in *Basic Principles of Curriculum and Instruction*, and as seen in Linda's room, the learners themselves were an important source of objectives. Kate had realized that her class needed help when "stuck" on a topic and designed a lesson to teach them a strategy for dealing with it. Linda judged that Joe needed an audience for his story about returning to his country in order to make revisions. The teachers not only encouraged and showed the children how to write about topics important to them but also diagnosed skill needs from their students' work.

Careful selection and organization of learning experiences are vital in planning curriculum. Both Kate and Linda designed lessons that were applicable to the needs of the entire group. Linda, when launching her writing workshop after two months of story starters, recognized that her class would need help and encouragement from her and from each other in choosing their own topics. The goal of her sharing meeting was clear, but the physical structure of the room and desks made it difficult for all children to be involved and to benefit. Because of this obstacle, I intended to discuss her room arrangement when we met.

Kate's room had been set up during August to accommodate her new approach to teaching writing. She had set up supply shelves, a publishing and conferencing table, and a group meeting area for instruction and sharing times. She had clear expectations for the way that she wanted routines and procedures to be handled by the children—smoothly and independently—in order to be able to focus on the content of workshop time rather than on discipline.

When I observed her, I noticed that after a smooth initial transition and a simple direct lesson on how to question each other, the children dispersed to their desks needing a bit more direction or reinforcement for their individual writing. Perhaps Kate would like to discuss one of the goals on her list: designing a sequence of lessons to help students develop the willingness and fluency to write daily.

I often refer to the ASCD chart, "Developmental Characteristics of Children and Youth" (1975) for help in designing appropriate and challenging lessons. In both lessons that I observed, concern for cognitive, social, and emotional development was evident.

For five- to seven-year-olds, "successful school experience is critical in establishing positive attitudes toward learning and later educational experience."[1] The children are "open to perceiving school as an exciting experience: are eager to participate and are aware of and influenced by teachers' social attitudes and values communicated through behavior." In both classes I observed, the teachers felt that the students' topic choice was important in tying school and home life together. I overheard Kate encourage a student toward this goal and toward building a positive attitude about writing. "You were in the hospital? What happened? That would make an interesting story. I'd love to hear about it." The hidden message given to all of the children in allotting a full period of writing daily is that writing, and what they have to contribute, is important.

Socially, the children's "ability to function independently is severely tested," explaining the need for both teachers to be clear and consistent about expectations coupled with constant affirmation of what the children were accomplishing. Kate would need to provide them with the chance to practice the new routines and procedures until they were internalized by the children. It was difficult for the 2nd graders to think independently; they already had a year of writing experience at school and were wed to erasers, dictionaries, making things come out "right," and a steady diet of story starters. ("Aren't you going to start me? How long does it have to be?") Getting these 2nd graders to think and write independently when their stage of social development indicated that this might be difficult was quite a challenge for Linda, and we could begin to plan the small steps necessary to build their confidence and change their attitudes.

---

[1]This and the other characteristics quoted in this section are all listed on the ASCD chart, "Developmental Characteristics of Children and Youth" (1975).

Other social patterns fit perfectly with the objectives of the writing program. During sharing meetings, because the students were able to express themselves freely, they were able to be friendly and candid critics of their own and each others' work. Their newly developing ability to delay gratification meant that while it was difficult, they were able to work on various other stories as they waited for their turn to "publish" another.

The two teachers structured their writing time in a similar fashion. Beginning with the class clustered on the meeting rug, Kate led a lesson on a specific skill everyone could try. Children then dispersed to their desks with folders and began writing, conferencing, illustrating, or publishing, all at various stages of the process. To pull things together at the end of this time, Kate called a sharing meeting with the children at their desks or once again on the rug. The structure was predictable but the content varied, and the physical moving around provided a chance for a change of pace.

As with many first-year teachers, Linda found her room wanting—she needed to arrange a group meeting space. The lessons, writing time, and sharing meeting were all taking place, but with the students at their individual desks throughout the period. Linda felt that the desks were a physical barrier and a distraction during the meetings: students often read in soft voices, losing the others' attention, and all needed the chance to stretch their legs.

Both teachers used modeling techniques, writing in front of the class, demonstrating how they chose new topics, modeling questions to ask of peers. Kate once remarked, "I hear myself in them, asking questions I've asked of them so many times, but if I listen longer, their own voice and opinions start to come through."

Conferencing, another technique long used in reading class, took place in a multiplicity of ways, varying with the purpose and the participants. Perhaps one student was ready to edit for mechanics and needed instruction about punctuation marks. Another was "stuck" and needed a pre-writing, brainstorming conference. Yet another time the entire class was ready to learn a capitalization rule.

In general, a wide variety of instructional practices occurred if one split the carefully integrated plans into discrete components. Modeling independent work, varied pacing, individualized learning, small-group and whole-class discussions, interviews and research on particular topics, and listening and responding to others' work were all used by Linda and Kate to help meet their goals.

Beliefs About Supervision

Because my situation was not a hypothetical one, I was able to interact with Kate and Linda about my observations. While I will use our work together as an example of peer collaboration, I would use a similar approach with other colleagues.

In addition to my beliefs about effective and high-quality teaching, my views about supervision influence my approach when working with teachers. To work effectively with colleagues, one must have a clear understanding of and commitment to the subject area, philosophies about good teaching and supervision, the trust and respect of one's colleagues, and strong communication skills, both as an empathetic listener and as a constructive consultant and advisor.

Assessing the Teacher's Needs

I have a responsibility to assess the teacher's needs: what we are going to work on or toward. I can learn about these in several ways. Most important is to ask the teacher about her own needs and goals. Kate was clear about hers: "I want help in getting the writing workshop going, in how to conference, how to publish, how to choose objectives for the lessons." Linda was more general, "I really want to start the writing in my class, but I want you to tell me about everything—the room, what I'm doing, anything that occurs to you." (A common need for a first-year teacher.) In my experience, most teachers can discuss areas they would like to improve, or that fall below their own expectations for their teaching.

A second source for determining a teacher's needs is my observation of the teacher's work based on my views of effective teaching. Linda, for example, was eager to structure the learning experiences to allow for lessons, writing, and sharing. However, her furniture restraints interferred with her goals. Developmentally, Kate's expectations for her 1st graders to work independently had to be adjusted from her memories of last year's class in June, and a plan had to be developed to lead the children toward increasingly independent behavior.

The third source is our discussions together in evaluating student work and our own teaching. It may be appropriate to design a sequence of goals for the children as they change and as the teacher learns more about a specific subject or instructional technique. Linda's immediate goal was to rearrange the room, but she would develop other goals once this one was met. Because I saw the teachers over time, teaching goals could evolve as a natural and desired result of daily discussion and analysis of the ongoing class workshops.

Assessing the Teacher's Philosophy About Help or Supervision

It is important to understand the teacher's previous experience with supervision or help and her attitude toward peer collaboration in genereal, in order to determine what role will be the most productive for me.

Kate

Kate, who is formally observed several times a year as required by our contract, saw our work together as quite different. She had invited me into her room and had ideas about how we would work together: planning for and modeling conferences and lessons, giving feedback when we observed each other, developing guidelines for editing and publishing, and providing general support for the program and the chance to discuss the children's growth in writing.

Among Kate's strengths are her ability to determine what she wants help with and her wide repertoire of instructional techniques. I could be a sounding board for her about what was going on in her classroom through my observations and careful evaluation of student-writing folders. The students were responding well to the physical set-up of the writing time and were beginning to take risks with "invented" spelling.

In her enthusiasm, Kate often felt impatient with their pace. After some discussion, we decided that she would keep the writing time short and successful for the students, lengthening it when they seemed more involved and ready. We focused on what kinds of lessons or short-term objectives would be appropriate for her class, ways of increasing their willingness to write, and on improving the climate and attitude in the room. We arranged to visit another writing class in the district to help establish a supportive network and to gain perspective on Kate's room.

Linda

As a student teacher, Linda had been observed and critiqued frequently by both her college supervisor and her cooperating teacher. This recent experience helped shape her attitude toward my role. She viewed my help as a continuation of this in that she left it up to me to determine her greatest needs and invited comment on "anything you see that I should change—anything."

As noted when Diallo and Joe were sharing, the physical set-up of the room interfered with Linda's goals that her students share their stories and help each other to improve their writing through peer response. We arranged with the principal for a meeting-area rug and discussed several room arrangements that would enhance writing time and also work toward Linda's goals in math, reading, science, and social studies.

Rather than relying on phrases like "nice work" when conferencing with students, Linda needed more direction and experience in judging how to expand, reinforce, question, or direct the students' work. In reading through their writing at night or listening during a conference, Linda would try to pinpoint a priority for that student, helping to focus her questions and to be specific. This concentration would also help focus the sharing meetings, which could be used as whole-class peer conferences, with Linda guiding the questions and responses.

The Future: Plans for Teacher Growth to Include Self-Sufficiency

In addition to working toward mutually agreed upon and incidental goals, part of our task together is to help the teacher develop strategies and resources that will continue after I have gone. In order to articulate their needs, teachers must develop their analytic and self-critiquing skills in the *context of writing* and learn which resources are appropriate for which needs.

Linda worried. "I don't know how I'll do it on my own with 25 of them or if I'll know which step comes next." She decides to attend inservice workshops when she can and to write down specific questions for me as she works with her class. With the principal's approval, we arrange a week-long return visit for me in a month.

Factors that Favor Peer Collaboration

After working as a writing facilitator for a year, I can identify several factors that have helped to make this colleagueship an effective means of improving instruction. First, the supervision is available because I have something to offer. I am seen as having expertise in a subject area, and my contribution is not a contractual, supervisory obligation. My authority is based solely on my colleagues' perception that I can help them with the teaching of writing, not on my institutional position. Second, the relationship is initiated by the teachers who wish to improve their writing instruction. Third, I bring empathy and credibility to my role. I understand the teachers' working conditions, *and* they are aware of writing programs in my classroom. Fourth, my daily release time and constant presence in the school building make me available for the frequent formal and informal contacts needed for teacher growth. Fifth and last, beyond careful analysis of our work together, there is no teacher evaluation involved. Such evaluation is often tied to—and clouds—the goal of improving instruction.

Some of these factors are situation-specific, while others are fairly universal.

Time as a Factor: Teacher Growth and Curricular Changes Need Time

Due to the complexities of today's schools, principals, who often act as supervisors, frequently find themselves faced with a multitude of unexpected situations. As a result, they become reactive rather than proactive. In the face of constant demands, many are increasingly forced to function as "educational managers" (Howell, 1981) rather than instructional leaders, no matter what their intentions or expertise.

Formal contractual supervision, which often occurs once or twice a year, does not serve to help teachers grow and learn over time. Acquiring a new teaching skill or attitude usually requires considerable trial and error. My daily release time as a facilitator reveals a classroom and a teacher's approach rarely seen by harried administrators: which variables are constant, which teacher strengths might be built upon. I also get the chance to discuss these with the teacher frequently. My role as facilitator has allowed me the time in my colleagues' rooms that my principal does not have.

Initiative and Motivation

When the initiative for improvement comes from teachers themselves, chances are that the attitudinal climate will encourage change, and the teachers will take responsibility for their own growth. As Kate said, "I feel I'm using you, taking advantage of something you know. I asked you to work with me because, in observing you last year, you had something specific that I wanted." Kate wanted me to function as what Eisner (1982) describes as a consultant: "Someone one talks to, someone who provides views to consider," noting, too, that "the initiative is with the individual who invites the consultant."

Empathy and Credibility

"Colleagues have the value of proximity, immediacy, and a first-hand knowledge of the other's work-space" (Alfonso, 1982). Kate and I wasted little time describing the frustrations and benefits of our open-space building and diverse student population, as we had worked together for over a year. Similarly, we had already developed the common vocabulary and compatibility of technical and educational jargon that evolves when teachers work together over time. Colleagues bring an empathy, an understanding of the impact of certain policies, and even a familiarity with the needs of specific children.

A Focus on Instructional Improvement

In addition to possessing empathy, time, and credibility, peer collaborators are freed of the typical obligation to merge evaluation with the charge of improving instruction, save for rigorous evaluation of the day's lessons in order to plan for the next. Formal observations, infrequent as they often are, may tempt teachers to repeat previous safe "performances." When the sole purpose of an observation is teacher growth, the freedom to take risks encourages the designing of lessons that might produce unexpected outcomes. Kate once remarked that she learned the most from our attempts that didn't work.

In addition to the factors listed above, the following conditions, designed for our project, have helped to facilitate our peer collaboration:

• Ongoing district workshops on teaching writing.

• Superintendent's and principal's financial support of release-time and an excellent teacher assistant to substitute for 45 minutes daily.

● Visiting days encouraged by the district.

● Periodic "spots" on agendas at faculty meetings for progress reports and presentations on the teaching of writing and general support from the principal.

● My own experience in teaching writing.

● The camaraderie of the teachers, their *option* to request my help, and their professional interest in instructional improvement.

As I work with other teachers, Kate and Linda have taken on the responsibility of working with colleagues, too, and the project has snowballed. Teachers who were on the periphery during initial stages of the project have found ways to become involved; discussions in the teachers' room often center around writing, as do recess-supervision conversations. A majority of the classroom teachers have asked for help in teaching writing, and in order to meet this encouraging demand and yet maintain the quality that time and high expectations can bring, we will have to develop a new structure for our peer collaboration. Perhaps, in our building, we are redefining teaching to include working with peers. We use our time together to improve instruction, and we begin to think of one another as resources. In helping each other, we not only improve our own teaching of writing but establish a grassroots structure for peer collaboration.

References

Alfonso, Robert J., and L. Goldsberry. "Colleagueship in Supervision." In *Supervision of Teaching*, edited by Thomas J. Sergiovanni. Alexandria, Va.: Association for Supervision and Curriculum Development, 1982 yearbook), 101.

Cogan, Morris L. *Clinical Supervision*. Boston: Houghton Mifflin, 1973.

"Developmental Characteristics of Children and Youth." Chart. Alexandria, Va.: Association for Supervision and Curriculum Development, 1975.

Eisner, Elliot W. "An Artistic Approach to Supervision." In *Supervision of Teaching*, edited by Thomas J. Sergiovanni. Alexandria, Va.: Association for Supervision and Curriculum Development, 1982 yearbook), 54.

Graves, Donald. *Writing: Teachers and Children at Work*. Exeter, N.H.: Heinemann Educational Books, 1983.

Howell, Bruce. "Profile of the Principalship." *Educational Leadership* 38 (January 1981): 333-336.

Ryan, Kevin, and others. *Biting the Apple: Accounts of First Year Teachers*. New York: Longman, Inc., 1980.

Stone, Joseph L., and Joseph Church. *Childhood and Adolescence: A Psychology of the Growing Person*. New York: Random House, Inc., 1973.

Tyler, Ralph W. *Basic Principles of Curriculum and Instruction*. Chicago: University of Chicago Press, 1949.

6. Teacher Expectations: A Framework for Exploring Classrooms

Thomas L. Good and Rhona S. Weinstein

Teachers' Expectations Are Important

We know that children's interest in and skills for academic scholarship begin to develop long before they enter school. Many educators and researchers have identified family practices (from symbolic appreciation for learning to actual instruction by parents) that contribute to early acquisition of basic academic skills. Preschool children vary in their ability to process information and exhibit different learning styles as well. As a result, students' innate capacities and early experiences, along with parents' beliefs and behaviors, affect students' abilities and interests in learning. In addition, we believe that teachers' expectations for students also affect how much students learn in school.

Teacher expectations are defined here as inferences that teachers make about the future academic achievement of students and about the types of

Thomas L. Good is Professor of Education, Center for Research in Social Behavior, University of Missouri, Columbia. Rhona S. Weinstein is Associate Professor of Psychology, Psychology Department, University of California-Berkeley.

Authors' note: We acknowledge the support provided by the Center for Research in Social Behavior, University of Missouri-Columbia, and thank Diane Chappell for typing the manuscript and Gail Hinkel for providing editorial advice. Both authors contributed equally to this chapter.

classroom assignments that students need, given their abilities. In particular, we are interested in the relationship between teacher expectations and classroom behavior that is a self-fulfilling prophecy. A self-fulfilling prophecy occurs when an erroneous belief leads to behavior that makes the original false belief become true. Self-fulfilling prophecies are the most dramatic effect of teacher expectation because they involve changes in a student's behavior. Sustaining expectations are also very important. Cooper and Good (1983) use this term to refer to situations in which teachers fail to see student potential and hence do not respond to some students in a way that encourages them to fulfill their potential. Thus, self-fulfilling expectations bring about changes in student performance, whereas sustaining expectations prevent change. Teachers need to be concerned about the influences on students of both types of expectations.

Expectations: A Framework

Both authors have had considerable experience conducting and interpreting research on classroom expectations. In the past this research focused on what teachers do in the classroom. More recent studies have examined student classroom behavior as well as how teachers and students interpret classroom behavior. We believe that the latter approach is a useful way to examine classroom behavior. An understanding of the literature on expectation aids in the identification of classroom conditions that may impede the academic performance of certain students and thus provides a basis upon which more, if not all, students can be successful in the classroom.

The concepts and findings associated with expectation research provide guidelines or frames of reference that allow teachers to think about and attempt to alter classroom environments. These classroom theories or concepts can help teachers to increase the number of dimensions they use in thinking about student performance and the number (and range) of alternative teaching strategies available. The concepts also encourage teachers to consider the possible consequences of selected actions on various students (Good and Power, 1976).

No Simple Answers

It is important to realize that classrooms are complex environments that involve a great deal of interpretation of ambiguous behavior by both teachers and students. In some classes, students can, with much agreement, identify differential patterns in teachers' interactions with different students (Weinstein et al., 1982). This awareness can be informative for students and suggest what the teacher expects from them. Students can also learn about differences in relative ability among students from such differential interactions. At other times, various students can differentially interpret similar teacher behaviors. For example, some students may perceive a teacher question during class discussion primarily as a chance to perform; other students may view the same question more negatively, emphasizing the teacher's evaluation.

Furthermore, in a single class, students' interpretations of what is meaningful and important can vary considerably, especially when students' social backgrounds are diverse. For example, students from some cultures have difficulty understanding that one can ask a question to evaluate understanding. In their cultures, one asks a question only to obtain an answer. Although many behaviors in the classroom do not involve such varied meanings, teachers and students often interpret the same behavior quite differently.

In this chapter we describe major findings concerning the dynamics of expectancy processes in the classroom. Following the development of a framework for thinking about expectations and how they function, we apply the framework to observations made of two classrooms during a reading and language arts lesson. Our purpose here is to suggest ways in which teachers can become more aware of how they may communicate inappropriately low expectations to students and how teachers might improve the conditions they create for student learning.

How Teachers Communicate Expectations

Brophy-Good Model

Various models describe how teacher performance expectations for students influence student behavior (see Brophy and Good, 1974; Rosenthal, 1974; Cooper, 1979; Cooper and Good, 1983; Marshall and Weinstein, 1984; Weinstein, 1985). Perhaps the earliest explicit model for studying the expectation communication chain in the classroom was described by Brophy and Good (1970a). The model they proposed follows: (1) The teacher expects specific behavior and achievement from particular students. (2) Because of these different expectations, the teacher behaves differently toward various students. (3) This treatment tells students what behavior and achievement the teacher expects from them and affects their self-concepts, achievement motivation, and aspirations. (4) If this treatment is consistent over time, and if students do not resist or change it in some way, it will shape their achievement and behavior. High-expectation students will be led to achieve at high levels, while the achievement of low-expectation students will decline. (5) With time, students' achievement and behavior will conform more and more closely to that originally expected of them.

Research on the Model

Research based on the Brophy and Good model clearly shows that many teachers vary sharply in their interaction with high- and low-achieving students. Good and Brophy (1984) summarize some of the common ways in which teachers have been found to differ in their behavior toward students believed to be more and less capable: (1) waiting less time for lows to answer; (2) giving lows answers or calling on someone else rather than trying to improve their responses by giving clues or additional opportunities to respond; (3) inappropriate reinforcement . . . rewarding inappropriate behavior or incorrect answers by lows; (4) criticizing lows more often for failure; (5) praising lows less frequently than highs for success; (6) failing to give feedback to the public responses of lows; (7) generally paying less attention to lows or interacting with them less frequently; (8) calling on lows less often to respond to questions; (9) seating lows further from the teacher; (10) demanding less from lows; (11) interacting with lows more privately than publicly and monitoring and structuring their activities more closely; (12) differential administration or grading of tests and assignments in which highs but not lows are given the benefit of the doubt in borderline cases; (13) less friendly interactions with lows, including less smiling and fewer other nonverbal indicators of support; (14) briefer and less informative feedback to the questions of lows; (15) less eye contact and other nonverbal communication of attention and responsiveness; (16) use of effective but time-consuming methods with lows when time is limited; (17) giving longer reading assignments, providing more time for discussion of the story, and generally demanding more from high than low groups; (18) interrupting lows more often when they make reading mistakes; (19) less often asking low groups higher-level comprehension questions.

These findings illustrate ways in which teachers may communicate inappropriate expectations in the classroom. Clearly, to bring about self-fulfilling or sustaining prophecies, it would not be necessary for teachers to exhibit all of the behaviors listed above. If teachers assign lows considerably less content than they can handle, that factor alone will reduce student learning (even if teachers call on lows frequently, etc.). Similarly, if teachers give low students less time to practice reading (or allow allocated time to be frequently interrupted), this could be a sufficient condition for reducing student achievement.

Implications of differential behavior. It is important to examine the implications of such teacher behaviors for low achievers. It seems that a good strategy for slow students who face such conditions would be not to volunteer or not to respond when called upon because such an instructional system discourages students from taking risks. To the extent that students are motivated to reduce risk and ambiguity—and many argue that students are strongly motivated to do so (see Doyle, 1979)—it seems that students would become more passive in order to reduce the risk of public failure.

Grouping Effects

We have seen that teachers often behave differently with high- and low-achieving students. Other studies suggest that teachers behave differently and have varied effects on the performance of students who are assigned to different ability groups in the same classroom. Weinstein (1976) noted in a study of three 1st grade classrooms that the reading group to which students were assigned contributed a significant increment of 25 percent to the prediction of mid-year achievement over what could be predicted on the basis of students' initial readiness scores. Although Weinstein did not find differences in teaching behavior that would account for the differential effects of group assignment, group placement may still represent an expectation effect that influences student achievement directly (by exposing students to poor or good reading models) or indirectly (by decreasing or increasing motivation).

Eder (1981) also studied 1st grade reading groups in one class and found that students who were likely to have difficulty in learning to read generally were assigned to groups whose social context was not conducive to learning. In part this was because assignments to 1st grade reading groups were based on kindergarten teachers' recommendations, and a major criterion of placement was the maturity of the students as well as their perceived ability.

Most of the students in Eder's study had similar academic abilities and socioeconomic backgrounds (middle class). None of the students could read prior to entering 1st grade; however, there were probably some important differences with respect to various reading-readiness skills. Still, their progress in reading could plausibly be related to the reading instruction they received in 1st grade. Despite the relative homogeneity of these pupils, the 1st grade teacher still grouped them differentially for reading instruction.

Because the most immature, inattentive students were assigned to low groups, it was almost certain that these groups would cause more managerial problems than others, especially early in the year. Indeed, because the teacher was often distracted from a student reader in the low group who was responding (because of the need to manage other students in the group), students often provided the correct word for the reader. Readers were not allowed time to ascertain words on their own, even though less than a third of the students interviewed reported that they liked to be helped and most thought this help interfered with their learning. Eder's work indicates that low students had less time than highs to correct their mistakes before other students or the teacher intervened.

Eder also found that students in the low group spent 40 percent of their listening time not attending to the lesson (versus 22 percent in the high group). Low students frequently read out of turn, adding to the general confusion. Eder reported twice as many teacher "managerial acts" in the low groups as in the high group (157 versus 61) and found that turn interruption increased over the course of the year. Due to management problems, frequent interruptions, and less actual teaching, low students may inadvertently have been encouraged to respond to social and procedural aspects of the reading group rather than to academic tasks.

Alloway (1984) found that favorable expectations expressed toward individual students in the classroom may have been undermined by low expectancy-related comments teachers made to *groups* of students. A systematic record of expressed expectation comments that occurred outside of the teacher-pupil dyad illustrates some of the *low-group* expectations that teachers communicated: (1) "You children are slower, so please get on with your work now" (low-expectancy group). (2) "I'll be over to help you slow ones in a moment. This group can go on by itself." (3) "You need this extra time, so pay attention to me, please." (4) "The blue group will find this hard." Alloway also pointed out low expectations in the form of labels teachers gave to individual students: "Hurry up, Robyn. Even you can get this right; Michelle, you're slow as it is. You haven't got time to look around the classroom." Utilizing a broader expectation framework, Alloway found other ways in which teachers communicated inappropriate expectations to individual students and groups of students.

As Hiebert (1983) and Borko and Eisenhart (in press) note, reading lessons for high-ability and low-ability students also show marked contrasts. For highs, the reading lesson is a loosely structured event with opportunities to read aloud or silently, give multiple answers, interpret reading passages, and answer meaningful questions. In contrast, low-ability students experience a more highly structured format in which decoding skills, short specific answers, and appropriate behavior are stressed. In a study of a single elementary school, Hart (1982) noted that reading for low-ability students was a group experience in which these students met at an earlier time, were part of a smaller group, had more special arrangements, and more extra helpers. With lows, teachers emphasized decoding rather than understanding language. In general, low students were kept busy during reading group, while highs had more fun and more often attempted to understand what they read.

Complex Interaction Variables

In addition to the influences of grouping and feedback to individual students, several general context variables affect how students will respond to these grouping and individual variables. Marshall and Weinstein (1984) provide a complex model specifying how a variety of classroom environment variables (that provide opportunities for students to observe differential teacher behavior) may reflect different teacher performance expectations that in turn influence students' own expectations and performance. Two of these general variables are discussed here, locus of responsibility for learning and evaluation.

Student choice. Teachers control the locus of responsibility for learning and evaluation in classroom, and they can share that responsibility to varying degrees with individual students. Marshall and Weinstein argue that the amount of responsibility students have may affect their susceptibility to teachers' expectations. Previous research has shown that students perceive that teachers offer more choices to high achievers than to low achievers and that teachers give more directions to low achievers. It may well be that when teachers allow high-achieving students to plan their own goals and projects, the goals that these students select and the procedures they follow in their work may show more variety and thus diminish the comparability of the products they are working on (Rosenholtz and Rosenholtz, 1981). It appears that in some classrooms, high achievers benefit from having more choices. First, their work is less open to comparison with others in their group. Second, the freedom to pursue to some extent *their own* learning activities in and of itself may motivate high achievers to work harder than they would if they had to follow a simple set of directions, as low-achieving students must often do.

Self-evaluation. Shared responsibility for evaluation is not a part of many classrooms. Teachers generally do most of the evaluation, and when students do have the opportunity to check answers it is usually against an answer sheet that the teacher has prepared. When the teacher is the evaluator, students are dependent upon the teacher for judgments about their ability, and their performance is more susceptible to teacher expectations.

In contrast, when the teacher encourages students to evaluate their own performance and to develop their own standards and criteria, evaluation may be more private and may be based on more varied criteria that are more realistic and understandable to students. Thus, students may be less vulnerable to external evaluation pressures. For example, being called on as frequently as other students to make public responses may be less important in a classroom in which students spend considerable time setting their own learning goals and engaging in self-evaluation. Clearly, the locus of responsibility for learning and evaluation will mediate grouping effects and the individual response opportunities that students receive.

Individual Differences in Expectation Communication

Why do some teachers noticeably differentiate their behavior toward high- and low-achieving students, while others show only minimal differences in their behavior? Following the work of Dweck and Elliott (1983), Marshall and Weinstein (1984) contend that teachers' beliefs about the nature of intelligence may influence their classroom behavior. Some teachers view intelligence as an entity and thus see it as relatively stable and singular in nature. Other teachers view intelligence as incremental, as a repertoire of skills and knowledge that can be increased.

Teachers who hold an entity view of intelligence would be more likely to place students in a stable hierarchy according to performance expectations and to treat these students differently on the basis of expectations. Marshall and Weinstein argue that low achievers in the classrooms of these teachers may use performance information to make detrimental social comparisons.

When such students perceive that they are treated differently according to their ability, they may use this information to compare themselves with other students and may see themselves as less capable and expect less of themselves. However, in classrooms where teachers hold an incremental view of intelligence, teacher statements and curriculum assignments communicate the belief that each student has the ability to improve regardless of current status, that individual differences in rates and modes of learning are normal, and that students can learn from those who have already acquired certain skills.

Good (1983) argues that a basic cause of differential teacher behavior is that classrooms are busy and complex environments that make it difficult for teachers to assess accurately the frequency and quality of their interactions with individual students. In addition, much classroom behavior has to be *interpreted* before it has meaning. Research suggests that once a teacher develops an expectation about a student, the teacher interprets subsequent ambiguous behavior or events in a way consistent with the original expectation (Anderson-Levitt, in press). Thus, teachers who have developed ways to monitor classroom behavior more systematically and more accurately and who are willing to examine classroom behavior from multiple viewpoints may be more likely to communicate rigorous expectations to all students.

According to Good (1983), a second reason why teachers differentiate more or less in their behavior toward high- and low-achieving students involves *causality*. Some teachers believe that they can and will influence student learning (for example, see Brophy and Evertson, 1976). Such teachers may interpret student failure as a need for more instruction, more clarification, and eventually increased opportunity to learn. Other teachers, because they assign blame rather than assume partial responsibility for student failure, may interpret failure as a need to provide less challenge and fewer opportunities to learn. This view considers teachers' self-efficacy beliefs. Teachers who have doubts about their ability to instruct certain types of students or to teach certain subject matter may communicate low expectations to students, just as teachers who hold low expectations for students may communicate these expectations.

A third explanation for differential teacher behavior involves the way in which students present themselves to the teacher. Because of linguistic deficiencies or lack of awareness of social cues, some students may have much more difficulty convincing teachers that they know the material than will other students. Thus, there are different reasons why teachers may hold and communicate low expectations, and each of these explanations applies in certain contexts.

If expectation-related problems are to be dealt with adequately in the classroom, teachers need the opportunity to see and to comprehend the effects of some of their decisions. Opportunities to observe other teachers and receive feedback about one's own teaching, the chance to interview students, and opportunities for reflection are all ways in which teachers can improve their understanding of classroom events (Good and Brophy, 1984).

Toward a Framework

In summary, we have reviewed a number of studies that suggest that *some* teachers behave differently toward students or groups of students they believe are high or low in ability. Students are often aware of differential teacher behavior, and such behavior can have direct (less opportunity to practice) and indirect effects (students not trying) on students' performance. The more complex and formal model that guided our thinking has been presented elsewhere (Marshall and Weinstein, 1984). The research findings on expectations are extremely complex. However, we attempted to present these findings as concisely as possible in the expectancy framework. Our classroom observations were guided by the major expectation dimensions presented in Table 6.1 (p.72).

Classroom Observations

We have stressed that research on teacher expectations yields findings and concepts that can help teachers to assess classroom communication and to be more sensitive to the ways in which they might express low expectations. To test this assumption, we observed a reading lesson in two classrooms (a 1st grade and a 5th/6th grade class) in a single school during one instructional day.

The communication of expectations for student performance can occur at a variety of levels: school standards and beliefs, norms for grade-level accomplishment, expectations for each classroom within a grade level, differential treatment of groups of children within a classroom, and differential treatment of individual children within a classroom. Our relatively brief observations did not permit a systematic look at the communication of expectations at each of these levels. However, we did learn that the school in which we observed had been chosen for participation in a school improvement project in the district, in part because of the low achievement of its students. This school practiced ability grouping at the classroom level, and thus the 1st grade we observed contained average achievers and the 5th/6th combination class consisted of high-ability 5th graders and low-ability 6th graders. This context provides an important frame for our observations.

There are also several limitations to our observations. First, we saw only a small sample of behavior that may not represent typical behavior in these classes. Second, both classrooms were in an inner-city school with predominantly black students and teachers. As white observers, we may have missed salient communication cues (both positive and negative) that would have been obvious to other observers. Furthermore, both classes were taught in whole-class settings, and thus it was not possible to explore some

Table 6.1. General Dimensions of Teachers' Communication of Differential Expectations and Selected Examples

	Students believed to be MORE capable have:	Students believed to be LESS capable have:
TASK ENVIRONMENT Curriculum, procedures, task definition, pacing, qualities of environment	More opportunity to perform publicly on meaningful tasks.	Less opportunity to perform publicly, especially on meaningful tasks (supplying alternate endings to a story vs. learning to pronounce a word correctly).
	More opportunity to think.	Less opportunity to think, analyze (since much work is aimed at practice).
GROUPING PRACTICES	More assignments that deal with comprehension, understanding (in higher-ability groups).	Less choice on curriculum assignments—more opportunity to work on drill-like assignments.
LOCUS OF RESPONSIBILITY FOR LEARNING	More autonomy (more choice in assignments, fewer interruptions).	Less autonomy (frequent teacher monitoring of work, frequent interruptions).
FEEDBACK AND EVALUATION PRACTICES	More opportunity for self-evaluation.	Less opportunity for self-evaluation.
MOTIVATIONAL STRATEGIES	More honest/contingent feedback.	Less honest/more gratuitous/less contingent feedback.
QUALITY OF TEACHER RELATIONSHIPS	More respect for the learner as an individual with unique interests and needs.	Less respect for the learner as an individual with unique interests and needs.

dimensions related to expectancy communication (such as different teacher interaction patterns with various ability groups).

1st Grade Reading Lesson

The lesson we observed involved whole-class instruction about the identification of beginning word sounds. Students then had the opportunity to identify "w" words in a free-response format (e.g., "Who can give me a w word? Who can give me another word that begins with a w?"). At another point in the lesson, the teacher read a poem (Star light, Star bright. . . .) and then asked students to name words in the poem that began with a particular sound. Finally, students had to complete "tree" charts (word trees) as a seat-work assignment.

During the public recitation part of the lesson, the teacher called on individual students for answers. learning was reinforced by repetition, either by the teacher or by the class in chorus. Children said letters aloud, held up their own copies of letters, and identified letters in a seatwork assignment that followed the class drill. The activity was highly teacher-directed and emphasized the rules of appropriate participation and responding. These rules appeared on lists on the wall and in the teacher's comments to the class. The teacher spoke loudly and clearly (with somewhat exaggerated enunciation). The teacher's unclear task directions and noise in the classroom complicated things. She frequently lapsed into long asides in the middle of class discussions: "Yes, that's a good word—that reminds me that vegetables are very important for you. If you want to be strong when you grow up, you have to eat a balanced diet. You know, when I was a little girl my father used to say. . . . Now, who can remember another word in the poem?" Furthermore, because the teaching segment was fragmented (often interrupted by the teacher's asides), students called on late in the discussion faced a more complex task than students who responded earlier. That is, after other students had identified a number of "w" words from the poem, and as the length of time since the poem was read and the number of teacher interruptions increased, it was more difficult for students to cite "w" words.

The students sat passively and whispered answers quietly when called upon. In this particular lesson, the narrowness of the task, its seeming unrelatedness to the act of reading, the slow pace, the heavy focus on rules rather than content, and the narrow range of student skills called upon, all decreased student involvement. The task students were engaged in did not involve a wide range of skills. Thus, opportunities to give a correct answer in front of the class were limited. Students were slouching and sleepy; many sat woodenly throughout the lesson. Though the teacher told the students they were "big boys and girls" and had given "wonderful sounds," the nature of the task and the teacher's tone implied instead that students needed a lot of drilling.

Seating assignments of the students around two tables were related to patterns of calling on the students. The teacher interacted more frequently with the students at the table closest to the front, although she was clearly aware of the need to engage all students. At times she walked to the back table and attempted to engage noninvolved children. The basis for these seating assignments was not clear.

Student choice in this lesson was limited. As a result, students' interest was low, and they were not required to use their full capabilities. The extensive direction also emphasized the teacher's version of right and wrong answers and behaviors. The whole-class activity heightened the publicness of the teacher's evaluation of students' answers. We observed attempts on the part of the teacher to soften the sting when a student was not able to answer a question; she noted that one child had been absent and asked him to pick another student to answer the question. Yet despite these interventions, the task at hand remained very narrow, limiting the ways children could succeed in the lesson.

With regard to feedback and evaluation, we could see that the teacher did not allow all students an equal opportunity to participate, she gave varied prompts after an incorrect answer or no answer, and that the quality of praise was different for various students. In one instance, we saw a child who was aware that he had been treated differently. The teacher did not recognize his answer, although it was clearly correct. Later in the lesson, the teacher became aware of her mistake and asked whether someone had given that answer. The student rose in his seat in anticipation, but she did not see him. She acknowledged that she had made a mistake and ended the interaction. He sat down, visibly disappointed. We cannot know what the pupil inferred from the interaction without interviewing him. However, this episode reveals the differential treatment that 1st graders appear to perceive, from forceful "very goods" (which this teacher used a lot of), to failure to recognize a right answer, with an accompanying admission of error but no positive feedback.

In summary, the teacher showed an awareness of the need to call on all the children, but the ways she did differed subtly. In one interaction, she turned to "someone I haven't heard from today." In identifying this student as someone she hadn't heard from and in asking "help me," perhaps in the context of the narrow repetitive task involving oral recitation, that call-on had a different feel. One wonders what the child felt about being "put on the spot."

The 5th/6th Grade Language Arts Class

This classroom environment also communicated low expectations for students' accomplishments. We were struck by the barren nature of the room. The wall clock was broken, there were few books around, virtually nothing was on the walls, and little student work was visible.

The lesson we observed also emphasized rules and procedures. The teacher dominated, quizzing the students about the meaning of topic sentences and main ideas and about the instructions for the class assignment. The task was narrowly defined. It seems inappropriate that students who had studied paragraphing and had been reviewing related material for several days were not required to write a paragraph, or at least to read several selections and identify which groups of sentences were paragraphs. Even the latter activity would have allowed active involvement and discussion among students with regard to why some groups of sentences were not paragraphs. This close monitoring of student behavior and attention to minor details (demanding procedural exactness—the precise words of the text in the precise order), and the lack of any discussion of the value or meaningfulness of the topic being studied, communicated low performance expectations for these students.

Furthermore, the pace was so painfully slow that the students (and observers) either became restless or sleepy. Although the teacher was aware of these symptoms, she attributed them to the students' lack of control and to students' lack of ability ("We've been on this a week"; "What am I fighting, City Hall?"). Only once did the teacher express an awareness that perhaps she was not making herself clear.

Further compounding the problem of an inappropriate task was the fact that the teacher expected students at both grade levels to cover the same material. From an inspection of the curriculum, we learned that both 5th and 6th graders completed the same task with similar instructions (although procedures were much clearer in the 5th grade text) in their textbooks. The teacher also pointed out that if the 5th grade students did not learn it now, they would have a second opportunity in 6th grade. This redundancy in curriculum, accompanied by a teacher-directed, highly passive mode of delivery, virtually assured that students would not be interested in the lesson, and they were not. Students' boredom was obvious, and it caused their failure to give the teacher the answers she wanted. Sadly, the teacher probably assumed that lack of ability caused the students' inadequate performance.

The focus was on the remediation of low reading achievement rather than on the support and stimulation of *expected* reading and writing accomplishments. This focus was also implied in the teacher's comment to the class as a whole: "If we are going to grow two years, what do we have to do to catch up, class? Run." It was difficult to understand the teacher's low expectations for above-grade-level 5th graders (according to the principal, and based on our own observations, they were better students than the 6th graders). It seems, then, that assigning high-achieving 5th-graders to this classroom with lower-achieving 6th graders resulted in lowered expectations for the younger students' performance.

That the teacher expected little from the students in general was also evidenced by her surprise at one student's excellent reading performance. The feeling that she believed that this was a class of students who "can't get answers" pervaded the lesson. In the context of lowered expectations for all students, the teacher also differentiated among students in the frequency and the quality of her interactions with them. She tended to call only on some students (the students were heterogeneously grouped according to ability at each table, an arrangement that the teacher noted to the class might not work because of disruption). In calling on students, she once announced, "I guess I have to go to a boy." The teacher was clearly conscious that she favored girls by providing them more opportunities to respond. However, in the pattern of interaction we observed, one girl received most of the performance opportunities. A male student expressed to the teacher his awareness of these differential opportunities for students to read aloud ("You don't call on me to read"). In addition, the teacher suggested that there were ability differences among students by comments such as, "I'm going too fast for some people," or "Some people haven't yet finished; you will hold us back."

Despite these distinctions the teacher made between students, the most striking aspect of what we saw during our observations was her communication of low expectations for all the students in the classroom.

The Need for Additional Information

The brevity of our observations and our lack of information about the teacher's and students' perceptions of the lesson put us at a disadvantage in our attempts to make sense of what we saw. There is much we cannot know from this segment. First, how the particular lesson we saw fits into the overall curriculum is a question of great importance. Whether or not the remedial tone we observed in both classrooms was a singular occurrence or a regular feature of instruction is unknown. Sustained observations of instruction in one subject over several weeks would provide important additional information.

Second, it would be useful to know *how* the teacher sees the achievement level and potential of this class relative to other classes she has taught or relative to other classes at the same grade level within this school. Knowing on what basis the teacher distinguishes between the students in the class would enable us to contrast the teacher's behavioral expressions of expectations. Is the teacher's behavior consistent with her beliefs about students and the class?

Third, it would be critical to examine the students' perceptions of the teacher's expectations for their performance, as a class, as 5th versus 6th graders within the class, and as individual students. We would need to examine the ways in which the students interpret the teacher behaviors we have discussed and how their experiences in these particular classrooms have made them aware of their teacher's expectations.

Finally, knowledge about how the school has affected the behaviors of these teachers during instruction in the subject matter in question would enlighten us about how much autonomy the teachers had in making choices about instruction. These additional sources of information would help to clarify whether or not our interpretation of the expectations that are communicated to students is correct and would indicate more clearly changes that are needed. Doubtlessly, the chance to interview students would make us sensitive to other important events that either did not occur during our brief visit or that we did not notice.

Improving Classroom Practice: Some General Reactions

Much of what we saw during the two lessons suggested low expectations for the class as a whole, although the teachers also expressed differential expectations for individual students. This occurred despite an administration report to us that classes were achieving at grade level. Aspects of what we observed in the lesson appeared to diminish most students' motivation and interest in learning. We infer this from students' drowsiness, restlessness, and lack of engagement in the tasks. Students frequently lost their places in the text and were slow getting started.

Our suggestions for change concern six issues. First, the goals of the lessons need to be broadened a great deal. Quizzing students on the meaning of a topic sentence or drilling them on identifying a single letter is too narrow a task to occupy an entire lesson. Students need to relate this information to eventual proficiency in reading and writing and to utilize the information in meaningful ways. Broadening the goals of a lesson speeds up the pace of the lesson. In these classes much time was wasted by the emphasis on procedures and rules of responding, particularly in the 5th/6th grade classroom. The students did not appear to be challenged by the instruction we observed.

Second, more attention needs to be paid to students' ideas and interests, and students need to play a larger role in assessing their own performance. The highly teacher-directed lessons we observed focused student attention on what the teachers thought about the material and on evaluation of students' performance. This did not promote students' feelings of competence. Increased student autonomy in instructional assignments would certainly be expected by 5th/6th grade, but we saw little in these classes. Indeed, if anything, 5th and 6th grade students had fewer opportunities for self-expression and open responding than did the 1st.

Third, opportunities for students to participate and utilize the materials in meaningful ways need to be increased. There was certainly more activity expected from the students in the 1st grade classroom in the form of recitation, holding up letter cards, and making word chart trees, but listening predominated in both classrooms. Students need opportunities to test and practice their knowledge and to be active and engaged.

Fourth, there were few opportunities for students to respond creatively and have their knowledge evaluated in the lessons observed. The questions asked of students required little thought or development of ideas and tapped a very limited part of their intellectual capacity. If the teachers had varied the tasks, the questions asked of students, and the criteria for evaluation, many more students could have experienced success, instead of the small but consistent group of high performers. By diversifying the opportunities for participating and broadening the criteria for assessing students' responses, one also broadens the chances of success.

Fifth, it is important to focus on the positive aspects of learning. Public sharing in a classroom community should affirm accomplishment of intended goals but not focus on any student's lack of success or limited chances of meeting goals. A basic and necessary assumption teachers must hold concerns the teachability of students—all students. Comments to the entire class or to individual students about failure to meet goals or the inability to do so lower students' self-images as readers or writers and reduce motivation. A focus on student success at differentiated tasks can build positive student self-images as learners.

Working With Teachers: A Hypothetical Discussion[1]

We have discussed our reaction to the teaching we observed and have emphasized the need to gather more data in order to verify our interpretations. We now discuss the next step in detail—how we would work with these two teachers to change their behavior. After first determining teachers' beliefs about students and instructional strategies (a procedure likely to produce only minor teacher defensiveness), we would recommend specific instructional alterations (which may threaten some teachers).

In working to improve classrooms it would be important first to measure the teachers' understanding of the lesson and to determine why they instructed as they did. We would want to establish a framework for interpreting their behavior, realizing that teachers can choose a particular instructional style for a variety of reasons. Considering the numerous problems we saw with instruction in the two classrooms, our goal would be to work with the teachers in order to radically change their behavior (that is, make classroom tasks more meaningful, demanding, and interesting for students).

However, if enduring change is to occur, it will be necessary to change the teachers' perceptions of student ability and their beliefs about what activities are most likely to stimulate academic growth. The first step is to determine how teachers perceive the observed lessons and how typical such lessons are. Then we would offer suggestions related specifically to the problems in these two lessons and also to the more general problem of low

---

[1] In writing this section, we assume that we have been asked to consult with a large school district to assist with the implementation of a major school effectiveness project. Individual teachers have the opportunity to be observed, to receive feedback and make decisions about continued assistance, if they choose to do so. Teachers may volunteer to participate for a variety of reasons (both positive and negative). We have no knowledge of why teachers volunteered or if they were pressured by the administration to participate.

expectations. There are countless practical ideas from motivational, developmental, and learning-theory work that we could offer to teachers. However, unless the basic problem of low expectation is solved, any improvement resulting from alterations in instruction is apt to be transitory.

In this exercise we will deal only with the 5th/6th grade teacher, although the 1st grade teacher would benefit immensely from reflective feedback about her teaching. For example, we suspect that the 1st grade teacher is largely unaware of how detrimental her long asides are. Information about the limited attention spans of young children would probably convince her that asking young children to think repeatedly about things other than the lesson causes them to be off-task. Furthermore, we believe that listening to a tape of her lesson would show her that she did not clearly communicate the focus of the lesson to students. She could also note instances of differential communication with high- and low-expectation students and with some coaching attempt to alter her behavior accordingly. In short, enhanced opportunities for reflection and an expanded repertoire of teaching strategies (such as visiting other teachers) would yield a broader perspective and improved instruction.

Intervention with the 5th/6th grade teacher would first need to find a starting point around which to organize a series of continuing efforts. This teacher seems to believe that students' intelligence is largely unalterable and that students in this class share low, limited potential (despite the obvious differences in ability between 5th and 6th grade students). We might begin to discuss the observed lesson at length with the teacher: why she chose it, was it appropriate for all students, how effective the lesson was, what would come next, how much students would learn, alternative lessons that could have been conducted, what students thought about the lesson.

We suspect that this discussion would indicate that the teacher holds low expectations for all students, and that she believes that there are no alternative ways to teach the lesson. If she did suggest alternatives, we would attempt to incorporate them into the intervention.

However, assuming the expression of low expectations and limited plans for dealing with students (low-level drill and structure), we would need to establish with the teacher some basis for altering her expectations. The important thing is that the teacher raise a question that she wants answered. We would organize the intervention in order to enable the teacher to act upon her concerns and insights in order to improve her perception of students' abilities as well as her self-efficacy. If, for example, the teacher actually wondered how much students learned in class, this would provide us a chance to demonstrate students' potential. We might interview three or four students to obtain data showing that students' problems are motivational and instructional, not intellectual. The interview would allow us to model teaching techniques for the teacher. For example, students might be asked to bring a favorite book with them to the interview, in order to show that when they are motivated, students can identify topic sentences. We could demonstrate the *social* value of learning by allowing two students to work together to find the topic sentence in each paragraph. After a few successful exercises, students could write their own topic sentences.

Similarly, the teacher might wonder how other teachers present the same material. In this case, intervention would consist of visiting the classes of competent teachers presenting the material, to show that students of similar ability can learn the material when the teacher presents it appropriately. If possible, the teacher should see two different teachers present a lesson, to illustrate that different approaches to the material can work and that although there are appropriate and inappropriate methods, there are different ways to teach successfully.

Similarly, the question, "How would you have taught the lesson?" would afford good opportunities to alter the teacher's expectations and teaching skills. *Working with the teacher*, it would be possible to develop a lesson outline that would be much more appealing to students than the instruction we observed (a 50-minute talk about what a topic sentence is). An outline may have resembled the following:

1. Ask students to find a favorite story.
2. Briefly review what a topic sentence is.
3. Read paragraphs and tell students what a topic sentence is and explain why.
4. Read two paragraphs that are on overhead projector and ask students to tell what the topic sentence is.
5. Read four paragraphs to students (not on screen). Following each paragraph, ask the students which topic sentence is best for the paragraph (show three or four possible sentences on board).
6. Have students read from their own books and make three or four topic sentences.
7. Discuss a general theme and have students write a topic sentence.
8. Ask them to interview another student and to write a topic sentence that would start their report of the interview.

Having done this, it might be useful to outline another approach to the lesson, showing that there are many ways to involve students and to motivate them appropriately. It would be important to stress that students should be expected to learn and to demostrate their understanding in practical ways (5th and 6th grade students could write monthly class reports). For example, the teacher could point out that after students learn to write paragraphs, they will write a class mystery story, and by the end of the year they will publish a newspaper. Whenever possible, students should have the chance to use new skills and knowledge in practical and enjoyable ways that are meaningful to them.

Other intervention opportunities might be presented if the teacher asks questions such as, "What should I do tomorrow?" or "Would you teach a lesson?" These questions allow constructive discussion about *future* alternatives, students' potential, and the types of learning assignments most likely to elicit student effort and learning.

A teacher's question about reading materials concerning pedagogy ("Can you recommend a good book?") would provide an opportunity to encourage the teacher to examine references that clearly describe appropriate instructional practice. Books such as *Looking in Classrooms* and selected articles from *Educational Leadership* and the *Elementary School Journal* would provide a useful starting point for more focused discussion. Much has been written about important individual differences that students bring to the classroom (Good and Stipek, 1983); however, it is important to realize and to act upon the assumption that teachers are unique and respond in different ways to similar opportunities.

Ultimately, the nature of interactions and recommended activities with this teacher would depend on what we learn about her beliefs. Strategies would have to be designed to fit the *individual* needs of this teacher. Her beliefs about what she can and cannot do in the classroom (efficacy beliefs) would be as important as her beliefs about teaching and students. Progress in changing teacher behavior and classroom plans can go only as fast as the teacher develops. This teacher might be willing to try certain instructional strategies but still cling to inappropriate beliefs about student ability that limit the range of opportunities presented to students. The starting point here is to begin to break the vicious self-defeating cycle of low expectations: the teacher expects little from students, and the insipid class assignment (talking about what topic sentences are for 50 minutes) guarantees that students will exhibit little motivation or performance. Hence, the teacher concludes that students have little potential and continues to make unchallenging assignments based on that assumption.

Conclusion

We believe that expectations play an important role in classroom learning. Various research studies illustrate ways in which some teachers communicate differently with students they believe to be of high and low potential. We summarized this literature, but also expressed our belief that such knowledge is useful only if it is used as a framework for thinking about classrooms rather than as a general definition of how teachers should behave in the classroom.

We knew that research on expectations does not yield an exhaustive set of dimensions or simple answers. However, we did not anticipate that our observations in these classrooms would illustrate this point so vividly. Although our case studies demonstrate a number of important expectation issues, it is interesting that few of these specific instances involving the communication of low expectations are directly comparable to those in the list presented earlier in the chapter. We were most sensitive to low teacher expectations that might be communicated to individuals or groups of students; however, in these classrooms the major problem was the expression of low expectations to *entire classes*. Many of these low class expectations were similar to the expectation communication variables that previous research had shown teachers to express to individuals and groups of students. Thus, it should be clear that lists of expectations are important but not definitive because there are many ways in which teachers can express low expectations. Teachers need to believe in students' ability to learn, strive to find positive ways to encourage student learning, and be sensitive to low expectations that can inhibit student motivation and performance.

We also found new variables in these classes. For instance, our observation convinced us that *when* a teacher calls on students during a class discussion may convey important performance expectations. Similarly, the failure of teachers to require students to use information (we talk about paragraphs but do not write them) and the redundancy of the curriculum from year to year ("If you don't learn this material now you will have a chance to do it again next year.") may unnecessarily erode students' interest and involvement in assigned work and consequently their performance.

We hope that this paper stimulates teachers' thinking about the role of expectations in the classroom and illustrates the need to adjust the expectation framework to particular aspects of individual classrooms. Expectations are expressed in so many ways (choice of curriculum topic, rationale given to students for curriculum topic, performance feedback) that it is not possible to suggest a single combination of behaviors that can lead to the communication of appropriate expectations. It is also difficult to provide advice to teachers, because the varied implications of teacher behavior (call-on, criticism, praise) depend not only on the *behavior* but also on the *context* in which it occurs (what is challenging to a 6th grader may be threatening to a 1st grader). The *quality* or style of the behavior, as well as students' interpretations of teacher behavior, are also important aspects that determine the effects of particular behaviors on students. For example, Brophy (1981) notes that praise may erode or enhance motivation, and Mitman (1985) reports that under some conditions, students may interpret teacher criticism favorably (teacher cares—expects good work).

Teachers must be decision makers and apply concepts and research findings to their own classrooms. For example, as we argued in the literature, there is ample evidence that some teachers call on low-achieving students less often than students they believe to be more capable. It makes little sense, however, to encourage *all* teachers to call on low-achieving students more frequently simply because *some* teachers call on low-achieving students infrequently.

Similarly, it does little good to call on low-achieving students more frequently if these students are generally asked only to answer simple factual questions or asked questions they cannot answer. Likewise, it is unproductive to increase the amount of time that a teacher waits for low-achieving students to respond, independent of a consideration of the particular context. If the teacher asks a factual question, simply waiting and providing clues may be an unproductive use of classroom time (the student either knows the answer or doesn't). However, in a situation involving judgment or analysis, more time to think, and more teacher clues may facilitate student response.

The task of observing, of trying to describe two class periods and to relate them to a broad and complex literature, has led us to ask a new question and to set a new task for ourselves. Is it possible to convey the vast set of findings associated with teacher expectations in a more concise way than we have here? How can we better summarize this literature so as to capture the critical aspects of extant findings and to encourage decision making on the part of those who use the report? Our question now is, can we state a succinct theory of classroom expectations? As we emphasize in this chapter, research that examines classrooms does not yield answers. It yields insights and improvements that are important, but it also presents new problems and challenges.

References

Alloway, N. "Teacher Expectations." Paper presented at the Australian Association for Research in Education Annual Conference, Perth, Australia, 1984.

Anderson-Levitt, K. "Teachers' Interpretations of Student Behavior: A Case Study and a Model." *Elementary School Journal* (in press).

Beckerman, T., and T. Good. "The Classroom Ratio of High- and Low-Aptitude Students and Its Effect on Achievement." *American Educational Research Journal* 18 (1981): 317-327.

Borko, H., and M. Eisenhart. "Students' Conceptions of Reading and Their Reading Experiences in School." *Elementary School Journal* (in press).

Brophy, J. "Teacher Praise: A Functional Analysis." *Review of Educational Research* 51 (1981): 5-32.

Brophy, J., and C. Evertson. *Learning From Teaching: A Developmental Perspective.* Boston: Allyn & Bacon, 1976.

Brophy, J. E., and T. L. Good. "Teachers' Communication of Differential Expectations for Children's Classroom Performance: Some Behavioral Data." *Journal of Educational Psychology* 61 (1970): 365-374.

Brophy, J. E., and T. L. Good. "The Brophy-Good Dyadic Interaction System." In *Mirrors for Behavior: An Anthology of Observation Instruments Continued*, 1970 Supplement (Vols. A and B). Philadelphia: Research for Better Schools, Inc., 1970.

Brophy, J. E., and T. L. Good. *Teacher-Student Relationships.* New York: Holt, Rinehart & Winston, 1974.

Confrey, J., and T. Good. "Academic Progress: Student and Teacher Perspectives." Research Proposal, Michigan State University, Institute for Research on Teaching, 1981.

Confrey, J., and T. Good. *A View From the Back of the Classroom: Integrating Student and Teacher Perspectives of Content With Observational and Clinical Interviews.* In progress.

Cooper, H. M. "Pygmalion Grows Up: A Model for Teacher Expectation Communication and Performance Influence." *Review of Educational Research* 49 (1979): 389-410.

Cooper, H. M., and T. L. Good. *Pygmalion Grows Up. Studies in the Expectation Communication Process.* New York: Longman, 1983.

Doyle, W. "Classroom Task and Students' Abilities." In *Research on Teaching: Concepts, Findings, and Implications*, edited by P. Peterson and H. Walberg. Berkeley, Calif.: McCutchan, 1979.

Dweck, C. S., and E. S. Elliott. "Achievement Motivation." In *Handbook of Child Psychology, IV: Socialization, Personality and Social Development*, edited by P. Mussen and E. M. Hetherington. New York: Wiley, 1983.

Eder, D. "Ability Grouping as a Self-Fulfilling Prophecy: A Microanalysis of Teacher-Student Interaction." *Sociology of Education* 54 (1981): 151-162.

Evertson, C., and J. Green. "Observation as Inquiry and Method." In *Third Handbook of Research on Teaching*, edited by M. Wittrock. Chicago: Rand McNally, in press.

Good T. "Listening to Students Talk About Classrooms." Paper presented at the annual meeting of the American Educational Research Association, Los Angeles, 1981.

Good, T. "Recent Classroom Research: Implications for Teacher Education." Address delivered at the annual meeting of the American Association of Colleges for Teacher Education, Chicago, 1983.

Good, T., and J. Brophy. *Educational Psychology: A Realistic Approach*, 1st ed. New York: Holt, Rinehart & Winston, 1977.

Good, T., and J. Brophy. *Looking in Classrooms*, 3rd ed. New York: Harper & Row, 1984.

Good, T., and C. Power. "Designing Successful Classroom Environments for Different Types of Students." *Journal of Curriculum Studies* 8 (1976): 1-16.

Good, T., and D. Stipek. "Individual Differences in the Classroom: A Psychological Perspective." In *1983 National Study of School Evaluation Yearbook*, edited by G. Fenstermacher and J. Goodlad. Chicago: University of Chicago Press, 1983.

Hart, S. "Analyzing the Social Organization for Reading in One Elementary School." In *Doing the Ethnography of Schooling*, edited by G. Spindler. New York: Holt, Rinehart & Winston, 1982.

Hiebert, E. "An Examination of Ability Grouping in Reading Instruction." *Reading Research Quarterly* 18, 2 (1983): 231-255.

Hunter, D. "Student On-Task Behavior During Reading Group Meetings." Doctoral diss., University of Missouri, 1978.

Levine, J. M. "Social Comparison and Education." In *Teacher and Student Perceptions: Implications for Learning*, edited by J. M. Levine and M. C. Wang. Hillsdale, N.J.: Erlbaum, 1983.

Marshall, H. H., and R. S. Weinstein. "Classrooms Where Students Perceive High and Low Amounts of Differential Teacher Treatment." Paper presented at the annual meeting of the American Educational Research Association, New Orleans, April 1984.

McDermott, R. "Kids Make Sense: An Ethnographic Account of the Interactional Management of Success and Failure in One First Grade Classroom." Doctoral diss., Stanford University, 1976.

Mitman, A. "Teachers' Differential Behavior Toward Higher- and Lower-Achieving Students and Its Relationship With Selected Teacher Characteristics." *Journal of Educational Psychology* 35 (1985): 149-161.

Nicholls, J. G. "Conceptions of Ability and Achievement Motivation: A Theory and Its Implications for Education." In *Learning and Motivation in the Classroom*, edited by S. G. Paris, G. M. Olson, and H. W. Stevenson. Hillsdale, N. J.: Erlbaum, in press.

Pepitone, E. "Social Comparison and Pupil Interaction: Effect of Homogeneous vs. Heterogeneous Classrooms." Paper presented at the annual meeting of the American Educational Research Association, New York, March 1982.

Rosenholtz, S. R., and Rosenholtz, S. J. "Classroom Organization and the Perception of Ability." *Sociology of Education* 54 (1981): 132-140.

Rosenthal, R. *On the Social Psychology of the Self-Fulfilling Prophecy: Further Evidence for Pygmalion Effects and Their Mediating Mechanisms*. New York: MSS Modular Publications, 1974.

Weinstein, R. S. "Reading Group Membership in First Grade: Teacher Behaviors and Pupil Experience Over Time." *Journal of Educational Psychology* 68 (1976): 103-116.

Weinstein, R. S. "Student Mediation of Classroom Expectancy Effects." In *Teacher Expectancies*, edited by J. B. Dusek. Hillsdale, N.J.: Erlbaum, 1985.

Weinstein, R. S., H. H. Marshall, K. A. Brattesani, and S. E. Middlestadt. "Student Perceptions of Differential Teacher Treatment in Open and Traditional Classrooms." *Journal of Educational Psychology* 74 (1982): 678-692.

Weinstein, R. S., and S. E. Middlestadt. "Student Perceptions of Teacher Interactions with Male High and Low Achievers." *Journal of Educational Psychology* 71 (1979): 421-431.

7. Staff Development Through a Collegial Support Group Model

Sam Rodriguez and Kathy Johnstone

The Role of the Site Administrator

Among their many roles and responsibilities, building administrators face the challenging task of providing for the professional development of the teachers at their sites. Often this responsibility is assigned to them because site administrators have ready access to data that provide a clear picture of the strengths and weaknesses of the individual staff members, the needs of the students, the weak areas of the curriculum, the values and desires of the community, and how their school measures up to district goals and objectives. In addition, site administrators know where their schools stand in relation to contractual limits (such as the number of minutes available and used each month for faculty and professional development meetings) and the dollars available for staff development through the local allocation of funds or from grants.

Armed with these data, and knowing they have the responsibility to provide for the professional development of the staff, site administrators are sometimes tempted to plan workshops, provide for attendance at conferences, hire speakers, and, in general, create activities that will address the areas that have been selected for improvement. However, research and experience have demonstrated that teachers often resist having others diag-

Sam Rodriguez is Principal, Potrero Hill Middle School, San Francisco Unified School District. Kathy Johnstone is Adjunct Professor, University of San Francisco.

nosing and prescribing for them. Because they are adults and because they are professionals, teachers know that they, too, should have some power in determining the professional development topics and activities which they need and in which they will participate (Sparks, 1983; Mazarella, 1980).

Such research has demonstrated that teachers want their building administrator to participate in, not provide for, their professional development activities. In addition, this research indicates that teachers have a better opportunity for long-term growth with a long-range program that provides for follow-up practice, coaching, and peer support in solving problems related to the implementation of new skills and behaviors.

Thus, although principals have ready access to data that are helpful in planning for staff development programs, it is clear that more than data is needed if long-term improvement in teachers' skills is to take place. Site administrators must also provide a process for involving teachers in the identification of professional skills that need to be improved and for involving them in the design of activities and programs to provide this skill development. And, since the role of staff development leader is only one of many responsibilities assigned to school principals, we see that principals, alone, cannot possibly provide the time, energy, and expertise needed for coaching and support of new skills and behaviors acquired by teachers.

Building administrators are therefore faced with a two-step challenge. First, they must find a means of sharing information not only about the school's strengths and weaknesses but also its financial and other resources for professional development and problem solving. Then, they must provide a process that enables both administration and faculty to work together to create a professional development program that uses the data regarding school and staff needs and that meets the criteria necessary for the program to demonstrate long-term effectiveness.

The following response to the simulation is written from the perspective of the site administrator. This response provides a review of the two classrooms visited and provides a proposed solution to the challenge described above. In response to the third part of this simulation, a proposal for a collegial support group model is presented that provides for a professional development program to give principals the means to share data about their schools' needs. It also provides them with a process for involving teachers in (1) assessing their own strengths and weaknesses; (2) planning activities that will help them improve their skills; and, (3) providing skills needed for peer coaching, which will facilitate long-term behavior changes.

Simulation Responses

In observing teaching, what are you looking at and for?

Two middle school teachers in a large, metropolitan school district were observed. Both teach 8th grade math in the same school district, yet the two situations are very different. The teachers do not use the same curriculum materials; the student achievement levels in the two locations are years apart; the resources apparently available to the two classrooms are unequal (one has an aide and many shelves full of additional curriculum materials; the other has no aide and appears to have only the basic text series from which to select learning materials); and the curriculum organization of the two teachers varies markedly.

Joseph H. teaches at an inner-city school. The majority of his class appeared to be students with limited fluency in English. There was an aide present during the entire class period. Although the teacher did not use a foreign language with the students, the aide spoke Spanish to the Spanish-speaking students in his group. The students were working at many levels of achievement, but they were all working below the normal level for 8th grade. The teacher had divided the students into three groups. The students appeared to be working in an outcome-based curriculum using a management system that allowed them to work independently of the teacher's guidance for portions of the class period.

Sally G. teaches at a suburban middle school. The lesson being presented appeared to be beyond the normal 8th grade curriculum. The students were not divided into subgroups; the teacher taught the entire class the same lesson at the same time.

Since this was the first observation of these teachers, and since the purpose of the observation was to answer the question, "What do you see?" it was decided to avoid the use of observation forms or instruments. It was believed that more data could be gathered if the observation process was kept as simple and open as possible. Thus, the data were simply an unstructured recording of what was observed.

In a situation other than a simulation such as this, the next step of the supervision cycle would use the data from the preliminary observation to determine (with the teacher's input) a specific area on which to focus subsequent observation and supervision. At that point, observation instruments might be used as an aid to focus both the supervisor and the teacher on the area or skills to be improved.

What do you see?

Although the data were collected in an unstructured, free-form process, examination of the notes taken during the observation revealed that the data appear to fall into three basic categories: the environment, student behavior, and delivery of instruction. Thus, without attempting to filter the actual notes taken during the observation, the data are now arranged under each of these categories. This superimposed structure would facilitate communication during the postobservation conferences with each teacher. The following are notes taken from each of the classroom observations.

OBSERVATION NOTES: JOSEPH H.

A. Environment

The room was divided into three work areas—a teacher-centered area, an aide-centered area, and an independent work area—with seating for about ten students in each area.

Student folders were clearly stored and labeled by period. Homework assignments and lesson topics for the week were listed on the chalkboard for each of the three groups. In the teacher's instruction area was an overhead projector and a chalkboard. In the aide's area was a chalkboard. And in the independent work area were clearly labeled work materials and a variety of resource materials such as compasses, pencils, paper, workbooks, additional texts, and reference books.

The room was clean, well-lit, and well-ventilated. There were colorful pictures on the walls and bulletin boards; although they were math-related, the pictures were unrelated to the math concepts being taught in any of the groups. Class rules regarding student behavior were clearly displayed. In addition, reminders of what to do after finishing tasks and assignments were clearly displayed.

B. Student Behavior

The students walked into the classroom laughing and joking with one another. They picked up their folders and consulted the chalkboard and one another for assignments. They then selected work materials and went to one of the three designated work areas. The teacher gave brief instructions to all three groups while the aide took attendance. Students listened to instructions and proceeded with their assignments.

When a student was disruptive, the teacher or aide walked to the chalkboard, wrote the student's name, and added whatever number of check marks were indicated according to the discipline policy posted on the wall. Student disruptions occurred only twice during the class period.

The students appeared to be on task during the 45-minute period and seemed to know how to use their time productively, even when they were waiting for information or instructions.

C. Lesson Delivery

After giving directions to the whole group for the period, the teacher spent the next 20 to 30 minutes with the group assigned to his teaching area. The teacher then began what was apparently a re-instruction lesson on the concept of borrowing and carrying in multiple-digit multiplication. He demonstrated the process through examples on the chalkboard. Next, he asked each of the seven students to work a problem on the overhead projector while the rest of the group worked the same problem at their desks. The teacher then passed out worksheets of additional problems, which the students completed while he monitored their work. To each student who was ready to work independently, the teacher provided a homework sheet with instructions calling for completion the following day.

While the teacher was monitoring the guided practice of his group, he also answered questions and gave directions to students in the independent work area.

About two minutes before the end of the period, the student monitors in each area signaled that the period was about to end. These monitors then collected work papers, put away materials, and prepared the area for the next group. At that time the teacher reminded the class of the assignments written on the chalkboard and of the group areas to which they would report on the following day.

OBSERVATION NOTES: SALLY G.

A. Environment

There were about 35 student desks arranged in six rows of five or six seats each. Student behavior rules were clearly posted on the wall. The room was clean, well-lit, and well-ventilated. The teacher's desk and work materials (lectern, overhead projector, papers) were at the front of the room.

Bulletin boards displayed school announcements and club flyers, not math materials or math-related displays. There was no apparent resource material or supply area available to the students.

B. Student Behavior

The students walked into the room laughing and joking with one another. They took their (apparently assigned) seats and a student took attendance. Students talked with one another for the first five to seven minutes while the teacher spoke privately with a few individual students who approached her desk; at this time she also reviewed her lesson plan.

Throughout the period, the students were expected to pay attention, ask questions, and monitor their own understanding. Some students were actively engaged with the lesson throughout the period; a few students appeared to daydream except when called on by the teacher. Some students spoke without being called on, others openly conversed with friends around them. The teacher did not excercise the discipline procedures noted on the chart on the wall; however, the student conversations did not appear to disrupt the lesson for those students remaining on task.

C. Lesson Delivery

The teacher began the lesson by asking all students to take out their homework from the previous night. She used the overhead projector to display solutions to the homework problems, and she asked the students to check their papers. After the students had done so, she asked if there were any questions regarding the assignments. Several students asked about a few of the problems; the teacher worked each one on the board; then she collected the homework papers.

Next, the teachers asked the students to open their books to a particular page in the text. She announced the topic of the lesson for the day. She explained the concepts involved with the lesson, did some sample problems on the chalkboard, and gave an assignment from the text as homework. The students spent the remaining 15 minutes working on their homework assignment. The teacher remained at her desk; students were free to go to her to ask questions or to request additional instruction.

Four or five minutes before the bell rang, the students cleared away their papers and were ready to leave when the period ended. As they left the room, the teacher reminded them of the assignment due the following day and announced a test to take place the following week on the chapter they were currently studying.

What kind of initial feedback would you give the teachers? Why? What kind of discussion/feedback would you hope would ensue?

Each of the postobservation conferences would include:

• An explanation of the process used to gather observation data and the rationale for superimposing the three categories (environment, student behavior, and lesson delivery) on the data.

• Sharing the notes taken during the observation. That is, each of the teachers would be given their observation notes exactly as they are presented above.

• Asking the teacher for any information regarding the class or lesson that the teacher believed to be necessary for the observer to know in order to achieve a complete understanding of the situation.

After the initial discussion, the teacher would be asked specific questions regarding the instructional decisions made in planning and delivering the lesson. For example:

• What was the objective of the lesson?

• How did you determine that this was the appropriate level of difficulty for these students?

• How did you select the materials used in the delivery of the lesson?

• (For Joseph H.) How did you determine what the aide would do? How did you communicate this plan to the aide?

• How did you determine which students needed additional guided or independent practice?

• What is your evaluation of the lesson? What went well?

• What would you like to see improved?

The goal for the postobservation conference is to provide the teachers with the motivation and tools to examine the plans and activities selected for their lessons. The questions posed to the teachers would serve as examples of questions they could and should be asking themselves in making instructional decisions and plans for their lessons. From the questioning process and through the examination of the observation data, teachers would be expected to see areas of weakness in their planning and delivery of instruction.

For example, when asked how she selected the materials she used for lesson delivery, Sally G. might respond that the materials came in sequence in the text. Thus, she would acknowledge that she had made no professionally based instructional decisions regarding what would be the most productive materials or activities for the lesson. Or, when asked how she had determined the appropriateness of the objectives for the class, she might say that she had not really considered needs and abilities of students, but rather that she had merely progressed in sequence from topic to topic through the text.

By the end of the conferences the teachers would be able to identify for themselves at least one area where there might be room for professional growth. They could then choose where they would like to have support in developing the skills necessary for improving their teaching. Next, having identified a skill area for improvement, teachers need some type of support system to help them work toward improved performance. This support is a form of staff development.

What research has shown to be critical elements of effective staff development must be included in support systems developed to help teachers such as Sally G. and Joseph H. Classroom teachers who are willing to identify areas in need of improvement deserve the most effective programs we can provide. Therefore, it is crucial that teachers be given the opportunity to see for themselves (and to have some power in determining for themselves) how they would like to improve their performance. This sharing of the responsibility for the improvement of instructional processes is the missing motivational element in many schools today. Adults need to see evidence of a need for change before they will act toward implementing the change. And they work harder to incorporate a change in behavior if they have had some opportunity to participate in planning staff development processes (Wood and Thompson, 1980).

If you were chosen to continue working with the teachers, in what kinds of ways (process and content) do you envision you would be working together?

One method of responding to this simulation assignment would have been to look for elements of Mastery Teaching, such as those described by Madeline Hunter: a five-step lesson plan, teaching to an objective, and so forth. We also could have used a clinical supervision model to observe and analyze the lesson. However, since our purpose is to find the best possible way to improve staff skills, focusing solely on classsroom observation and delivery of instruction is too limited an approach. Mastery Teaching and clinical supervision are effective tools for improving instruction. However, they alone do not provide a solution to low test scores or to the problems of low teacher morale and lack of motivation to participate fully in the school organization. While classroom observation and instructional supervision provide many elements that help teachers to improve their instructional processes, in reality these activities affect only one area of teacher behavior: delivery of instruction. There is no question that the improvement of instruction is critically important to increasing student achievement, but it is also true that teachers who are not encouraged (nor even allowed) to participate in the school's goal setting, decision making, and planning are not going to be motivated to perform at their highest potential.

If schools are to increase student achievement, they must stop ignoring the primary sources of student learning: teachers. Research and professional literature today carries the message that until we treat teachers as professionals, we cannot expect them to contribute as professionals to the school organization (Sergiovanni and Carver, 1980). Furthermore, if teachers are to become partners (rather than adversaries) in efforts to create improved learning conditions in our schools, they must be involved in planning, decision making, and goal setting. For their involvement to be meaningful, teachers must first be provided staff development programs and opportunities that will prepare them for this participation and motivate them toward higher levels of self-actualization.

However, current staff development programs are not meeting the needs of school districts or their personnel. This problem is more crucial than ever now that declining enrollment and the consequent reductions in staff result in a lack of "new blood" in the schools.

Problems and weaknesses in staff development programs today include the following:

• Failure to involve teachers in the processes of identifying staff needs and selecting appropriate programs for remediation and growth.

• Lack of a solid conceptual model. Programs often consist of a series of unrelated topics presented for teacher training.

• Emphasis on "training" teachers, not on "educating" them. That is, teachers are given a recipe for a new technique or behavior, but they are not given the time to think through it, to try it, to work with colleagues to solve problems of implementation, or to get support in adapting the techniques or behaviors to their situation.

• Use of standardized themes or topics. There is no provision for individualization according to needs or interests within the district or within the schools.

• Reliance on monetary rewards for teachers who seek professional growth (for example, increases on the district salary scale for professional growth units earned). Districts fail to provide intrinsic rewards for professional growth, such as recognition, achievement, and increased responsibility. As educators, we are all aware of the importance of intrinsic rewards in effecting long-term changes in behavior.

Programs ignore what research has shown to be necessary elements of adult learning, such as participant involvement in the selection of objectives, the need to see results of their activities and receive feedback on their progress, and the need for concrete experiences that give participants the opportunity to try what is being learned (guided and independent practice).

Two very diverse situations were observed in this simulation. Any professional development program designed for a staff with such variance in talent and skills must be individualized. Otherwise, as happens in so many districts, a single program will fail to meet the needs of many staff members. Teachers then ·become frustrated and angry when they are required to spend valuable time (and district funds) on activities that are of value only to certain individuals.

A Model for Staff Development

In an effort to avoid the problems and weaknesses of past practices, to provide for individual needs and interests, and to take advantage of effective elements of adult-learning programs, the following model is proposed as a framework for staff development. This approach is based on building collegiality among teachers and between teachers and administrators. This collegial support model would not only correct weaknesses in the present structure of staff development programs but also help teachers reach higher levels of professionalism and self-satisfaction by encouraging them to become involved in problem solving, decision making, and goal setting for themselves, their departments, and their schools.

This proposal to develop and implement collegial support groups provides for professional growth on two levels: process and content. Process skills include those needed to identify personal/professional and school (or department, subject area, or grade level) weaknesses and needs and to create goals and plans to remedy those weaknesses and needs. Brainstorming, reaching consensus, problem solving, prioritizing, long-range planning, team building, and collegial support are among the process skills that are modeled and practiced by participants throughout the program and throughout the monthly content presentations. The program content evolves from the Personal/Professional Plans (P/P Plans) and School Improvement Plans (SIP) developed by the participants. Thus, the content of this program is relevant and motivating to the participants because they themselves have chosen it.

The collegial support group model proposed here involves two stages of program development. Stage I is the period of introducing participants to the program and to one another. This stage takes approximately three or four day-long meetings, spread over a period of two months. (After the first year of the program, only one meeting is needed at the beginning of each year to complete the Stage I activities.) During the meetings included in Stage I, teachers are involved in team-building activities; they review district and building goals; they engage in self-evaluation and interest studies; and they use this information for developing their individual Personal/Professional and School Improvement Plans. During this period the large group is broken down into support groups of eight to ten participants. Team building and sharing take place within these small groups; the support groups are then used to help participants evaluate and refine the P/Ps and SIPs being developed. An example of a Personal/Professional plan that might be developed by Sally G. is provided in Figure 7.1. A School Improvement Plan that might be created by Joseph H. is provided in Figure 7.2.

At the end of Stage I, the participants' P/Ps and SIPs are prioritized, and the participants use this list to choose themes for each of the monthly meetings. (See Figure 7.3.) Stage II continues and reinforces the skills and processes developed during Stage I. During Stage II participants meet monthly,

---

Figure 7.1. Sample Personal/Professional Plan for Sally G.

Objectives

1. This school year I will create a management system for my 8th grade math classes. This system will include:

   A. Assessing individual student mastery of concepts to make sure that the objectives of the lessons being taught are appropriate to each learner.

   B. Creating a communication system with the students so they can be responsible for knowing assignments and for planning their time appropriately.

2. This year I will manage instructional time carefully so that students spend a minimum of 85 percent of their class time on task.

Activities

1A. Appropriateness of Objectives

   (1) Talk with other teachers in this subject area to see how they plan for individual needs and mastery (by October).

   (2) Design pretests for each concept to be taught (by the beginning of each unit).

   (3) Design alternate enrichment activities for those students who pretest at mastery level (by the beginning of each unit).

1B. Communication system

   (1) Talk with other teachers to see what they use as communication processes (by September).

   (2) Design communication plan and put into practice (by October).

2. Time management

   (1) Design a class period time-management chart to include each activity in any class (by October).

   (2) Plan and communicate to students a class period schedule of procedures so that they know exactly what they should be doing from the time they enter the classroom door (by October).

Evaluation

[In this section Sally G. keeps notes regarding the process, difficulties, problems, successes, and any reactions she has to this Personal/Professional Plan.]

Figure 7.2. Sample Department Improvement Plan for Joseph H.

Objectives:
    1. This year I will create a workshop on the proper management techniques to be used when supervising a classroom aide. This workshop will be given to members of the math department at this school.
    2. This year I will create a math resources center that will include a catalogue of all of the reference and enrichment materials we have in the department. It will include a file of each of our course descriptions, outlines, worksheets, tests, quizzes, and any other artifacts department members are willing to share.

Activities
    1. Workshop
        A. Research proper management techniques appropriate for teacher-aide relations (by October).
        B. Design a department workshop for the November inservice.
        C. Create a follow-up evaluation instrument to be administered to the teachers in February in order to evaluate whether the workshop techniques are being used and if they are effective.
    2. Resource Center
        A. Inventory the materials available (by October).
        B. Find a location for the center and necessary storage equipment or furniture (by November).
        C. Create a catalogue or index of the materials available (by December).
        D. Facilitate a departmental meeting at which the department members will put the center together and create any procedures or rules they believe necessary for managing the material flow through the center.

Evaluation
[In this section, Joseph H. will keep notes regarding the progress, problems, successes, suggestions, and reactions he has to his Department Improvement Plans.]

Figure 7.3. Stage I of the Staff Development Model

To be carried out in three or four meetings over two months:

1. Divide participants into groups of eight to ten.
2. Conduct team-building activities.
3. Conduct self-assessment activities.
4. Review district and building activities.
5. Participants set individual SIP and P/P Plans.
6. Introduce the processes of brainstorming, consensus, inbasket, planning, evaluating.
7. Using individual SIP and P/P Plans, plan program contents for remainder of the year.

rotating the chairmanship of the meetings. Each month's meeting contains the following elements: collegial-support activities (sharing processes, "inbasket" problem-sharing and solving), content presentations, P/P and SIP updates, and a commitment by each individual to implement some aspect of the content presented at the meeting. In addition, time is scheduled at the end of the year (or at the midpoint) for program evaluation and future planning. (See Figure 7.4.)

Figure 7.4. Stage II of the Staff Development Model

1. Meet monthly away from school for all day, if possible.
2. Rotate chair responsibilities among participants.
3. Provide the opportunity at each meeting to:
    a. Share successes
    b. Share problems
    c. Update reports on SIP and P/P Plans
    d. Participate in content presentations (scheduled from SIP and P/P Plans; can use outside speakers or delegate responsibility for presentation to group members)
4. Reserve final meeting of the year (or semester) for evaluation and planning.

The basic needs for implementation of this program are few. (Figure 7.5.) The key element is a facilitator. This person should be someone from outside the district so that the role is not clouded by the person's position within the school or district. Next, participants need released time. Ideally, they would be released for three or four days at the beginning of the year for Stage I activities. Later, they would be released one day per month for the regular meetings of the group. However, if participants can't be released for this much time, elements of this model can be selected for incorporation into regular staff or faculty meetings. This limited implementation of the

---

Figure 7.5. Program Needs (Flexible)

Facilitator
Release time for participants
Clerk time
Meeting place

---

model is not ideal, but even a minimum amount of sharing and problem solving among participants is better than nothing. A minimal amount of time for reflection on school programs, needs, and goals is better than no time for reflection. The third necessary element is a place to meet. The ideal program would meet away from the school site. The geographical distance from the school helps the participants to separate themselves from the mundane tasks, frustrations, and problems they face regularly and enables them to view the school more objectively and creatively. The last essential element is a small amount of clerical time for typing and duplicating agendas, minutes, and other written documents generated by the program participants.

This model is based on the I/D/E/A (Institure for the Development of Educational Activities) program, an affiliate of the Charles F. Kettering Foundation. The I/D/E/A program was developed as a model for principals' inservice. However, the adapted form presented here works as well for teachers, administrators, superintendents, or even students. In fact, one of the strengths of this program is its flexibility. It can be used whole or in part and as a framework within which any areas of need or interest in professional growth or problem solving can be incorporated. For example, if the district were focusing on improvement of student test scores, it is certain that this topic would appear in one or more participants' SIP or P/P Plans. This then would be rated high during the prioritizing activities and would likely be chosen as the content topic for at least one of the monthly meetings. (Of course, it is possible that the topic might not be selected if the participants already felt competent with the skills.) Thus, any area of district or school programs and plans could be included in this overall development framework. In addition, the framework builds in the opportunity for sharing questions, concerns, problems, and successes. This is important, because it includes the guided and independent practice elements that are currently missing from most staff development programs.

Teaching can be a very lonely profession. Sporadic classroom observations by site administrators do not provide an efficient process for revitalizing, motivating, and improving teacher performance. We must build a framework for productive problem solving and professional sharing among staff members. If we fail in this task, we are guilty of ignoring an incredibly rich resource of talent and skill in our schools; and we are guilty of not providing the opportunities for professional growth that will create productive, self-actualizing professionals for our classrooms.

Bibliography

Firth, Gerald R. "Ten Issues on Staff Development." *Educational Leadership* 35 (December 1977): 215-220.

LaPlant, James. "Principals' Inservice Program." Institute for the Development of Educational Activities, Inc., an affiliate of the Charles F. Kettering Foundation, Dayton, Ohio, 1979.

Mazarella, Jo Ann. "Synthesis of Research on Staff Development." *Educational Leadership* 38 (November 1980): 182-185.

McLaughlin, Milbrey, and Paul Berman. "Retooling Staff Development in a Period of Retrenchment." *Educational Leadership* 35 (December 1977): 191-194.

Miller, William C. "What's Wrong with In-service Education? It's Topless!" *Educational Leadership* 35 (October 1977): 31-34.

Sergiovanni, Thomas J., ed. *Supervision of Teaching.* Alexandria, Va.: Association for Supervision and Curriculum Development, 1982.

Sergiovanni, Thomas J., and Fred D. Carver. *The New School Executive: A Theory of Administration.* San Francisco: Harper and Row, 1980.

Sparks, Georgea Mohlman. "Synthesis of Research on Staff Development for Effective Teaching." *Educational Leadership* 41 (November 1983): 65-72.

Wood, Fred H., and Steven R. Thompson. "Guidelines for Better Staff Development." *Educational Leadership* 37 (February 1980): 374-378.

8. Thinking About Teaching

Gary A. Griffin

Carol: If I get through this year, I'll probably make old bones after all.

Elaine: How can you bear taking all those notes about this stuff? Even *I* get bored listening to me!

THE COMMENTS BY CAROL AND ELAINE ARE TYPICAL OF THE WAYS THEY THINK about their teaching. Carol's wry expressiveness suggests, of course, that she *will* get through the school year, despite the pressures and complexities she faces, while Elaine deprecates her teaching because, it seems, she suspects that the visitor will find it considerably less than stimulating.

What prevents these teachers from realizing their expectations? What demands must Carol meet instead of teaching as she sees fit? If Elaine finds her approach boring, why doesn't she change it?

This chapter describes one way of learning about teaching by talking with and observing teachers and then using that knowledge to plan ways of working with them.

Looking/Seeing

Most of us have a conception of teaching that guides our response to what we see. This belief in what teaching is, whether an inchoate set of snapshots or a full-blown, detailed tapestry, also guides how we *judge* what we see. If our vision of teaching is controlled by stereotypes such as Mr. Chips or Miss Dove, we will visit different classrooms with varying degrees of sat-

---

Gary A. Griffin is Dean and Professor of Education, College of Education, University of Illinois at Chicago.

isfaction. If we think that classrooms should be communities of interest and interaction, individualized settings will be unsettling and unsatisfying. If we believe that student choices and decision making are important to learning, teacher- or curriculum-dominated classrooms will dismay us. In short, we look and see, but more often than not we are looking *for* something, and when we don't see it, we are disappointed.

What was I looking for in Carol and Elaine's teaching? What did I see? The responses to those two questions raised important questions for me and, I hope, for the two teachers.

Teacher as Victim: *Carol*

Carol teaches in an inner-city school. The approach to the school is littered with debris. There's an abandoned car nearby, and in front of the small stores in the area knots of people talk, argue, and drink from bottles wrapped in brown paper bags. The entrance to the old brick school building is formidable, more like a fortress to be assaulted than a place of welcome. Windows are covered with wire mesh, outside walls are covered with graffiti, and there is not a blade of grass in sight.

Inside the school, however, are well-swept corridors, colorful hallway bulletin boards, and a prevailing sense of order and well-being. Of course, there are times when a crying child or a harassed teacher will intrude upon the calm. But those times are few, and the quiet, somewhat unsettling perhaps because of its unexpectedness, returns.

Carol's classroom is "down the hall, turn right, and there you are" from the school office. It, too, is quiet and orderly. It is hard to believe that 28 5th graders and two adults (Carol and a teacher aide) are crammed together in a room no larger than 25 by 30 feet. The children sit in neatly arranged rows of desks; student work is stacked according to assignment and subject; bulletin boards tend to be made up of schedules, timetables, checklists. Perhaps because of the size of the room, there are no learning centers, no student library, no puzzles, games, easels, or phonograph with earphones.

Carol has arranged a semicircle of chairs facing a chalkboard. She sits in front of the chalkboard with a chartrack; within reach is a low table stacked with materials. Eight students, five boys and three girls, have reading texts open in their laps. The students take turns, in sequence from left to right, reading what appears to be a primary-level basal reader.

When the students complete the story, Carol points to questions on a chart. She asks a question, selects a student to respond, moves on if the response is correct, redirects the question to another student if it is not, and accompanies this activity with a rhythmic clicking of her fingers. When all of the questions are answered, the students are asked to open their folders (which have been placed under their chairs), and Carol explains what is expected of them as they complete a "worksheet." The ease of the pacing and the absence of any clarification or substantive questions from the students suggest that this activity is a typical one in Carol's classroom.

Carol reaches over to the small table, shifts one book and stack of papers to the back and another to the front, rings a small handbell once, and watches while the reading group students return to their desks and another group moves to the chairs. With the exception of the level of difficulty of the reading text (this one appears to be about 5th grade level), the routine is the same.

In fact, this is the routine for all reading, language arts, and mathematics instruction observed on two occasions. Examination of notes taken during the visits and analysis of the "worksheets" given to children reveal the following:

- All instruction occurred as a consequence of direct influence from Carol.
- All teacher questions could be classified at the recall or comprehension level.
- The timing of student movement was precise and did not vary from a schedule posted at the front of the classroom.
- Unless students were moving to or from a teacher-led group, there was little physical movement about the classroom.
- Carol's adherance to the routine was almost absolute; she varied it only when a student became ill and when students talked with one another during seat work (a rare occurrence).
- Instruction materials were as constant in nature and use as the instructional routine, consisting of text, prepared worksheets, and what appeared to be commercially designed charts.
- Students were consistently attentive to the teacher and completed their assignments with an apparent high rate of success.
- Carol occasionally showed a sense of humor, but her dominant style was businesslike and systematic.
- Talking with Carol before and after school revealed another side to her personality and unearthed a somewhat unexpected point-of-view about teaching. Here are a few excerpts from our conversations:

Gary: Your classroom looks to an outsider a bit like a well-oiled precision instrument. I can't remember seeing anything like it before.

Carol: Thanks, I guess. We've worked hard to get where we are. You should have seen us when we started the new curriculum—it was all fits and starts. Jackie [another teacher in the school] and I would just sort of collapse into heaps in the lounge at lunchtime. But we finally got the hang of it. It's all in the timing, y'know.

Gary: What's all in the timing?

Carol: Getting it right.

Gary: Getting what right?

Carol: The curriculum . . . all the stuff we teach in the basics. Of course, that's *all* we teach now. Y'know, I've been thinking. I've been teaching for 13 years now, and I've seen the bandwagons come and go. . . . This one's been around for a few years, but I don't see that the kids are really reading or writing any better.

Gary: Is that what we're talking about, a bandwagon?

Carol: I think so. All this business with testing and retesting and objectives and worksheets and so on. I wonder what would happen if we just set the kids to reading again. You know, don't you, that they never *really* read.

Gary: What do you mean by "really read?"

Carol: Sit down with a book and just read . . . until they have a problem.

Gary: Then what?

Carol: Then you teach them something that'll solve the problem.

Gary: Do you think that would work, to teach them to read, I mean?

Carol: I'm not certain of it. But I used to do that and life seemed simpler, somehow.

Gary: Simpler?

Carol: Well, now that you ask, I guess not. I really mean *better.*

Gary: Why don't you give it a try?

Carol: Are you kidding? [The teachers] are all up to their eyeballs in forms to be completed, checklists to get to the office, lesson plans to write, and stuff like that; we don't have the time to do what we want.

Gary: What's the difference between what you want and what you think is right?

Carol: I'd never thought about it that way.

In another conversation Carol said, "I think I'm a good teacher. Nope, I know I'm a good teacher. But I feel sort of like no one will let me teach or really wants me to teach. It's kind of like being caught up in something you can't get hold of, like being in an undertow at the beach. You know you've got to get out, but you end up just drifting along. Oh, I don't know."

But I think she did know. She knew that she was more than vaguely dissatisfied. She knew that she was feeling pressure to teach in certain ways that might not be as good as her ways. And, sadly, she knew, or believed she knew, that she couldn't really make changes. In her words, she was just "drifting along."

Teacher as Buffer: *Elaine*

Elaine is also in an inner-city school, also teaches 5th grade, and also is a bit, as she put it, ". . . singed around the edges, if not quite burned out." There are some important differences between the two schools, though. Whereas Carol is in what can only be termed a harsh environment, Elaine does her work in a pocket of relative affluence. The outside of the school building is clean and attractive, and some effort has been made to provide landscaping and to otherwise suggest an invitation to the passerby.

Inside, Elaine's school is newly painted, and there is a good deal of children's art displayed on bulletin boards. There appear to be more students in the halls than in Carol's school, and there is a more obvious hum of children's voices.

Elaine's classroom, though, is arranged much like Carol's, although there is ample space for it to be more informal. Interestingly, many of the same materials (charts, lists, schedules) are replicated in Elaine's room. The similarity is striking.

Elaine is moving around the classroom, glancing at students' papers and occasionally asking a question or making a suggestion. The boys and girls, 26 in all, are correcting answers to short questions posed about stories that have been read in reading groups. (Elaine or the instructional aide have already made corrections on the students' papers as well as specific comments.)

Elaine stops in the center of the classroom and, raising her voice a bit above a conversational level, says, "Is anyone stuck? Remember, you can ask me or someone near you for help. But, and I know you know this, we mustn't talk too loudly or we'll disturb each other." Two hands are raised for Elaine, and three pairs of students move together and talk quietly.

Elaine greets me and says, "Don't tell anyone I do this. The kids aren't supposed to help one another but I like to have them do it anyway. Sometimes they talk about something besides the work, but who wouldn't?"

She moves away, motioning me to sit by the circle of chairs at the front of the room. She, too, moves to the reading circle and says in a soft voice, "Blue group." Seven students, four girls and three boys, move to the circle. Each is carrying a set of papers in a blue folder, a pen or pencil, a textbook, and what appears to be a book from a library. There is some good-natured bickering about who gets to sit next to Elaine, who gives a mock grimace and moves her chair to the other side of the group. She says, "So there!"

"Everyone has read the story," says Elaine. "If not, it's too late." She distributes a page of short-answer questions related to the story in the text. As with Carol, she moves through the questions in rapid order, stopping only once when a student drops a pencil. After all of the questions have been read aloud, she asks if there are any problems that she can help solve. No one has a problem.

She then asks the students to open their textbooks to page 86. She proceeds to move through the next story at a quick pace. She occasionally works out the sound of a new word with a student, but that is unnecessary for five of the students. When the story is completed, the students close their books, and Elaine asks a series of comprehension questions. The students are quick with their answers, and the entire exercise is completed in less than ten minutes, including the brief overview of questions related to the previous story.

Elaine then asks one student, Jennifer, to tell the group about the book she is reading. Jennifer launches into an enthusiastic recounting of one of the tales in the *Little House* series. A classmate asks how the book is different from the reruns of the television series. Jennifer says, "Well, it's sort of the same but . . . I don't know, with the book I can make the people and the places look the way I want 'em to look. And the book lets you stop when you want to or go way ahead if you have time."

Elaine interrupts to lead a brief discussion about television and what it requires of the viewer in terms of time, suspension of imagination, and commercial interruptions. All of the students participate.

Each student tells something about his or her book. (I find out later that Elaine has discarded—"short-circuited" is her phrase—the schedule she is supposed to follow in reading group instruction. She has substituted the regular reading of library books for a set of follow-up activities to be used when the teacher is with the groups.)

While the groups switch places, there is a bit more jostling and talking than I had seen in Carol's room. There also appears to be some confusion about who is to do what next. Several students ask procedural questions of Elaine. Given that the semester is several months along, the questions seem to be unnecessary interruptions.

The two observations of Elaine's class suggest these conclusions:

- In place are most elements of the direct instruction strategy that is so routinized in Carol's classroom.
- The students are less certain of what to do than the students in Carol's classroom.
- About a third of reading instruction time is spent on the use of library books (or books brought from home).
- Commercial curriculum materials are supplemented with teacher-made ones.
- Students are regularly expected to work together.
- There is an observable amount of off-task student behavior.
- The use of routines is somewhat sporadic, and there are frequent stops and starts when routines are put into operation.
- Elaine alternates humorous and businesslike approaches to working with students.

As I did with Carol, I talked with Elaine about her students, the school, the reading and language arts curriculum, and, ultimately, her views about her own teaching:

Gary: There seems to be district curriculum in place here.
Elaine: Oh boy, is there! I manage to get around it, though.
Gary: How?
Elaine: It ain't easy. All of the money gets spent on the district curriculum, so I have to bootleg other stuff. My public library thinks I'm hooked on children's books, I check out so many of them every two weeks.
Gary: Why do you do that?
Elaine: It just seems *wrong* for kids not to read for pleasure. Did you no-

tice that the kids race through the standard reading lessons to get to the discussion of library books?

Gary: Are they rushing or are you?

Elaine: You got me there. I think it's really all of us. In fact, I sometimes think I might be shortchanging the kids by not doing exactly what the reading curriculum requires. But, still. . . .

Gary: Putting aside the library books for a minute, what do you think about the curriculum you're expected to use?

Elaine: It's okay, I guess. I really haven't gotten the hang of it, especially the routines. It just doesn't seem important that everything hop along like clockwork, although I admit that there are times when I wish that I could push a magic button and all confusion would stop.

Gary: How do you decide how and when to "short-circuit" the required curriculum?

Elaine: I guess it depends on what I'm thinking about at the time. *I* learned how to read, and read well, by going through hundreds and hundreds of books. I learned how to teach reading in college according to a lot of phonics rules and then did my student teaching in a classroom where the regular teacher used the old word recognition method. And now the district has produced all of these lesson plans for us to use. Sometimes I do phonics, sometimes I use the lesson plans, but I always use the library books.

Gary: Do you mean that you know how to teach the various methods but decide when to use them because of something that happens in the classroom?

Elaine: I'd like to think so. I'm not sure.

Later, Elaine said, "Your questions kind of bothered me. You seem to think that I have a plan, a method to my madness. Actually, I probably do what I do without a lot of thinking, sort of like an automatic reflex. I seem to be pushed and pulled between what the district says, what I've been taught, and what I sort of know. I worry that I just take the easiest way out most of the time."

When I reflect upon what I was looking for in these two classrooms, a dilemma emerges. On the one hand, my own predilection for teaching tends toward the activity-oriented, experience-based mode. I value highly student decision making, student cooperation around academic tasks, and a problem-solving atmosphere. On the other hand, my recent work has, in part, focused on the introduction of the direct instruction model in classrooms as a means to test the effects of that way of teaching on classroom climate, teacher behavior, and student outcomes. Yet, I cannot say that either mode of teaching is entirely satisfying to me for all instruction in all classrooms. I most admire teaching that is the result of a blend of styles, a "mix-and-match" amalgam whose parts are suited to specific curricula, student groups, and purposes of instruction. This form of teaching requires teachers to think precisely about the relationships among the components of a classroom and to have at hand a repertoire of teaching skills and styles.

In Carol's classroom for the most part, I saw solid instruction rooted in smooth routines; it was a somewhat uneasy blend of direct instruction and flexibility in Elaine's. In neither instance could an observer find major fault with the teaching. I might, for instance, have been more impressed by greater attention to student choice in Carol's class and a smoother shift from pattern to looser structure in Elaine's. But, all in all, teaching styles and strategies could be defended for both.

Yet, I find that the teachers themselves are unsure of their competence. This was particularly evident when they talked about decision making. Carol believes that she is expected to teach in certain ways and does, although she doesn't seem to be happy with the fit between her own beliefs and the curricular requirements. Elaine acts almost guilty about her inability to rationalize her decisions about how and when to engage in certain teaching strategies.

These observations and conversations lead me to think about how I might talk with the teachers about their teaching.

Initial Feedback

My initial feedback to the teachers occurred during our conversations, some parts of which have already been reported. Even these almost casual exchanges provide part of a foundation upon which to build a professional relationship. In the same way that I formed initial impressions about Elaine and Carol as educators, I am sure that they formed preliminary judgments about me as a possible colleague based on my questions and responses.

Carol and Elaine, in different ways, appear to be caught up in some of the perennial problems associated with teachers and teaching. It might be useful to ask them, in a relatively formal feedback session, the following questions:

- Is teaching a professional activity or is it technique? Is it art or science?
- What degree of autonomy or freedom in decision making do you think you have?
- What knowledge is most important to you in making decisions about teaching?
- How do you compare with others who teach at your level?
- What methods of teaching are most effective for you? For the students with whom you work? How do you know?
- What influence do you have upon curricular and instructional decisions made at district and school levels? What influence do you want?
- What changes do you make as you move from year to year? Why? To what effect?
- How much time do you spend thinking, alone or out loud with others, about teaching and schooling?

These questions might spark Elaine and Carol to think more deeply about what they do and *how* they think about what they do. In light of these perceptions of how their classrooms work, it seems necessary for them to find more coherent ways to think about teaching.

In other words, Carol and Elaine must become empowered as teachers. To a large degree, that will help them to gain control over teaching activity. That will counteract Carol's sense that she is "in an undertow." And Elaine could become more articulate about how she decides to deviate from district expectations.

It is also important for teachers like Carol and Elaine to participate more meaningfully in school decision making and other activities *beyond* their classroom walls. Clearly, these experienced teachers are more than minimally capable. However, they both seem to have accepted a teacher role that is more technical than professional, more immediately responsive than reflective, and more individualistic than participatory.

Notes taken during the classroom observations suggest ways to raise and answer the more general questions above. For instance, Carol could provide greater detail about her decision to use the district curriculum instead of her own ideas. Elaine, too, could be asked to amplify on her apparently intuitive approach to decisions about abandoning the same curriculum. By comparing my notes on their teaching with their *views* of teaching, we could begin to clarify some of the sources of discomfort that both are experiencing and, perhaps, articulate more sharply conceptualized expectations for classroom life. Asking about teaching as art or as science might give Elaine a more coherent view and help Carol realize that her stance on pedagogy, now only dimly perceived, may be defensible.

A central issue for me is that these teachers appear to be demonstrating, in varying degrees, what happens as teaching becomes more centralized, more technically oriented. Carol seems to have caved in to district decisions, whereas Elaine pushes back a bit but probably would not be able to withstand an all-out assault on her methods. This is not the same as saying that the district is wrong and the teachers, Elaine in particular, are right. It *is* to suggest that a professional need not engage in automaton-like behavior or act out a role as though it were punched out of a template.

Also, it is probable that the teachers have no real frame of reference for talking and thinking about their work in relation to others who do the same or similar work. Carol has the routines down pat. If Elaine wanted to develop that same proficiency, a visit to Carol's classroom would probably contribute greatly to that end. If Carol wished to act on her idea about "just reading," some time with Elaine might help her make that adjustment in her classroom.

This last point, seeing and talking across classroom boundaries, would be the central focus of any sustained work I would do with these teachers and others like them.

Working and Thinking Together

Over the years, certain principles that seem to undergird successful professional development have shown their worth again and again. In working with teachers, I would keep in mind the following:

• Teachers learn and grow when they focus on a "technical core" of activity, the stuff of which teaching is made (Williams, 1982).

• Teachers change more readily as a consequence of interacting with one another around common problems than when they are told to change by administrators or "experts" (Bentzen, 1975).

• When teachers believe, on the basis of real evidence, that they are primary decision makers in professional activity, they are more responsive to change, experimentation, and taking chances (Tikunoff et al., 1981).

• Continuing education of teachers is most effective when it focuses on issues indentified by teachers rather than by others (Schiffer, 1978).

• Teacher growth is enhanced by support in both material and ceremonial ways (Schlechty and Joslin, 1984).

• Teachers respond more positively to expectations for excellence than minimum competence.

• The complexities of teaching often prevent teachers from seeing their real problems; they focus on the symptom rather than the problem.

• Teachers are seldom asked to think in radically different ways of what they do. When they do, they are often surprised at the array of options that are open to them (Tikunoff et al., 1980).

• Teachers have come to accept the low status that is assigned to them by the media and, often, by their own clients and patrons. Overcoming this acceptance is a first goal in initiating change.

• Teachers assess the world through their daily activities rather than through systematic examination and analysis (Lieberman and Miller, 1984).

What might this mean for Carol and Elaine? First, we would talk together about teaching, particularly about the similarities and differences in Carol's and Elaine's teaching. We would work from my field notes and then, when we were comfortable with one another, I would arrange for the two teachers to observe each other and talk over what they had seen. My hunch is that they would find specific aspects of teaching that they could "borrow" and adapt for their own uses. Carol, for instance, might find Elaine's use of library books an attractive idea. Elaine, on the other hand, might pick up on some of the cues, signals, and other techniques that help Carol's routines to move so smoothly. If no other provision for substitutes were possible (and I would hope that such would be the case, in terms of district support for our activity), I would teach the classes of the observer teacher.

If it did not arise naturally, I would suggest that we identify a problem or issue of interest to all of us, myself included. We could then develop a plan to attack the issue, a set of procedures that would lead us to conclusions about teaching, either in terms of its raw activity or, better, in terms of its effects. This activity would force us to think systematically, to provide evidence, to test out ideas with one another, and to move together toward some resolution, calling into question our biases, ingrained beliefs, and expectations.

As suggested above, it is important that this activity be legitimated beyond the interests that the two teachers and I might bring to it. This legitimization could come from the district in the form of released time, financial support, salary schedule credit for participation, and other material ways. Further, the district could offer what might be termed "ceremonial" support, such as by asking the teachers to share their experiences with others, recognition in newsletters and other communications, and so on. The important issue is that the activity is clearly valued by the system in which it takes place.

At this point, it may appear that the only intellectual and human resources brought to our work come from the three of us. Teachers, like other professionals, need access to powerful assistance to deal with the problems they face (Griffin and Barnes, in press). Unfortunately, in matters of education, that technical assistance, though often of high quality, may be not only inaccessible to teachers but also unintelligible to them (such as technical research reports and scholarly journals published by learned societies) (Griffin, 1983). It is important for Carol and Elaine to discover how others have thought about their concerns, how both scholars and practitioners have dealt with their dilemmas, and how complex problems have been treated outside the boundaries of classroom walls.

My role in such an exploration would be to act as translator and *marriage* broker. Because of my experiences over the years and because of my personal predilections, I think I can make the research studies meaningful and understandable. Also, I have developed a network of professional colleagues and friends who would be interested in working with teachers like Carol and Elaine. I would call upon this network as appropriate.

As a start, I believe that the two teachers would respond positively to knowing how other teachers, working in small groups with researchers and teacher educators, discovered that they could make differences in their classrooms and their schools (Tikunoff et al., 1981). I believe they would find the teacher-driven studies interesting and useful and would want to begin the action research procedures themselves.

To help legitimate Carol's superb use of rules and procedures and to give some authority to Elaine's search for the same level of classroom efficiency, I would suggest an examination of syntheses of direct instruction research (Barnes, 1981; Good, 1981; Rosenshine, 1983). In particular, I would emphasize academic research findings since a number of these studies dealt with inner-city classrooms and the teaching of reading and mathematics, an apparent preoccupation of the curriculum decision makers in Elaine and Carol's system (Good and Grouws, 1979).

I noted earlier that my view of teaching is more comprehensive than the usual specification of teacher-student interactions. It is this view that drives my preoccupation with the ways teachers think about their important work and the ways in which they influence the settings in which that work takes place. Carol and Elaine could be encouraged to think about these perspectives, about teaching and the teacher's role in schooling in general, and to consider the findings from Goodlad's (1983) study, the results of Little's (1981) investigation of workplace norms associated with school success, Eisner's (1985) propositions about curriculum evaluation, and Raywid's (1984) study of schools of choice. These attempts to understand schooling might trigger a sense of the empowerment mentioned earlier.

Because I am anticipating that the teachers will discover the limitations of research findings as prescriptions for practice, a healthy dose of theory and proposition would be part of our interactions. The appeal of Greene's (1978) essays in this regard seems to me unquestionable. Also, both teachers' vague discontent, rooted in a conception of teaching as dull and routine, suggests that Dewey's (1963) ideas about experience and education would be welcome. The testing of these propositions against the realities of the teachers' settings would, I suspect, create a set of dilemmas that the teachers would want to understand, investigate, and resolve.

The series of interactions proposed here with Carol and Elaine might be pictured as a set of concentric circles of information. Attention is given to the innermost circle through the research and propositions about teaching as interaction with students. That activity, in turn, is surrounded by a growing understanding of the school and the system, the more general but still powerful influences upon life in classrooms. These physical and organizational contexts are placed within an even more comprehensive intellectual environment composed of ideological, theoretical, and propositional knowledge. The hope is that these ways of understanding classroom activity will be helpful in clarifying the teachers' expectations for teaching and that the clarification will be accompanied by an increased ability to take articulated stands on teaching, learning, and schooling issues.

It is important to set forth briefly some of the conditions necessary for this work to go forward. I would urge the teachers to include their colleagues in the effort. This develops a group of cohorts for intellectual, personal, and institutional support—a network of concern and activity. The ultimate manifestation of this would be, of course, a schoolwide effort affecting all schooling activities. This "spread" of activity would require intellectual and material support from school and district leadership. Teachers, in my view, must reconsider and revitalize their *professionalism*. To do this, they must be able to resist the growing tide of paraprofessionalism that threatens to reduce teaching activity to that which is easily taught to teachers, readily observed, and mechanistically remediated (Griffin, 1985). My view of teaching is much more comprehensive and complex and, I believe, most teachers would agree with it. To be influential, however, that agreement must be buttressed by teachers' practical *and* intellectual knowledge and skills. All of us who are concerned about the quality of life for teachers and students need to develop ways of thinking about teaching that lead us toward the creation of the best possible learning situations for our nation's young people.

References

Barnes, S. *Synthesis of Selected Research on Teaching Findings.* Austin: Research and Development Center for Teacher Education, The University of Texas at Austin, 1981.

Bentzen, M. M. *Changing Schools: The Magic Feather Principle.* New York: McGraw-Hill, 1975.

Dewey, J. *Experience and Education.* New York: Collier Books, 1963.

Eisner, E. W. *The Educational Imagination.* New York: Macmillan, 1985.

Good, T. L. *Classroom Research: What We Know and What We Need to Know.* Austin: Research and Development Center for Teacher Education, The University of Texas at Austin, 1981.

Good, T. L., and D. A. Grouws. "The Missouri Mathematics Effectiveness Project: An Experimental Study in Fourth-Grade Classrooms." *Journal of Educational Psychology* 71, 3 (1979): 335-362.

Goodlad, J. I. *A Place Called School.* New York: McGraw-Hill, 1973.

Greene, M. *Landscapes of Learning.* New York: Teachers College Press, 1978.

Griffin, G. A. "Implications of Research for Staff Development Programs." *Elementary School Journal* 83, 4 (1983): 414-427.

Griffin, G. A. "The Paraprofessionalization of Teaching." Paper presented at the annual meeting of the American Educational Research Association, Chicago, April 1985.

Griffin, G. A., and S. Barnes. "Changing Teacher Practice: A Research-Based School Improvement Study." In *School Effectiveness Research and the Teaching of Reading,* edited by J. Hoffman and G. Duffy. Newark, Del.: International Reading Association, in press.

Lieberman, A., and L. Miller. "School Improvement: Themes and Variations." *Teachers College Record* 86, 1 (1984): 4-19.

Little, J. W. *School Success and Staff Development: The Role of Staff Development in Urban Desegregated Schools.* Boulder, Colo.: Center for Action Research, 1981.

Raywid, M. *The Current Status of Schools of Choice.* Hempstead, N.Y.: Hofstra University, 1984.

Rosenshine, B. "Teaching Functions in Instructional Programs." *The Elementary School Journal* 83, 4 (1983): 335-352.

Schiffer, J. "A Framework for Staff Development." In *Staff Development: New Demands, New Realities, New Perspectives,* edited by A. Lieberman and L. Miller. New York: Teachers College Press, 1978.

Schlechty, P. C., and A. W. Joslin. "Images of Schools." *Teachers College Record* 86, 1 (1984): 156-170.

Tikunoff, W. J.; B. A. Ward; and G. A. Griffin. "Interactive Research and Development as a Form of Professional Growth." In *School-Focused Inservice: Descriptions and Discussions,* edited by K. R. Bents and D. Corrigan. Reston, Va.: Association of Teacher Educators, 1981.

Tikunoff, W. J.; B. A. Ward; and G. A. Griffin. *The IR&DT Experience.* San Francisco: Far West Laboratory for Educational Research and Development, 1980.

Williams, R. "Changing Teacher Behaviors: From Symbolism to Reality." In *Changing Teacher Practices: Proceedings of a National Conference* (R&D Report No. 9017), edited by M. Defino and H. Carter. Austin: Research and Development Center for Teacher Education, The University of Texas at Austin, 1983, pp. 25-46.

9. Working with Teachers: The Advisory Approach

Maja Apelman

From 1971 to 1979 I was a staff member of the Mountain View Center, an independently funded, university-sponsored teachers' center. In an occasional paper published by the Teachers' Center Exchange, Amity Buxton, then director of one of the oldest teachers' centers in the country, defines teachers' centers as "places and programs for staff development that are designed and used by teachers on their own volition to fill their self-identified training and curriculum needs" (Buxton, 1979, p. 1). Buxton states that teachers' centers operate from the assumption that teachers have the most accurate information for assessing their professional needs, based on direct individual experience in their classrooms, schools, and community. She further asserts that the centers represent "a distinctive option for staff development"; "[a teachers' center] is *developmental* in its view of how teachers learn; *integrated* and *substantive* in its choice of curriculum; and *supportive, active, nonevaluative* and *professional* in its style of working with teachers" (p. 7). I approached my work with teachers from this point of view.

At least half my time at the Mountain View Center was spent in classrooms working with teachers as an advisor. Many of the early, privately funded teachers' centers had advisors on their staffs. In the late 1970s and early 1980s, many teachers working in and being served by federally funded teachers' centers expressed considerable interest in the work of advisors.

Maja Apelman is an educational consultant who is currently teaching at Bank Street College and the University of Colorado in Denver.

The following definition of an advisor summarizes the most important and generally accepted characteristics of this role. An advisor:

1. Provides assistance only upon the request of the teacher.

2. Has no evaluative or supervisory function.

3. Has no predetermined agenda and does not impose or implement mandated programs.

4. Provides assistance in terms of teachers' needs, goals, and objectives.

5. Acts as a support and resource person for the professional growth of teachers and helps them develop more effective educational programs for children.

6. Respects teachers' autonomy and works toward strengthening teachers' independence.

7. Develops long-term collegial relationships based on mutual trust and respect.

Working with Teachers—Some Assumptions

When teachers ask me to visit their classrooms and give them feedback on their teaching, I make several assumptions. First, teachers who ask an outsider to observe them are most often experienced teachers whose classrooms are functioning well but who are dissatisfied with or have questions about some aspects of their day-to-day teaching or their professional lives. Beginners tend to be more hesitant about asking for assistance. Those who do ask are secure enough to understand that asking for help is not a sign of weakness. My second assumption is that teachers who ask for input are ready for some kind of change. They may not know exactly in what direction they want to move, but they know, even if only vaguely, that some growth and change will take place as a result of their working with an advisor. Third, teachers who ask an outside resource person to guide and support them in their professional development goals have some knowledge of the educational beliefs and the style of work of this resource person. The teachers whose classrooms I describe here knew, if only in general terms, what I believed about children and their school education.

My Educational Beliefs

When young children come to school, they have developed distinct ways of coping with the world, of asking questions and seeking answers, of dealing with situations and relating to people. Certain patterns have been established in the constant interaction between the child and his or her environment. This interaction continues as the child enters school. The teacher, the other children in the class, the physical environment and the atmosphere of the classroom and the school, and the subject matter all constitute a new world confronting the young child. What kind of learning will take place depends on how well the child can use and adapt this new world to his or her individual needs, interests, and learning styles.

To create an environment in which children learn well, teachers must be broadly educated in both child development and curriculum. They must be able to create an atmosphere of both emotional trust and intellectual excitement, and they must know how to make diverse subject matter accessible to children of widely differing backgrounds. Healthy children have an inborn drive to learn. To nurture this drive, to guide, uncover, or reawaken it is the ultimate challenge of every teacher. To help teachers meet this challenge by supporting them in their own continuing education becomes the challenge of the advisor.

Observing in Classrooms

When teachers ask me to observe them in their classrooms, I first ask for permission to take notes, explaining that I wish to write down the things that I will want to discuss after the observation. Later, when we sit down together, I put my open notebook on the table and use my remarks as starting points for our discussion. I always share my classroom notes with teachers, though I may make additional notes for myself at a later time.

What am I looking for when I go into a classroom? I look at the room arrangement, the organization and set-up of materials, the teacher/child interaction, the involvement of the children in their work. I take note of classroom routines, time schedules, bulletin boards, noise level, and amount of movement. I want to see if this is a classroom that is intellectually stimulating, gives children emotional support, and allows for positive social interaction. I pay special attention to areas of teacher strengths because I always want to give some positive feedback and because I will want to use these strengths later to move into areas of needed change. After my initial scanning of the room, I generally become a participant observer. It is almost impossible for me to be in a classroom with young children and not in some way become involved in what they are doing. I may participate in a class discussion; I may help a child with reading or math; talk to a group about an art or science project; lend a helping hand, even give assistance with classroom routines if the teacher indicates that that would be welcome. I may ask the teacher some questions and make some simple suggestions, and I generally act as a friendly, supportive co-teacher. Having worked mostly in informal, primary classrooms made this approach possible.

It is important for the teachers to know, however, that an observation, however unstructured, will never be neutral. I bring with me my practical experience and my theoretical knowledge about teaching and learning. What I notice and pay attention to will be determined to a large degree by what I think constitutes a good life for young children in school. I may look at a classroom without a specific plan, but what I *see* is organized and analyzed according to my personal beliefs.

Classroom Observations

The following account of actual classroom observations illustrates my method and approach. I observed twice in two different classrooms and talked with teachers after each visit. Patterns for further work began to emerge after these observations and discussions.

Broadway School

Broadway School, located at the edge of a university campus, is housed in an old two-story brick building with large, high-ceilinged rooms and wonderfully wide staircases and halls. After several years of negotiation between Broadway School and both the school administration and the Board of Education, Broadway School has recently been recognized as a K-6 alternative school within the district.

The school's Follow Through program, sponsored by Bank Street College of Education in New York City, is described in a letter to parents as "activity-oriented with individualized programs which encourage children to be self-directed learners." The school's principal has been most supportive of the Follow Through program, and over the years the school has attracted teachers who hold a similar teaching philosophy. Broadway has two classes at each grade level and currently has a traditional and an alternative strand in addition to the Follow Through classes. As a result of Broadway's designation as an alternative school in the district, the traditional strand is being phased out over the next two years. Several of the current "traditional" teachers already have classrooms with individualized programs quite similar to those in the Follow Through and alternative classes.

Broadway is a comfortable school to visit. There is an overall friendliness and warmth, and there is obvious respect for the children from every staff person, from principal down to custodian. The teachers are exceptionally hard working and committed to making the alternative school a success in the community. The school population is probably the most diverse of all the elementary schools in the district, partly because of the many minority children (Hispanic, Asian, and black) who are bused into the Follow Through classes and partly because of the school's proximity to the university, which always has foreign graduate students and visiting faculty with young children.

The Kindergarten Classroom. George, the Follow Through kindergarten teacher, is in his first full year of teaching. He took over the kindergarten class in the middle of last year after finishing his student teaching in a 1st-2nd grade classroom in the same school. George had a variety of interesting work experiences before he turned to elementary school teaching. Most recently he taught at a residential facility for emotionally disturbed adolescents. He is a mature person, quiet, open, warm, and relaxed. He has a lovely way of relating to the children, who are obviously very fond of him. He works with an assistant teacher who has been in the Follow Through program for many years and who clearly appreciates George's qualities.

For my first visit I arrived right after the morning meeting. The children were already at work. I was immediately struck by an atmosphere of busy involvement. Children were building with blocks, working with clay, experimenting at the water table, and playing in the housekeeping area. A group sat around a table with Mary, the assistant, making alphabet books. George was in the hall, part of which was set up for additional activities. There was a terrarium with growing plants, a woodworking bench, and a couple of tables. George was playing a game with a small group of children. The children in the class were friendly, easily approachable, and responsive. Those not engaged with the two teachers worked quite independently.

The room itself was relatively small but was sensibly arranged. A large area in the middle was left open. Children took games and puzzles there during the work period and met there in a circle for group meetings and snacks.

After about 40 mintues, the noise level in the room began to rise, little arguments occurred here and there, and a number of children seemed to be drifting around. George had left his group in the hall and was in the room now, helping to settle arguments and directing children to other activities. Cleanup was a little hectic. Many children were wandering around, and some needed to be reminded repeatedly to do their share. In the end, everything did get put away. Children sat in a circle on the floor to have a snack which had been prepared by Mary with the help of some children. Two children passed out the snack, the others ate and chatted with each other. Then there was some singing of Spanish songs, led by Mary, after which the group went outside to the playground. George had asked me to observe only during the morning work period, so I returned after the children left, at 1:30, to talk.

While I had lunch I thought about what I had seen and made some notes:

1. George seems to care strongly about relationships. His way of handling conflicts among children showed him as an arbitrator who expected the children to think and talk about their problems and, whenever possible, to come up with their own solutions. However, he gave them enough support to make them feel secure and confident that they could deal themselves with many of their little problems.

2. When I saw George interacting with children around materials, I did not see quite the same commitment. He expressed interest but did not really get involved. Except when he was working with his own group out in the hall, he was more of a benevolent overseer going around the room, checking to see how everything was going. That is often the role of the classroom teacher in an informal setting, but I could not tell whether George's investment in the intellectual discoveries and learning of the children was as deep as his interest in the children's interpersonal relationships. At first that sur-

prised me. I know the teacher with whom he student-taught, and she is outstanding in her support of children's learning. Then I had to remind myself that this was only George's first year of teaching. Perhaps because of his maturity and calm manner and because Mary helps to make the program run smoothly, my expectations for George may be unrealistic. The kind of investment in children's learning that I have in mind is rarely evident in a beginning teacher.

After George's children left, we talked for about an hour. It was not hard for me to give him positive feedback. I complimented him on his way of interacting with the children and on his good relationship with his assistant. I told him how well the room was functioning when I arrived and how much I enjoyed talking and working with different children. I then asked him if this was a typical day. "Fairly typical," he said, "though not all days are so calm." I mentioned the restlessness I noticed toward the end of the work period, and George said he was aware of it and that was typical. We then discussed cleanup. He was not happy with it. That enabled me to make some suggestions on how to organize it differently, mentioning that transition times are always hard for young children and need a lot of attention. I also thought he could be a little more persistent in following through with cleanup demands and expectations.

I asked George if he ever found time to talk with groups of children who were working in various parts of the room. "Not as much as I would like to," he answered. "I miss many teachable moments and often wake up in the middle of the night thinking of things I could have said or done." George said that he is just as committed to supporting children's intellectual learning as he is to supporting their social and emotional growth, but he doesn't know how to do it, how to get to all the children in the class. We then talked about how he could *make* time to give more input, perhaps concentrating on a different area each week, and taking notes on children's activities, discoveries, questions, and conversations. George's top priority, however, was clearly the children's interpersonal relationships. He told me that he cares deeply about how children feel and that he wants to help them with their self-concepts and their attitude toward school. "I will feel successful," he said, "if the kids walk out of here anxious to go to 1st grade."

My second visit to George's classroom a month later was shorter because of an all-school event that I did not know about. The water table now had sand in it, and again it was a popular place, although there was some fighting about equipment and space. Some girls were engaged in intense dramatic play with puppets, and a group of boys in the block corner were playing with their television characters brought from home. Mary was at a table giving help to children who were drawing and writing in their journals. A prospective student teacher from the university took a group out to the hall to work on place value with craft sticks and beans. Not surprisingly, the children were rather confused.

George seemed tired when we sat down to talk at the end of the day. I mentioned the fighting at the sand table and suggested he add more equipment such as funnels, strainers, and containers. I asked about the student teacher's place-value lesson. "As soon as I saw which children she was taking out," George said, "I knew it would be above their heads. Yesterday she took another group who were much more ready for it." I questioned the point of teaching place value to *any* kindergarten children and then shifted the conversation to George's role as teacher and his responsibility to make decisions on behalf of the children. I commented on the block-corner activities; on both my visits I had noticed interesting structures that had been built on a previous day, but the play around these structures tended to get out of hand. I wondered whether some input from George might not improve the quality of the play. Yet I also witnessed a lovely incident in the block area: a little boy was trying to comfort another child, at the same time urging the group that had excluded him from play to let him participate. I told George about it and he was pleased. His attention to working on relationships is obviously paying off.

Later I made some notes on possible long-range goals for work with George. He is exceptionally tuned-in to children's feelings, but I would like to help him understand what intense involvement with materials can do for children's self-concepts. I would like to have more conversations with him about the teacher's role in providing for such involvement and for interacting with the children to stimulate their learning. I wondered whether I needed to help George differentiate between intervening to settle arguments and intervening to further children's learning. In a long-range working relationship, we could clarify these issues.

Jefferson School

Jefferson School is located in a small community about 12 miles east of Broadway School, in the same school district. Due to recent rapid population growth in this part of the county, two additions to the school were built in the last five years, and now more space is again desperately needed. A new elementary school opened nearby this past fall, and another new one will open next fall. Until that school is completed, Jefferson will continue to be overcrowded. It is the largest elementary school in the district, with 30 classrooms and over 700 children in grades K-5.

Like Broadway School, Jefferson has had a Follow Through program for many years, but unlike Broadway, the program has not had much influence on the rest of the school. On the whole, the Follow Through staff has kept to itself when not involved in all-school activities.

Jefferson has a very different atmosphere from Broadway. It is a much larger school, more spread out, and it also has so many specialists and programs that it is hard to get a feeling for the school as a whole. At Broadway, the reading and special education teachers, the librarian and the art, music, and P.E. specialists all support the goals of the teachers. At Jefferson, perhaps because of the larger number of teachers and the greater diversity of teaching styles, there seems to be less communication among the staff. (The principal told me that every day there are about 110 adults in the building, counting teachers, assistants, and program specialists.) Jefferson's wide range of teaching approaches is fairly typical of large elementary schools, but the new principal is working hard to develop a more cohesive faculty.

The Kindergarten Classroom. This is Sherin's second year as Follow Through kindergarten teacher at Jefferson. Last year she took two months' maternity leave in the middle of the winter. In addition to her baby boy, Sherin also has a six-year-old daughter. Her previous teaching experience includes a variety of early childhood positions, including teaching in the university's daycare center and in a local half-day kindergarten program.

Like George, Sherin is with the children from 8:30 to 1:30 and then has 1½ hours—until 3 p.m.—for preparation time. She has a full-time assistant, a woman who has been with the Follow Through program for many years. There are 25 children in her class, of whom over a third are Hispanic. Sherin's Hispanic children come from English-speaking homes. Monolingual Spanish-speaking children go to Jefferson's bilingual-bicultural program.

Sherin's kindergarten room is much more spacious than George's at Broadway. She has basically the same equipment—blocks, water and sand tables, woodworking bench, dramatic-play area, art materials, and table toys—but because there is much more space, more things can be put out without cluttering the room. Sherin also has animals—right now there is a pregnant guinea pig, and later in the spring she plans to incubate chicken eggs.

The room arrangement is pleasing and sensible. I had only one question about it: the block area did not seem sufficiently closed off to allow buildings to remain up for several days, nor did it give the children the kind of privacy and protection that tends to enhance the quality of the block play.

The children had been on a walk the day before I visited, looking at houses and yards in the neighborhood. When I arrived, they were just gathering in a circle on the floor to start a discussion on what they had seen. Expectations for circle-time behavior must have been made very clear in this class; there was none of the pushing and shoving that so often takes place when young children are in a large group. Sherin has excellent controls. With her quiet and calm voice, she communicates authority without being in the least bit authoritarian.

I liked Sherin's way of leading the discussion. Her interest in the children's ideas and her respect for their ways of expressing thoughts and feelings were obvious. Every statement made by a child was accepted, sometimes clarified for the sake of other children, sometimes extended, but always responded to in an honest way. I thought, however, that the discussion went on too long; quite a few children became restless after about 20 minutes.

Around the room were some charts that reflected another topic the children had been studying: families. One chart, titled "What is a family?" contained the following statements:

BEING TOGETHER MAKES A FAMILY.

SHARING THINGS (TOYS, FOOD) MAKES A FAMILY.

WORKING TOGETHER MAKES A FAMILY.

BEING NICE TO EACH OTHER MAKES A FAMILY.

FRIENDS CAN BE PART OF A FAMILY.

TALKING TO EACH OTHER, SHARING YOUR FEELINGS IS PART OF BEING A FAMILY.

I liked the charts but wondered whether they might not be more appropriate for a 1st grade class. (They reminded me of what a 1st grade teacher once said to me. She had done a lot of work with measurement and had displayed many graphs and charts on the walls of her room. But she was wondering why she was doing "all these little 'Nuffield' charts. They look good on the walls of my room, but they aren't used very much after they are put up.")

After the discussion, the children went to various activities. Sherin took a group to the block area. She had a blueprint of a house. I think she wanted the children to see that people build houses according to a plan, but the children seemed more interested in doing their own building. Another group was doing some cooking with Jenny, the assistant, and the rest of the children dispersed to the water table, the play house, the table toys, etc. Clay had been set out at one table, and two or three children were working there intensely. I gave some technical help to one little boy, making a mental note to show Sherin how to do this later on.

The work period was busy and productive. Cleanup was orderly and unrushed. Then there was snack, outdoor play, and story time, after which the children went to lunch. I had some other business to attend to in the school and returned at 1:30 to talk with Sherin. What kind of feedback did I give her?

First I mentioned all the things I liked about her class—and there were many: the excellent organization of the classroom and the smooth flow of the day's activities; the lack of discipline and management problems; the children's discussion on houses and Sherin's calm yet focused way of leading the discussion; and the evidence of interesting activities going on in her classroom. Then I raised some questions: How did she feel about the children's response to the blueprint? "It was a bit over their head," she said. "I don't think they are quite ready for this kind of planning."

I agreed, though I said it was a nice idea. I asked Sherin how much experience she had working with clay, and she said not too much. I showed her some things she needed to know so that the children's products would not fall apart when the clay dried. I also suggested she consult the art specialist, and I promised to loan her some books on children's art. I mentioned the restlessness of some of the children during the latter part of the discussion; Sherin said she realized that the discussion was too long and that she often tends to go on too long. We talked about possibly dividing up the group for some discussions so that children would not have to wait so long for their turn to talk and so that shyer children would have a better chance to participate.

I then asked her to tell me about the topic the children had been studying, families. Sherin said that this was an area in which she would like more input: how do you develop a unit, how long should it last, what are appropriate subjects for this age, etc. She wanted to study growth and development next and wanted some ideas. We made a date to meet for another talk in about two weeks.

That meeting took place in a coffee shop—I like meeting away from school for longer talks—and we spent a wonderful couple of hours talking. We started out with Sherin's theme, growth and development, then branched out and discussed curriculum development in general as well as the district's curriculum expectations in social studies and mathematics; we talked about children and their various interests, about the difference between the Follow Through program and some of the more traditional classrooms at Jefferson, and about other school-related topics. We covered a lot of ground, and I wondered, at the end, whether our talk had been too diffuse to be of help to Sherin. "No," she said, "it gets me thinking, and then I have to sit down and put it together for myself."

After Sherin left, I made some notes: Sherin is a perceptive, sensitive, thoughtful teacher who is anxious to grow and who welcomes questions that stimulate her thinking. She needs no help with the day-to-day routines of her class. She is open to suggestions and secure enough to take them, leave them, or put them aside for a while. A combination of classroom observations and away-from-school curriculum talks would probably work well for her.

On my second visit to Sherin's class, two weeks after our talk, the children were discussing their trip to a hospital. We had talked about that trip in the coffee shop. I had alerted Sherin to the fears that such a visit can arouse in young children, and I also encouraged her to find out ahead of time what the people at the hospital were planning to show the children and to decide if it was appropriate. I don't know if she had time to make this previsit. She now had mixed feelings about the trip itself. After the discussion, a group of children went to the dramatic-play area, which had been equipped with some hospital-related playthings. Jenny went with the children, guiding their play.

I would have preferred to see the children on their own, but Sherin said that they have a hard time with dramatic play, that it easily gets silly or out of hand. I went over to the woodworking area and watched two boys make an airplane. I was impressed by their skills. I also spent some time with a group of children in the block area. They had started their building by grabbing all the large blocks, and they were competing to see who could build the highest structure. I talked to them about making different kinds of buildings and tried to get them interested in using blocks of all sizes and shapes.

Snack time was fun. Sherin had prepared several plates with a variety of fruits and vegetables: grapefruit sections, pieces of avocado and kiwi fruit, raw potatoes and turnips, and some peanuts in their shells. The children ate the samples, compared taste and texture, talked about the various shapes and colors, and commented on skins and seeds. I participated in the discussion, raising some additional questions for the children to think about. Sherin had told me that she likes this sort of input from me. It extends her curriculum and gives her ideas. Both of us got interested in the topic of seeds: Why does an avocado have such a large seed, and why does the kiwi fruit have so many little seeds? What is the reason for the distribution pattern of seeds in the fruit? Which seeds could we plant in the classroom? Could we classify fruits and vegetables according to their seeds—large/small, one/many, edible/inedible? Sherin is always open to this sort of talk. She enjoys learning herself and does not have much opportunity to think with a colleague.

I liked all the activities that Sherin planned for her class, but after my second visit I began to wonder whether perhaps she plans a little too much. Were the more standard classroom activities like block-building, painting, or sand and water-play being neglected? Should Sherin have fewer special activities and pay more attention to the regular curriculum? Might that help to give the children more continuity and independence? Would they work with greater involvement and become more self-directed? I shared these questions with Sherin. I said that my general feelings about her program were very positive, but if we continued to work together I would want to explore these questions with her. She was eager to do so.

Long-Range Goals

General Goals

I have described how I work with teachers and how directions for continued work developed from my observations and from our subsequent talks. Although my initial visits with George and Sherin did not have a specific focus, the pattern for our mutual work soon became clear. If I were to continue to work with them, what would be my goals, and how would I go about implementing them?

My long-range goals reflect my general beliefs about the kind of education that best stimulates and facilitates children's learning. My aim, therefore, would be to help George and Sherin create the best possible learning environment for their children. I would try to make it possible, for instance, for George to spend some uninterrupted time working with small groups or individuals while I looked after the rest of the class. This would help him to experience the children's learning in a different way and give him a chance to see what sustained teacher input can accomplish. In Sherin's room I might propose to come in temporarily as an additional teacher to help with a gradual shift from teacher-directed to more child-initiated activities. We would always talk afterwards to reflect on what happened, to analyze successes and failures, and to plan for further work.

My overall goal is broad and does not change. Getting there, however, rarely proceeds on a straight and simple path. George wanted me to continue coming to his classroom to give him feedback on his teaching. He liked the combination of observation and talk, since it gave him an opportunity to think in greater depth about the children and their activities. Sherin, on the other hand, preferred to spend more time talking with me. She enjoyed having me in her class—most teachers appreciate feedback from an interested, nonevaluative observer—but she was at a different stage of development from George, more interested in her own growth and learning, eager to think about curriculum development and to gain a better understanding of that process.

The teachers' expressed needs would provide the starting point for our joint work, but as other needs became apparent and as changes in the classroom situation occurred, the directions of our work would be adapted to the new demands, and shifts in emphasis might become necessary. The success of advisory work depends on a relationship of mutual trust and respect that develops gradually as teachers and advisors work and learn together through their attempt to solve the problems of daily teaching.

Cook and Mack (1975) expressed concern that advisors sometimes lose sight of their long-range goals by emphasizing only the concrete, practical day-to-day help in the classroom:

While advisory programs must allow teachers to develop at their own pace and draw on their personal strengths and individual starting points, they must also emphasize the need for growth and introspection over a long period of time. Without question, it is simpler to teach teachers how to use a new piece of equipment or material, to arrange a classroom, even to ask different kinds of questions, than to be thoughtful, analytical and independent professionals relying on their own initiative and critical judgment (p. 7).

What methods, besides my work in classrooms, do I employ to help teachers develop into "thoughtful, analytical and independent professionals?" Following are some examples.

Methods

Networking. Teachers often feel isolated in their classrooms. One of my goals is to help break down this isolation. I encourage teachers to *visit other classrooms*, both in their own and other schools. I may propose that they visit a class where a different approach is being used; I may recommend a specific classroom because I want to put two teachers in touch with one another; I may suggest a visit simply to give a teacher a chance to get out of her school and spend some time in a classroom without being in charge. Almost always, teachers find these visits useful, stimulating, and reassuring.

I may organize *discussion groups* for teachers with similar interests and·concerns. We may meet only once or for several weeks or months. In some parts of the country, such informal meetings have developed into seminars on children's thinking that continued over many years.

While a staff member at the Mountain View Center, I would invite teachers to come to the Center to work with materials and to meet other staff with expertise different from mine. Without the backup of a teachers' center, I would still try to organize *workshops and classes* on various curriculum topics as well as on child growth and development. If I could not teach these classes myself, I would try to find people in the community to do so. I would encourage teachers to use each others' expertise freely and to start building a local network of support. Greater use of community resources would also be one of my goals.

Journals. I would encourage teachers to keep journals in order to become more reflective about their teaching. Although time-consuming, the discipline of writing requires you to organize your thoughts and helps you to focus on the most important events of the day. I ask teachers to make their journal entries in a loose-leaf notebook and to give me their journal pages once a week. I always respond to the journal entries, sometimes in considerable detail. Journals provide both teachers and me with a permanent record of their thinking and learning and of my reactions and suggestions. They can always be used as a reference, to observe progress, and to check on past events. This kind of written dialogue offers possibilities of working with teachers even if there is not enough time for an advisor to make regular classroom visits.

Notes. I find that once I start focusing on a topic, I often get additional ideas after I talk with a teacher. Sometimes I write down these ideas after leaving school. Teachers appreciate the fact that I continue to think about their classrooms—just as they do—and they find my personalized curriculum suggestions most helpful. These notes can be shared with other teachers working on the same themes, and they also provide me with a record of suggestions I have made.

Curriculum development. Unfortunately many teachers are trained to use curriculum guides or texts as their only curriculum resource materials. A 3rd grade teacher once told me that she didn't want to "just teach from the book," but she didn't know how to develop her own social studies curriculum. If teachers want a curriculum that is appropriate for a particular group of children living in a particular setting, they need to learn where to find other resources. They need to learn how to use, select from, and adapt a wide variety of available materials in order to develop studies suited to the age level and experiential background of their children.

Since I am interested in helping teachers become curriculum developers, I always encourage them to do their own thinking and to rely on their knowledge and intuition about children when making programming decisions. One year I worked with an experienced traditional teacher who wanted to change her approach but who was having problems with a more individualized, experience-based curriculum. I worked intensely with her at the beginning of the school year. Later, she told an interviewer: "I was going to phone Maja one day but then decided not to because I realized I knew what she was going to say. I thought: Oh boy, that is the beginning of doing it myself." Without doing your own thinking, you cannot solve your problems or make informed decisions about the content of children's learning.

Conclusion

The kind of teaching I am encouraging and supporting demands intelligent, creative, and sensitive individuals who will approach their task with energy and compassion and who will be committed to their own continued learning and growth. These are professional teachers. Over 30 years ago, Lucy Sprague Mitchell expressed concern about the lack of professionalism in public school teachers. She wrote:

Teachers' whole experience within the administrative setup of a big school system has been away from their taking the responsibility for planning individually for their particular children, away from experimentation and initiative in their classrooms, away from trusting their own judgments based on their own experiences, away from taking part in or even following educational efforts which do not affect them personally—in short away from *taking their teaching job as a profession*. It is an anomaly inherent in this form of administration that the teachers, who are on the lowest level both in responsibility for educational decisions and in salary, are the ones who really control the school lives of the children (1951, p. 329).

Although efforts have been made to change this situation, the problems described by Mitchell still exist. I believe that only when teachers are given full responsibility for their job, and learn to *take* this responsibility, will teaching become a respected profession. The main goal of advisors is to support teachers in their quest for professional growth.

References

Buxton, A. P. "A Distinctive Option in Inservice. The Teachers' Center Meets Individual Needs and Institutional Goals." Occasional Paper No. 5. San Francisco: Teachers'

Center Exchange, Far West Laboratory for Educational Research and Development, June 1979.

Cook, A., and H. Mack. *The Word and the Thing: Ways of Seeing the Teacher*. Grand Forks, N.D.: North Dakota Study Group for Evaluation, University of North Dakota, 1975.

Mitchell, L. S. *Our Children and Our Schools*. New York: Simon and Schuster, 1951.

10. Tasks in Times: Objects of Study in a Natural History of Teaching

Frederick Erickson

THIS CHAPTER HAS TWO MAIN SECTIONS. IN THE FIRST, I DISCUSS A STAFF DEVELopment project that has just begun,[1] describing what I notice when visiting a classroom. I sketch the process of written and oral dialogue that ensues with the teacher and briefly mention the topics of inquiry that emerge from our discussions. In the second section, I provide more background on the perspective that underlies my work with experienced teachers. This section presents a social-constructivist view of work and tasks in classrooms and concludes with a model of the social and academic dimensions of classroom task environments. This sociocognitive model of teaching and learning informs the approach to classroom observation and staff development that is described in the first part of the chapter.

---

[1]The staff development and research effort described in this chapter is a project of the Institute for Research on Teaching, "Teachers' Conceptual Change." For further information, contact the author at the Institute for Research on Teaching, College of Education, Michigan State University, East Lansing, MI 48824.

Frederick Erickson is Professor, Department of Teacher Education and Institute for Research on Teaching, Michigan State University, East Lansing.

Author's note: I wish to thank Cherie Wilcox for editorial assistance and her husband, William Natho, for advice on the kinds of arithmetic reasoning involved in the example of a classroom task. Preparation of this chapter was supported in part by the Institute for Research on Teaching, Michigan State University. The Institute is funded primarily by the Program for Teaching and Instruction of the National Institute of Education, U.S. Department of Education (Contract No. 400-81-0014). The opinions expressed in this chapter do not necessarily reflect the position, policy, or endorsement of the NIE.

Looking in Classrooms with Teachers

A Staff Development Project

A few months ago I began working with a 1st grade teacher, who I shall refer to as Mrs. Smith. The work was being conducted with a group of colleagues under the auspices of the Institute for Research on Teaching. We worked with three other 1st grade teachers from the same building, their principal, and central administrators in a suburban school system with a diverse student population. The elementary school in which we began our project was one of the two schools in the district that had the highest percentages of children from working-class families. The aims of our project were to conduct a new kind of staff development with classroom teachers and administrators, to study the process of implementation as it took place, and to document and reflect on what personnel from the university and the school district were learning during the course of the project.

A distinctive feature of this attempt at staff development was that we did not have a predetermined set of skills or insights to teach. Rather, we wanted the teachers and administrators to look at and reflect on what was happening routinely in the classrooms. This inductive approach to staff development stemmed from presuppositions about the nature of teaching and about classrooms as learning environments.

The Content of Observation Notes

My visits to Mrs. Smith's classroom occurred almost weekly. The notes are typical of those of researchers who study teaching from a qualitative, or ethnographic, point of view.

Certain kinds of information always appear: the events that occur, the times and places of those events, the cast of characters, patterns of social relationships among the characters. In the past, my notes contained little information about subject matter and much about social relations (see the discussion in Erickson, 1982b). I now include much more information about the content of instruction.

On the first day of an observation, I draw a map of the classroom, identifying the seats of the children and the major places in which various kinds of action take place. In Mrs. Smith's room these places included the main chalkboard, her desk, the trays into which students' written work was deposited, the students' large rectangular tables, a round reading table, a row of coat hooks along the wall, and a long shelf holding cardboard cylinders in which the students stored written work and school memos to be taken home.

As the children enter the room, I begin to jot down the times that major activities begin. For Mrs. Smith's room, major activities at the beginning of the day include the Pledge of Allegiance, updating a weather chart, taking lunch count, explaining seatwork and the first reading group. Sometimes, as the action happens thick and fast, I just sit and watch and listen. I may video-tape on the first day, or I may help an individual child or two. Usually, how-ever, I keep writing, even if the video camera is recording.

When writing, I note major phases with the named events. Boundaries between phases of events occur as rearrangements take place, either in the subject matter focus or in patterns of social participation (or in both simul-taneously, as is often the case). Often, the teacher and children do not label these phases or attend consciously to them, although there are expectations of this, such as the clean-up phase at the end of an art activity.

An example of phases within an activity occurred on the first day I vis-ited, which happened to be Lincoln's birthday. The overall activity was ex-plaining seatwork. A few sentences about Lincoln had been written on the board. The children were to copy these on the lined bottom half of a large piece of paper and draw a picture on the unlined top half to illustrate the sentences. The first phase within the activity was general discussion, appar-ently continued from the previous day, about who Lincoln was. During this discussion, children volunteered comments without raising hands, and the teacher did not designate speakers. The next phase was a question-answer sequence about which war occurred when Lincoln was president. Here the children volunteered to answer, and the teacher called on individuals by name. There was more than one answerer in the sequence because the first child designated to answer said, "World War II?"

After the question-answer sequence, the next phase was reading aloud the sentences about Lincoln. This was done as choral recitation, with the teacher reading with the children and pointing to each word with a pointer. In the next phase, the teacher explained the procedure for using the paper to copy the sentences on the board and draw their illustrations. In the final phase of the activity, the teacher explained a word recognition ditto sheet that the children were to fill out.

In recording whole activities, phases within them, and action within the phases, I note the time the activity begins and the time of each new phase within the activity. During each phase, I transcribe as much as possible of the children's speech—their exact words, timing, and intonation. I also de-scribe salient nonverbal actions by the teacher and students—in detailed be-havioral terms rather than in terms that imply intent. For example, I would write, "Sam picked up Mary's worksheet, folded it in half, and put it back down on the table." I would not write, "Sam was annoying Mary." Nor would I write, "Sam was annoying Mary by messing around with her worksheet."

I attempt to avoid paraphrases of either the verbal or the nonverbal be-havior, not in order to write a disembodied, so-called "objective record," but because I assume, especially at the outset of working with a teacher, that I do not know what is going on. I also assume that the teacher doesn't know fully what is going on, either, not because he or she is incompetent or irre-sponsible but because of information overload and time press in the class-room. Experienced teachers respond to the surplus of information and shortage of time for reflection in two ways. One is to let routine perform-ance become invisible. The other way is to look very briefly at what is hap-pening—a quick scan of a student or a group. Let us think about what the teacher sees and hears while teaching.

Limits in Teachers' Routine Awareness

Consider first the significance of our basic human ability to allow the content and process of customary actions to become invisible to us as we perform them. A psychologist might say that overlearning enables us to per-form routines preconsciously, without reflection. An anthropologist or lin-guist might say that most of the cultural and linguistic rules (or better, op-erating principles) basic to everyday life are implicit and outside awareness rather than explicit and inside awareness. Cultural learning teaches us what not to see and hear as well as what to notice consciously.

Our capacity to perform customary action intuitively is a tremendous asset as well as a significant liability. We cannot reflect continuously from moment to moment or we would be overwhelmed with information and for-ever immersed in decision making. But there are costs in being freed from too much information. Sometimes we need to look carefully at our activities in a distanced and reflective way. If we never subject the taken-for-granted to scrutiny, we are unable to deliberate on it when we need to.

One kind of scrutiny in the classroom is the quick scan—the experi-enced teacher's intuitive radar. There are trade-offs inherent in the use of the quick scan. While it is economical in terms of time, it only produces snapshot views of behavior. They may be clear and vivid and thus easy to re-call later, but they do not provide information on what was happening be-fore and after the observed behavior. In reality, action happens in connected sequences. To understand an action, we must look longer than a split second.

Both because of the invisibility of routines and because of the tendency to scrutinize bits of routines by using the quick scan, there are serious lim-its on what the teacher can attend to while teaching. Experienced teachers have learned ways of processing intuitively much of the buzzing and confu-sion of daily classroom life. This means they have learned how *not to see* the content of learning environments in their classroom—the structure of sub-ject matter and social relations that makes up the enacted curriculum.

Recent research on teaching has pointed to the importance of student time-on-task (see for example, Denham and Lieberman, 1980, and Brophy and Good, 1985) or, in a more felicitous phrase, "active learning time" (Har-nischfeger and Wiley, 1985). If that time is crucial for mastery, it is especially important that the teacher be able to look at and think about what is going on during active learning time—what portion of the curriculum the child is working on and what the child is learning, including the preconceptions, in-terests, and feelings the child brings to the task.

In working with experienced teachers, I have found some aspects of the enacted curriculum are invisible to them, precisely because they have learned to put their attention on "automatic pilot." The main thing I have to offer the experienced teacher is a way of looking that stretches the attention span across longer time. When teachers do this, they begin to raise new questions about sequences of action and about more complex patterns of ecology involving the various actors and objects in classroom activities. This way of looking with new eyes makes the familiar strange; it makes the commonplace problematic and interesting again. But what is interesting is often also a bit scary. We enter the threshold of reflective awareness with profound ambivalence between approach and avoidance.

Learning to tell stories about one's everyday experience is one means of crossing the threshold of awareness. These stories have often been dismissed by academics as "merely anecdotal." Yet they are a means of gaining an interpretive sense of our experience that can be called *narrative understanding*.

Remembering as Narration

Let us think about the nature of a narrative understanding of events and ask what insights such an understanding might have to offer teachers. Personal narratives take the form of stories about what happened to us and to those around us. It might seem that awareness must precede narration, but that is not necessarily so, for telling stories is a means of thinking. Etymology points to the significance of narration as a mode of thought. The terms *story* and *history* are related. In the original Greek, *history* means inquiry into events as well as a report of the events. This is true for personal history as well. As we render an account of past events, we take one step back from our experience. That is a point at which reflection can begin. Thus the very act of telling a story about what happened—producing an account of sequences of actions that occurred in the past—can be a means of developing deeper understanding of the organization of those action sequences.

A key factor of this deeper understanding is its narrative character. There is considerable evidence from schema theory and the subsequent empirical work in contemporary cognitive psychology and cognitively oriented linguistics that we use narratives as a way of making sense both in remembering past events and in anticipating immediate next moments in our current experience (Bartlett, 1932; Schank and Abelson, 1977; Becker, 1979; Chafe, 1980; and Tannen, 1984).

Narratives have a story line—a plot. It is an old notion that clear knowledge of plot is important for making sense. For example, Aristotle in the *Poetics* saw plot as the essential foundation of drama. He defined plot as a sequence of necessarily connected actions (i.e., reasonably expectable patterns of succession). Literary critic Kenneth Burke (1969) has influenced linguistics and social scientists in the development of a "dramatistic" theory of social action in which plot and scene are central concepts. Rosen (1984), the English literary critic, has recommended that teachers learn to write narrative accounts of life in their classrooms as a means of developing deeper insight into their teaching.

From a variety of disciplinary points of view, research suggests that a sense of story seems to be the way by which we cognitively organize our culturally learned knowledge of the routines of daily life. For example, when we see a knife, we place it in a sequence of actions, social relationships, place, and time—something being cut, someone doing the cutting. The same holds for a pencil and paper. Who is writing? What is being written, to whom, toward what end? These are elements of a story—the who, what, when, where, and why of daily life.

To use another metaphor, it seems that in remembering we interpret the meaning of the snapshot view of isolated objects and actions in terms of the place of that snapshot in a home movie. The home movie version—recording a succession of events before and after the snapshot—answers more completely for us the story questions of who, what, when, where, and why. The snapshot by itself cannot tell us all of that. The home movie provides a more comprehensive view. As we reflect on the movie, we derive a more powerful and coherent understanding of the event than we could by looking at a few snapshots. Moreover, with a short movie shot, we can do instant replays of strategically significant sequences. We can even freeze the frame to stop the action. The freeze is a snapshot, but it is a snapshot in context, and it is one chosen deliberately after some reflection. It is apparent, then, that the home movie makes available a different order of understanding than the snapshot does. The movie version tells a story, while the snapshot only points to one.

The Natural History of Enacted Curriculum as a Focus for Staff Development

Why is telling stories as a mode of inquiry especially appropriate for experienced teachers as a means of staff development? Because a narrative understanding of classroom events can become a way of making visible the invisible routines of the enacted curriculum. By this transformation, the enacted curriculum as experienced by students can be seen more clearly and fully. It becomes available for deliberation and for redesign, if and when that is appropriate.

The teacher is responsible for seeing to it that students are actually engaged by the curriculum, i.e., that they spend active learning time interacting in environments that have certain substantive contents. For the individual student, the curriculum as enacted consists of concrete tasks concretely engaged in within daily classroom events. Those aspects of curriculum that are not actually engaged by a student do not exist for that student.

An approach to staff development can be grounded on these insights. The approach presumes that the ability of the teacher to look at and deliberate on the enacted curriculum of the classroom—its content and process—is pedagogically crucial for the teacher (unless one assumes that curriculum can really be student-proof and teacher-proof, an assumption I find unwarranted). Experienced teachers can quite readily learn to see the enacted curriculum that has become invisible to them. They do this by learning to take longer looks—moving from the quick scan and the behavioral snapshot to the short home movie as a way of remembering classroom events.

Some stimulation is needed to begin taking longer looks at classroom life in order to consider as a project of natural history the enacted curriculum in the room. Stimulating the teacher into becoming a natural historian, a more observant participant, is the central point of the staff development effort in which I am currently engaged.

Beginning and Continuing Conversations with Teachers

The preceding discussion set forth a perspective that guided what I did as Mrs. Smith and I began to discuss what I saw in her room on the first days I visited. I asked her to write her recollections of what happened in a classroom event that she thought was interesting. I wrote my recollections of the same event. Then, through exchange of dialogue journal entries and discussion, we compared our versions. Neither account was treated as superior or more objective. Her narratives were in first person, mine were in third person. Using an heuristic device, we focused on the similarities and differences in the contents of our stories.

Out of our scrutiny a theme emerged—noise. What was classroom noise, we asked? It wasn't just any sound—some hearable phenomena were noise and others weren't. In later visits and dialogue, it became apparent that students' movements could sometimes be "noisy" even though no decibels would appear on an audiometer. Noise, it seemed, was disruption. That led us to ask about the nature of the order that was being disrupted. At that point, we were talking and writing about classroom task environments in the places and times of their enactment.

We have only just started to work together. Likely next steps will include videotaping events of interest and reviewing them, separately and together. The teacher is already taking longer looks than before. I will continue to ask her to look and remember as she stretches her span of attention to connected sequences of activity. Reading and writing instruction has emerged as a theme, and I will give her a set of articles that outline options for organizing time spent on reading, as well as outlining opinions on the nature of reading-skill acquisition. I expect we will begin to look closely at the kinds of text activities that occur in the room. We will consider changing some of the task environments involving reading. But first we will look a lot.

Some of this looking is being done by the other two teachers on the team. They have been writing narratives in dialogue journals and discussing the journal entries with other staff on the project. Next steps in coordinating these personal histories will involve visiting one another's rooms to observe and exchanging videotapes of routine events.

None of us knows where all this will lead, so I will stop here the discussion of our staff development work. In the next section, I sketch in more detail some notions about education that are basic to our efforts. I emphasize certain aspects of the classroom task environments that can become visible through a natural history approach to narrative inquiry. However, it should be obvious that the kind of staff development we have initiated must start with the immediate interests and questions of the teacher and must proceed quite slowly. This approach is not a brief workshop, but an attempt to begin inquiry with teachers that they will continue on their own and with others. Such inquiry takes time, and that is a short commodity for teachers. Released time for such deliberation through peer consultation is one of the organizational rearrangements that must accompany this sort of staff development. To provide time for reflection each week, as well as to hold teachers accountable for systematic study of their own practice would fundamentally change the role of the schoolteacher as a professional. Such change will not come easily. It may well be necessary, however, if the quality of teaching is to improve and if teachers are to find their profession worthy of continued interest and effort.

I believe there is no quick fix if we are to help experienced teachers help one another to develop more powerful reasoning about their teaching. The work we have begun is a bit like psychotherapy, and our experience recalls the joke about the therapist and client:

Q: How many psychiatrists does it take to change a light bulb?
A: Only one, but the light bulb has to really want to change.

Social Constructivist Perspectives on Classroom Tasks and Teaching

There are various ways of thinking about the tasks in which teachers and students are engaged. During the late 1960s and early 1970s, a model of teaching emerged from the teacher effectiveness literature. Over the 1970s and into the 1980s, the job of the teacher was seen as keeping learners on task. Yet there continues an older tradition, one that considers the social construction of teaching and learning in the classroom—the genesis of tasks, time, and place in social relationships.

This tradition looks at teaching and learning dialectically, as John Dewey (1939) and others did. They were learning to think systematically about the ways people constitute environments for each other. Dewey's colleague, George Herbert Mead, was thinking those same thoughts as early as the 1890s. In the 1930s, Mead gave a series of lectures at the University of Chicago that were published posthumously under the title *Mind, Self and Society* (1934). In the 1920s and '30s, the Soviet psychologists Vygotsky and Luria and their students saw that what was called "thinking" is not simply internal action, but is present in the transaction between the individual and the immediate environment: people, objects, learned values, signal systems, and communication systems (see Vygotsky, 1978).

In the 1960s and '70s, process-product research on teaching was developing its technology and accumulating a substantial body of empirical data and conclusions. About the same time, cognitive psychology, under the leadership of Herbert Simon, was developing some new conceptions about thinking that came from work in computer science and artificial intelligence. Under the leadership of Michael Cole, cognitive psychology was discovering the Soviet psychologists. Part of the reintroduced thinking about mind was the social constructivist theory. Walter Doyle, in his review "Paradigms in Research on Teaching" (1977), said that education was actually undergoing a paradigm shift toward a cognitive approach. Doyle's point has been reiterated and extended by Shulman and Carey (1984).

Axioms and Questions as Grounds for Staff Development

As a social constructivist, I propose the following axioms regarding the nature of classroom work by students and teachers. These are conceptions that I believe are necessary to teachers and university-based researchers. They have not been addressed in the research literature on teacher effectiveness nor in the staff development approaches derived from that research.

1. Every child and teacher is on task 100 percent of the time. Consequently, there is no such thing as off-task behavior. A fundamental question for teachers thus becomes, "What's the task environment and the work that the learner is busy at?"

2. Everybody is someplace. No one is ever no place. A question for teachers thus becomes, "Where are the places in time and space that tasks are being worked on?"

3. Everybody makes sense. It is not that some people make more sense than others or that the teacher is making sense and the children are learning how to make sense; everybody is making sense all the time. A question for teachers becomes, "What sense is this learner (and I as a teacher) making of the task at hand?"

4. Everybody teaches and learns. Teachers learn from students and students teach one another as well as the teacher. A question for teachers becomes, "Who's teaching whom what, when, and where?"

5. Everything is potentially invisible. Some aspects of the complex work of teaching and learning are visible. Other aspects are outside the actors' awareness. However, there is always more going on than anybody could consciously attend to. A question for the teacher becomes, "What's visible and invisible in this scene for the learner and for me?"

6. At any moment more than one thing is happening. A question for teachers becomes, "What's going on in subject matter while this is going on

in social relations?" Another question is, "What's happening over there while this is happening here?"

7. Some very important things are not seen at all because they happen in different places and times. Some past actions in separate places—policy decisions by administrators or legislators or work with a previous class—may be influencing the teacher's choices at the moment. Other past actions from the same place—what a particular child or group did yesterday or last month or at the beginning of the year—may influence the teacher's choices. Some future actions, as anticipated by the teacher or child, may also influence choices—what they see as the likely consequences of what they are doing now (e.g., what the teacher envisages as a potential reaction by the principal or fellow teachers to what the teacher plans to do).

The choices of teacher and student are made in the context of lived history—such diachronic information is not available to the intermittent observer who can only take a synchronic look at any point in time. Teachers need to ask, "What do we need to know from outside this classroom and this point in time in order to make sense of what we see going on now?"

Contrast this way of thinking about teaching with the view that one gets from the literature on learning time. It is an elegant literature in some ways, and the original formulation by John Carrol (1963) is elegant as well. There is intuitive appeal, aesthetic attractiveness, coherence, and power in the assertion that people must spend time as a necessary condition for learning. This points to the importance of the curriculum as it is actually enacted. There does, indeed, seem to be a very clear correlation between the kinds of time that students spend on certain activities and the kinds of learning that they are able to demonstrate at the end of the year on standardized tests. However, such findings do not tell us anything about the tasks themselves, and it is those tasks and the people doing them with which teachers are chiefly concerned. Teachers are not able to live in a world of elegant abstraction. They live in a world of time and space and people and materials and social relations—a world of top dogs and bottom dogs, insiders and outsiders, listening and not listening. The list could go on and on.

Reduction of these complex concerns to a metric of time on task has all the problems that reduction carries with it. There are costs that accompany the benefits of elegance and coherence. I believe that one of these costs is to deskill the teacher and to ignore the teacher's own way of thinking about what he or she is doing. If the fundamental problem is reduced to keeping people spending time on task, then the teacher learns less and less about how to understand people, activities, and tasks. This is fatal for teachers, especially for those in elementary schools.

Another of the costs is meaning-stripping. When one abstracts behaviors analytically from their use, counts them up, reassembles the frequencies statistically, and subjects the tabulations to correlational analysis, the situated meaning of the original behavior gets lost in the process. According to one kind of philosophy of social-scientific inquiry, meaning-stripping is a deliberate strategy. From that research perspective, it is seen as necessary to separate meaning from the point of view of the actors and the scientists. But this becomes a fundamental problem in research on teaching, since the world in which the teacher lives is the world of those situated meanings— what does it mean when this child, rather than that one, looks out the window now? Who is on task and who is off task?

The point here is that work and its meaningfulness are not always obvious from a quick reading of surface behavior. Rather, to understand the meaning, one must determine what the behavior does in specific situations. This implies looking for meaning in context. On this point, many contemporary anthropologists, linguists, sociologists, and cognitive psychologists, as well as Mead, Vygotsky, and Dewey, are in agreement (see, for example, the discussion in Mishler, 1979).

If we want to think about meaning in context, we must first think carefully about the notion of context itself. The term "context" is used quite differently in different research perspectives. Process-product researchers use context when they look at reading groups, at large-group instruction, and at transitions between named classroom events. In contrast, social constructivist researchers use context to mean more than that which surrounds a behavior—that which stands outside the text. Just as modern literary criticism is reconstruing the notion of the relation between text and context, so current social scientific research suggests that we do not simply see an action and then a context around it; we look at the set of relations between actions that mutually construct the context. In Latin, *contexere* is a performative verb meaning "to weave together separate strands." That is what people are doing. As my colleague Ray McDermott puts it, people in interaction create environments for one another (see McDermott, Gospodinoff, and Aron, 1978). In other words, the disparate strands of social action are woven together into an ecosystem, and the ecosystem itself is the context from a social constructivist point of view.

As a researcher in the classroom, I look for the task environments that teachers and students create for each other. These are task environments within which teachers learn as well as teach, and students teach as well as learn. I focus on the nature of the classroom tasks that are enacted—on their implicit and explicit content and process. In doing that special kind of task analysis, I try to consider how two related strands of curriculum are woven together in enactment. These two strands are the structure and content of subject matter and the structure and content of social relations by which the learners and the teacher engage the subject matter. We can now consider in detail what is involved in doing this special kind of task analysis.

A Social Constructivist Model of Classroom Task Structure

The academic tasks or activities within which people create environments for each other can be thought of as having a subject matter task structure (SMTS) and a social participation task structure (SPTS). Because people construct these contexts in real time, there is always a sequential set of steps in a subject matter task. Some cognitive scientists have become very good at showing flowcharts of successive steps (decision points) in subject matter task processes. There is also always a corresponding sequential set of steps in the social participation task, because there is always some set of social relationships. Even if the subject matter task involves reading a book alone or looking at an interesting bug, there is still a social relation. Part of the meaning one attributes to a passage in a book depends on what one knows of the meaning of that passage to other people who have read it. Furthermore, the participant in a task holds culturally learned notions about what it means for a person to be doing the task—reading a book, looking at a bug, or chipping a piece of flint. All of the task environments across the last few million years of human evolution have entailed some social relationship(s) at any given step in performing the task. (For more extended discussion, see Erickson, 1982a and 1982b.)

As an example of how, in academic tasks, the SMTS and the SPTS operate together, I will use a task environment that is simple compared to much of what we do in the classroom. Consider the children who are given the following 1st grade math worksheet. They need to know all of the steps and concepts involved in successfully completing the task.

	Math Worksheet	**Name:** _____
2 +3	4 +5	7 +4
4 +3	9 +8	2 +8
6 +7	6 +0	1 +6

There must be an awareness of the propriety of identification by placing one's name in the blank. Then there is a set of items to be completed, not necessarily in order, but there must be some response given to each. To do the first of these items, there must be recognition of the fact that the written symbols are numerals and that they stand in a problematic relationship to each other. There must be numeration (i.e., class inclusion and one-to-one correspondence) and assessment of the quantities represented by the numerals, in this case, twoness and threeness. There must also be an understanding of the operation of combining and a recognition of the sign (+) that cues this operation. There must be understanding of the appropriate location of the answer under the problem and familiarity with the numerals needed to represent that answer.

The next step is to go on to another of these items and go through the same process recursively both in the logical sense and in the purely mathematical sense of repeating the steps. The third item requires additionally that one know the conventional way (place value system, modulo 10) to represent numbers greater than nine.

The social participation task structure also has a set of rules that go along with these steps. There must be paper and pencil (not to be dropped on floor) and an awareness of the propriety of working at one's own desk. When the teacher says to "start the workbooks," there is usually a protocol to be followed, such as: write your name and then keep going, finish everything, and do it quietly. Then there are the procedures for what can be done if one gets stuck. Is it permissible to ask a neighbor for help? Is there a monitor or other designated person to ask for help, or is the teacher the only person who may be asked? If the teacher is at the reading table, when is an appropriate time to ask a question?

This is just one example of the fairly concrete practical knowledge needed to accomplish a seemingly simple classroom task. There is a local world full of conventions for task performance. Beyond that, there are non-locally derived sets of conventions and meanings, in this instance extending all the way back to the Arabs who invented the symbol system from which these relationships and quantities are communicated. Language is another such nonlocally derived symbol system. One student may ask another for help using English or Spanish or Chinese, depending upon who is in the room. If a student's primary language is Spanish and somebody else in the room speaks Spanish well, the student is more likely to ask the person who speaks Spanish.

Sometimes a new child comes in and another of the children says, "Pssst, you can ask your neighbor." That is teaching done by the student. Sometimes the children run out of worksheets to do, so they start other asks that may not be what the teacher wants them to do. (Remember, everybody is always 100 percent on task.) These children are not off task; it is just that the task they are on is not the one assigned by the teacher. If enough of them start doing that, collectively they may begin to teach the teacher. For example, two subsets of social actors, those at the reading table and those walking back and forth, may be creating environments for each other that the teacher needs to deal with. The teacher may stand up and turn the lights out and say, "Everybody quiet," or "I like the way Sammy has almost finished his math worksheet." Those are the behaviors that process-product researchers count. Rather than asking, "How can I keep more students on task?" the teacher may take a more fundamental look and ask, "How am I going to get enough work available so that the people who finish their work more rapidly than others have a place to go—or should I just not worry about it since everybody is on task?"

However, the teacher may have problems if the definition of effective teaching is that everybody looks like a Calvinist Protestant; if they are not only doing work but also doing work that looks as if it hurts. Multidimensional work is not taken into account in discussions of time on task. Elizabeth Cohen (1976) and Robert Slavin (1980) have been working for a number of years on creating additional kinds of task environments. These are environments of people and subunits for cooperative work groups for children. Peer tutoring is only one of the many under-used resources for increasing active learning time. If we were to think about increasing students' active learning time by increasing the range and number of possible places to be in the classroom while still working within the curriculum, then we could bridge a false dichotomy; between management and instruction. The staff development literature separates management and instruction, as if curriculum were one thing and keeping students involved in curriculum were something entirely different. If we see them as different, our attention is being directed away from curriculum in its fullest sense and toward such things as management moves—separate reinforcements that we can offer learners. We do not look at the way the learner is teaching us how to relate to students. We also do not look for the task environments already in the scene.

Such an emphasis also draws our attention away from the necessary "wiggle" that needs to be built into task environments. Engineers do not build bridges with totally fixed connections because the slightest stress would cause such a bridge to fall apart. Similarly, within learning task environments, if there is not room for some wiggling, then the slightest deviation from what is supposed to happen becomes a big problem. Such wiggle could allow for the kind of slack that relieves the stress that occurs when people encounter intellectual difficulty or as social relations get tougher. For example, if we want to teach a complex turn-taking system for conversation, the teacher may choose subject matter that is not as demanding. Thus the points of difficulty in the SMTS and the SPTS will not occur at the same time. The teacher needs to be able to work back and forth between the two structures and their relations. Having that wiggle in the task environment creates a qualitatively different task than if the wiggle is not there.

An example of qualitative differences in the nature of learning tasks is found in a recent chapter by Lave on the striking difference between arithmetic tasks learned in school and the computations that people do in the grocery store (Lave, Murtaugh, and de la Rocha, 1984: 67-94). The researchers had fieldworkers ask shoppers to explain how they computed and how they made shopping decisions. The subjects were subsequently given a written test, and many had trouble with arithmetic operations that they used accurately in the store. Lave's analysis shows that in the grocery store we help construct the arithmetic task. We have ways of setting it up so that we can solve it, and we become very creative in thinking in terms of chunks—this can at this price, those four boxes at another price—so that we come to the correct solution. That means we can wiggle this part of the task. Nobody in the store tells us that there is a set of algorithms that we must use.

It is not a new idea in education that the teacher's role is to provide for the necessary wiggle in tasks, thus allowing students to construct the task for themselves. In a classic article by Wood and others (1976), teaching is characterized as providing a scaffold. Engaging the student at the zone of proximal development, the teacher builds a scaffold of connections to where the student's understanding and interests are. As the student's capacity for independent work grows, the teacher takes the scaffold down and builds another, higher one or builds it someplace else. A teacher's capacity to determine where the student is and adjust the social arrangements or subject matter to get to the zone of proximal development is what Wertsch (1979) calls "proleptic instruction," or instruction that reaches out to students in order to draw them on to the next steps.

That's what people used to call good teaching. But it presumes some things about society as well as about cognition. It presumes that both the teacher and learner have the authority to be flexible with tasks. This is a matter of the allocation of power in society. If the teacher does not have the authority or the opportunity to reconstruct these tasks so as to build scaffolding and engage the learner's zone of proximal development, then both the teacher and the learners are stuck spending time on tasks they didn't help to construct. That makes for very alienating work. The beautifully colored instructional textbooks, workbooks, and dittoes, as well as the tests that accompany them, remove the opportunity to construct tasks. In recent attempts to monitor the implementation of teaching materials that are designed to be both learner proof and teacher proof, we may have inadvertently backed ourselves into a corner in which severe constraints are placed on the capacity of teacher and students to negotiate proleptic instruction together. Staff development efforts that try to be teacher proof and learner proof only exacerbate this problem.

Since learning and teaching are a matter of social relations as well as cognition, we need a way of thinking about them together. In addition, we need to look at the micro-politics of teaching. We can see the teacher as a politician in the best sense: the manager of the allocation of desired goods, the manager of places to be in the world. Good politicians manage access to places that people enjoy. It follows that teachers might well read Machiavelli or Aristotle if they wish to become more effective. Issues of safety and risk, of morality and love, of honor and justice are the stuff of everyday life in classrooms. These issues are the domain of Aristotle's politics—a domain not of theory but or *praxis*, practice. The practice of teaching can be seen as the practice of politics.

As teachers, we need ways to see complex social relations operating along with cognitive relations, to see distinctive local meanings-in-context along with meanings derived from nonlocal sources. We need to be able to make more visible those invisible parts of total learning environments, and to include in our analysis the things that affect people's behavior but which cannot be seen because they occur in different places and times, some of which are outside the classroom. The research literature on teaching has overlooked some very important aspects of teaching and learning: that everybody is on task 100 percent of the time; that everybody is some place in particular; that everybody is making sense; that task environments need to be flexible enough to withstand stress and to allow for mutual scaffolding work by the teacher and learner.

I have presented three sets of ideas as foundations for staff development. First to be presented was the notion that narration of classroom events could be a form of natural historical inquiry into the organization of those events as enacted curriculum. Next to be presented were seven dicta on teaching and learning, which I proposed as axiomatic sources of questions the teacher might ask about the enacted curriculum as it happens in routine classroom life. Last came the model of the task environment as enacted curriculum. This is a model that takes account of the ever-present connections between the social and academic dimensions of classroom tasks. By its emphasis on the sequential organization of routines across the time of their enactment, the model allows one to develop a narrative understanding of the specific structure and content of the task environments that students customarily experience.

This discussion raises many issues. Some are old for me and no doubt for readers as well; some are quite new for both of us. My colleagues and I are beginning to test these ideas in staff development work. We do not know whether or not our efforts will lead to higher student achievement on standardized tests. But there are important aims of teaching that reach beyond what those tests can measure. In attempting to achieve those broader aims of teaching, and of education, I believe it is time for teachers to look closely at their work as natural historians who scrutinize the enacted curriculum. For the experienced teacher, staff development can consist of learning to deliberate on classroom tasks as they occur in the concrete times and places of daily life in the teacher's own room.

References

Bartlett, F. C. *Remembering: A Study in Experimental and Social Psychology.* Cambridge, England: Cambridge University Press, 1932.

Becker, A. L. "Text-building, Epistemology, and Aesthetics in Javanese Shadow Theatre." In *The Imagination of Reality: Essays in Southeast Asian Coherence Systems,* edited by A. L. Becker and A. Yengoyan. Norwood, N. J.: Ablex, 1979.

Brophy, J., and T. Good. "Teacher Behavior and Student Achievement." In *Handbook of Research on Teaching,* 3rd ed., edited by M. Wittrock. New York: Macmillan, 1985.

Burke, K. *A Grammar of Motives*, 3rd ed. Berkeley: University of California Press, 1969.

Carroll, J. "A Model for School Learning." *Teachers College Record* 64 (1963): 723-733.

Chafe, Wallace L., ed. *The Pear Stories: Cognitive, Cultural, and Linguistic Aspects of Narrative Production*. Norwood, N.J.: Ablex, 1980.

Cohen, E. G. "Problems and Prospects of Teaming." *Educational Research Quarterly* 1, 2 (1976): 49-63

Denham and Lieberman, eds. *Time to Learn*. Washington, D.C.: National Institute of Education, 1980.

Dewey, John. *Experience and Education*. New York: Macmillan, 1939.

Doyle, W. "Paradigms for Research on Teacher Effectiveness." In *Review of Research in Education* 28, 5 (1977): 51-55

Erickson, F. "Classroom Discourse as Improvisation: Relationships Between Academic Task Structure and Social Participation Structure." In *Communicating in the Classroom*, edited by L. C. Wilkinson. New York: Academic Press, 1982.

Erickson, F. "Taught Cognitive Learning in Its Immediate Environments: A Neglected Topic in the Anthropology of Education." *Anthropology and Education Quarterly* 13, 2 (1982): 149-180.

Harnischfeger, A., and D. Wiley. "The Origins of Active Learning Time." In *Perspectives on Instructional Time*, edited by C. Fisher and D. Berliner. New York: Longman, 1985.

Lave, J.; M. Murtaugh; and O. de la Rocha. "The Dialectic of Arithmetic in Grocery Shopping." In *Everyday Cognition: Its Development in Social Context*, edited by B. Rogoff and O. de la Rocha. Cambridge: Harvard University Press, 1984.

McDermott, R. P.; K. Gospodinoff; and J. Aron. "Criteria for an Ethnographically Adequate Description of Concerted Activities and Their Contexts." *Semiotica* 24, 3/4 (1978): 245-275.

Mead, G. H. *Mind, Self, and Society*, edited by C. W. Morris. Chicago: University of Chicago Press, 1934.

Mishler, E. G. "Meaning in Context: Is There Any Other Kind?" *Harvard Educational Review* 49, 1 (1979): 1-19.

Pike, K. *Language in Relation to a Unified Theory of the Structure of Human Behavior*, 2nd ed. The Hague: Mouton, 1967.

Rosen, H. *Stories and Meanings*. Sheffield, England: National Association for the Teaching of English, 1984.

Schank, R.C., and R.P. Abelson. *Scripts, Plans, Goals, and Understanding*. Hillsdale, N.J.: Lawrence Erlbaum Associates, 1977.

Shulman, L.S., and N.B. Carey. "Psychology and the Limitations of Individual Rationality: Implications for the Study of Reasoning and Civility." *Review of Educational Research* 54, 4 (1984): 501-524.

Slavin, Robert. "Cooperative Learning." *Review of Educational Research* 50 (1980): 315-342.

Tannen, Deborah. *Conversational Style: Analyzing Talk Among Friends*. Norwood, N.J.: Ablex, 1984.

Vygotsky, L. S. *Mind in Society: The Development of Higher Psychological Processes*. Cambridge: Harvard University Press, 1978.

Wertsch, J. "From Social Interaction to Higher Psychological Processes." *Human Development* 22 (1979): 1-22.

Wood, B.; J. S. Bruner; and G. Ross. "The Role of Tutoring in Problem Solving." *Journal of Child Psychology and Psychiatry* 17 (1976): 89-100.

11. The Classroom Teacher and Curriculum Developer: A Sharing Relationship

Kathleen Dunlevy Morin

FOR A FREE-LANCE CURRICULUM DEVELOPER, THE INITIAL WALK UP TO THE FRONT door of a school is a thought-filled journey. With each passing step, the mind is jogged by question. It is the answers to these questions that eventually shape the way teachers and consultant will work together.

What are the educational and social needs and interests of the diverse members of the school community? What is the nature of the existing curricular content, and what changes are desired or needed? What range of instructional resources is available? Will the consultant's educational philosophy and change strategies jibe with those of others? What is the social system within the school which formally and/or informally governs the day-to-day interactions of students, parents, administration, and staff? Within that system, how is the prospect of change—and the role of an outside consultant—perceived? And, ultimately, who will control the answers to the questions which undergird all curricular decision-making and frame the task at hand: *What* should students experience and learn? *When, how, why,* and at what *expense?* (Foshay, 1975, p. 172.)

Kathleen Dunlevy Morin is a free-lance educational consultant from New York City.

As the school door swings open, only clues become immediately manifest. The answers will begin to surface later through personal observation, reflective analysis, and active participation within the school community. But where does one begin the search for answers? With the teacher is a logical starting point. It is through the teaching process that the classroom teacher breathes life into the curriculum. And, in the final analysis, it is the classroom teachers who implement the curriculum, adapt it to the needs of the students, and inject into it their individual teaching styles. Quite simply, in the long run "the curriculum is what the teacher makes of it" (Michaelis et al., 1975, p. 459). Clearly, direct observation of and continued discussion with classroom teachers are basic steps within the curriculum development process.

But a curriculum developer never arrives at a classroom door empty-handed. "Baggage" is in tote in the form of assumptions, priorities, and philosophy about teaching and education. Baggage drawn from years of personal and professional experiences both in and out of the classroom. Baggage that will temper judgments about what the consultant looks for and sees in the observation of teaching. Such baggage must be opened, aired, sorted, sifted, adjusted, and repacked prior to and periodically throughout the curriculum development process.

In a profession all too often fraught with uncertainties, it is essential for curriculum consultants to be able to articulate to potential clients what they "stand for," why, and how this stance might well influence professional observations, judgments, and products. Then, the free-lance consultant must be prepared for the consequences of such forthrightness—the job may or may not be offered.

A Vantage Point

The reader is now invited to take part in a journey into the curriculum-development process, to walk along with me into a hypothetical situation that touches base with reality through a preliminary observation of three classroom teachers.

As background information, you should know that the baggage I carry is drawn primarily from my experiences: teaching at the elementary and junior high school levels in the Blue Ridge Mountains and in Spanish Harlem; supervising and instructing supervisory interns and preservice students affiliated with a graduate school of education; and working for seven years as a free-lance curricular consultant at grade levels K-12.

My professional perceptions are also colored by a constructionist philosophy and constructivist psychology of schooling. These perceptions draw upon a tradition that views individuals as capable of constructing knowledge through experiences both in and out of school and which rests upon the tenet that democratic, reflective, group problem-solving experiences are central to education and even to social progress.

I also carry with me a corollary set of experiential assumptions which includes the belief that education is inherently an optimistic process rooted in the premise that positive changes can take place. Schools can and should be enjoyable, productive places for both students and teachers; teachers deserve more resources, rewards, recognition, and respect; teachers should have more freedom and greater control over local curricular decisions; and outside consultants are all too often viewed, legitimately, as importing more woes and work than pleasures and productivity.

A Reality Base: Three Classroom Observations

The three classrooms selected to provide an observational base reflect a diversity of grade levels and socioeconomic settings.[1] The common thread binding the three is that all were studying housing and neighborhood improvement. More specifically, each teacher was employing as a curricular resource the "House Sense" program, for which I serve as a consultant.

The Curricular Content

"House Sense" is an interdisciplinary program sponsored by the New York City Department of Housing Preservation and Development in cooperation with the city's Board of Education and with the help of 11 other city agencies.[2] A goal of "House Sense" is to provide teachers with instructional resources about the nature of and strategies for housing and community improvement. The resources include: (a) a network of guest speakers and field experiences and (b) a 650-page collection of readings, suggested activities, and student activity sheets designed to assist teachers in developing one or more of 28 housing topics. The range of topics, all of which are laced with local history, includes the concepts of "house" and "home"; types of housing; landlord-tenant relations; household systems, safety, and security; pest control; consumer strategies; careers; architecture; and city planning. The program primarily is designed to encourage teachers to assume active roles as curriculum developers by determining if, when, and how the House Sense resources should be used or adapted.

---

[1]Credit and gratitude are extended to the three observed teachers and their school communities: *Observation #1*, Myra Langford, P.S. 145 M, New York, New York (Selma Katz, principal); *Observation #2*, Joni Christie, Specialized Instructional Environment VI, Teacher Moms Program, P.S. 224 Q at P.S. 191 Q, Floral Park, New York (Nathan Kuznitz, principal); *Observation #3*, Eugenia Scott Redmond, St. Catherine's School, Richmond, Virginia (Suzanne P. Wiltshire, director of the lower school).

[2]The 11 other New York City agencies that contributed to its development were the Department of Environmental Protection, the Department of Buildings, the Fire Department, the Health Department, the Housing Authority, the Commission on Human Rights, the Landmark Preservation Commission, the Department of Parks and Recreation, the Planning Commission, the Police Department, and the Sanitation Department.

A Broad Perspective

For a free-lance curriculum developer, it is useful first to view the teaching process broadly and then to narrow the focus as familiarity with the setting increases. Thus, the act of teaching must be observed not only within the context of the classroom but also within the context of the other communities upon which it draws, serves, and is influenced. This is especially important when the curricular content centers on a societal issue such as housing. For a curriculum developer the contextual observation of teaching begins long before reaching the classroom door and continues long after leaving the school building.

Factors upon which the curriculum developer should focus include:

● *Community at large*: types and conditions of housing; nearby resources (human, manmade, and natural); the nature of and degree to which public spaces and facilities are used by various sectors of the community; the socioeconomic needs and interests of the community; local history; and the geographical range from which students are drawn and how they are transported to and from school.

● *School community*: the architectural design of the school plant (such as open-space, traditional closed corridors); the range of available resources and facilities for students, faculty, and staff; how and when members of the school community use the space and facilities; the organization of time, which delimits the school day/week/year; curricular requirements; and formal or informal evidence of a prevalent school philosophy.

● *Classroom community*: the physical setting and its flexibility given the constraints of the number of students, the types of furniture available, and related traffic patterns; the age and special needs/interests of the student population; the scope and depth of content developed; seating and grouping patterns; how and by whom the room is decorated; the range and availability of resources; the nature, tone, and degree of participation evidenced by observed verbal and nonverbal interactions (child-child, child-teacher, child-resource, teacher-resource, and so forth); the diversity of instructional strategies and formats employed; evidence of teacher and student enjoyment of an engagement in the learning experiences; how time and resources are organized and used; and even the view from the window, especially if it enriches the study of housing and community issues.

Through analysis and discussion, the consultant and the teacher can use this broad data base to draw preliminary inferences about several aspects of the teacher's work: instructional and management styles; command of, interest in, and ease with the subject matter; employment of theories of learning and child development; congruence among goals, intentions, and practices; and the social and bureaucratic forces that affect the instructional factors.

Clearly, this broad view of teaching provides only a sweeping survey of needs, interests, and resources. Such a perspective raises more questions than it answers. It requires *continued* observation, inquiry, and refinement of data collected and generalizations drawn. But it reduces the chance of tunnel vision, which so often limits a consultant's initial view of the environmental connectedness of child, classroom, and community. Perhaps even more significantly, an initially broad contextual view of teaching reminds the outside consultant of the inherent complexity of the day-to-day teaching endeavor—a reminder that should humble any consultant who works with classroom teachers.

What Was Seen

In the supervision literature, it is often suggested that an observer schedule a pre-observation conference with the teacher. In a supervisory relationship, such opportunity for advanced planning, analysis, and communication is often helpful even if not mandatory. However, in the evaluation of the relationship between a teacher and a free-lance curriculum developer, which should not be supervisory, it can be useful to maintain an open mind and, thus, to forego a conference until *after* the first classroom observation. Moreover, to keep an open mind during the observation, I purposefully use a reportorial rather than an analytical approach in gathering initial data.

In the three observations that serve as a base for this case study, data were collected from time-sample notes, information discussions with teachers, walking and automobile tours of the surrounding community, audiotapes, and photographs. Highlights of the observations follow.

Observation 1. Friday, October 19, 1984, 1:15-2:15 P.M.

Teacher. Twenty-two years of teaching experience at the same school; involved in the House Sense program since its inception in 1981.

Grade/class. Fifth and sixth grade; a designated Gifted and Talented class of 30 students.

The school. Public elementary, K-6; inner-city setting; traditional closed-corridor modern facility; specialists in art, math, science, bilingual, and special education on staff.

The community. Students drawn primarily from a five-block radius of the school; nearby housing is diverse, including tenements, brownstones, converted mansions, traditional pre-war buildings, high-rise public housing projects; evidence of neighborhood gentrification despite many abandoned buildings; two nearby parks; a public library within an easy walk.

Classroom setting. Third floor; windows overlook a church, tenements, and a sealed-up vacant building; classroom decorated with student work; evidence of ongoing projects in diverse subject areas; an abundance of reference materials, books, charts, newspapers, a globe, art supplies readily available and evidence of frequent use.

Seating pattern. Desks arranged to form six large "table" formations.

Synopsis of Classroom Observation. 1:15 PM: The teacher gives each child a two-page letter written to "Harry," a hypothetical friend of the class. The author is anonymous but writes to let off steam about his/her housing problems: lack of heat, hot water, window guards, and smoke detectors; mice and roaches; broken toilet; neighbors who "air mail" garbage out of windows; stop and no-go elevators; faulty security; rickety steps and no fire escape; and a superintendent who turns off all the water when tenants complain about leaky pipes. The teacher (who stands or walks along the side/front of the class and maintains direct eye contact with the class throughout the lesson) explains that everything in the letter is based on fact and asks the students to determine whose apartment it is. Upon reading the letter silently, some students challenge, "This letter cannot be true!"

1:20. Hands swing up around the room when volunteers are asked to read sections of the letter. As it is read, students offer and defend their guesses as to who wrote the letter. [Throughout the lesson, the teacher listens to responses and through questions helps students to build upon and draw linkages between their ideas and those of others.]

1:30. A student suggests that the letter is a composite of the class's *own* housing problems. The teacher confirms she wrote the letter based on lists of problems previously identified by the students about their own housing conditions: "This apartment represents *your* own housing concerns," says the teacher. "Imagine if they [the problems] were all in one building. There are some buildings like that! Imagine you lived in this composite apartment. What would you do?" All hands bounce up. Responses include: move out; don't pay the rent; organize a rent strike; take the landlord to Housing Court. A whole-class discussion focusing on potential actions and related consequences ensues.

1:40. A student gasps, "The whole building is a mess—you can't live in it!" The teacher then asks, "What can we do about it? Let's explore some strategies by role-playing." Hands go up as teacher asks for participants; students suggest the roles be that of landlord and tenant. [Students appear to be very familiar with the role-play format.]

1:42. [First Role-Play. Front of Room.] Tenant complains of grafitti and lack of heat. Landlord suggests he *"Move"* and argues, "When you moved in, the building *was* clean. It was better than those downtown condos. It is you and the other tenants causing the problems." Tenant snaps that his apartment *is* clean! The problems are not his fault! Argument continues.

1:46. Whole class evaluates the role-play and alternative strategies. One student says: "The landlord was a good actor but a bad landlord." Another: "Many landlords are like that." Two others note that "there are also bad tenants."

1:52. [Second Role-Play. Same roles, different participants.] The tenant asks the landlord why he doesn't repair the building. The landlord claims ignorance. Tenant and landlord argue over economic hardships of rent, moving, and maintenance. The teacher interjects, "Hey, Mr. Landlord, why don't you fix our broken window?" The landlord retorts, "Are you talking to me?" Teacher, "Yes." Landlord, "Cause tenants just continue to break it whenever they play ball!" End of role-play. Spontaneous applause erupts.

1:57. Whole class evaluates and compares role-plays. For each problem cited in the letter, the students determine the locus of responsibility for maintenance and repair. The teacher lists their conclusions in two columns on the board. [Through questions, the teacher draws from students that both landlords and tenants have rights and responsibilities, many defined by law.]

2:12. The teacher asks, "What will Harry tell his friend to do?" Responses include: work with other tenants to improve their building; organize a rent strike; tell the landlord to set an example by repairing the building and then the tenants will follow suit. Smiling, the teacher asks if the class wants her to convey its sentiments to Harry the next time she hears from him. "YES"—a unanimous response.

Preparing the class for a visit to Housing Court, she instructs them to listen to the tenants and landlords; to analyze whose rights and responsibilities are in question; to consider the roles of the judge and others; to evaluate how they would determine the case if they were the judge. [*Note:* Observation included trip to court and follow-up classroom discussion. The judge actively engaged students in a discussion of court traditions and roles, education, and development of some case law. Class observed two real cases involving landlords seeking possession of tenant-occupied apartments (one for alleged property damage).]

Observation 2. Monday, October 29, 1984, 9:20-9:55 A.M.

Teacher. Two-and-a-half years teaching experience; first year teaching in a new language-based unit in this school; second year using House Sense; first visit for observer.

Class. Four- and five-year-olds, nine boys (seven present); two paraprofessionals.

School. Special education "mini-school," Specialized Instructional Environment Unit housed within a public school; the children have a regular school day with intensive social and communication instruction; the students require full-time special instructional services as a result of severe language or emotional disabilities; activities are supervised intensively within the classroom, the school building, and the community.

Community. Middle-class suburban New York City public school in Queens; tree-lined streets edged by neat rows of single-family houses; nearby main street; all students in this program travel by bus from other communities with greatly diverse housing conditions.

Classroom setting. Second floor; gaily decorated with students' work including Halloween mobiles and various posters including shapes, colors, and vocabulary, a "trip corner," puppets, and a tape recorder.

Seating pattern. U-formation of desks; activity areas in front and back of room.

Synopsis of Classroom Observation. [In recent weeks, the students had studied neighborhood people, places, and housing and had taken a "house" walk.]

9:20. Arms reach high above heads in stretches led by teacher. "Now let's put on our thinking caps" signals group to sit. Hands touch heads, smiles etch faces. Teacher sits snug within the U of desks. "Today we are going to talk more about houses. Tell me about *your* house," she instructs, guiding responses with "MY HOUSE IS . . ." and asking for its size and color. [Full sentences are encouraged and teacher follow-up questions extend responses.]

9:25. Teacher shows a picture book of houses, including a dome house. "What shape is this house?" she asks. A child swings rounded arms over head and proclaims "Round!" "Yes, and what shape is your house?" she asks each child. Tracing the shape with each child on his desk, she repeats with the class "square" or "rectangle." "What shape is a window?" she probes. One child responds "Glass." "Well, they're made of glass, but what shape are they?" Another voice: "Square!" "Right, square or sometimes they are rectangles," she clarifies.

9:30. Reaching to her side and never losing eye contact with the class, she hands each child a book, *The House*, a "brand new book!" Teacher and students point to title as they say "THE HOUSE." "What color is this house?" she asks, holding the book up. "Orange!" a child observes. "Good," and "What do you see on the first page?" she asks, circulating to assist each child in locating and focusing upon the page. "I see a roof," another child exclaims. "Let's all make the shape of that roof," she instructs. All swing arms above their heads to form a peak. "What is this shape?" "Wood" another announces. [Brief discussion about men now working on school roof.]

The teacher gives each child a sheet of paper on which there is a large square outline for drawing a house. [On the board, she draws a square and adds parts to the house as children suggest them.] "What will you put on your house?" she asks. "A roof!"/"A door" are two quick responses. "What if we are inside and want to look out to see if it is raining?" she asks. "Windows!" several respond. "Yes, and where does smoke come from?" she probes. "A chimney," one child responds, explaining that his house has a fireplace. Another child suggests drawing a mailbox on the door. The teacher asks each child what color he wants his house to be and gives each a matching crayon. [The students color and finish their houses with varying degrees of speed, thoroughness, and peer interaction. One student draws harsh lines across paper.] As they work, the teacher circulates, questioning each about the color, size, shape, and names of parts of their houses. As each student dictates "My house is . . .," she writes the sentence below the drawing.

9:50. Having collected the drawings, the teacher shows them to the group. She asks who made each drawing and asks each student to tell about his house including its parts, color, shape, and size. [All students participate, some more vocally than others.] The teacher highlights details overlooked by students (such as automobiles and trees). [Throughout the lesson, the teacher emphasizes, assists, enforces, and reinforces on-task behaviors through eye contact, reiteration of expectations, positive feedback, and supportive body language (silence, smiles, postures). Paraprofessionals assist mainly in focusing students in close proximity to them.]

Observation 3. Monday, November 12, 1984, 10:30-11:20 A.M.

Teacher. Science teacher, part-time; 11 years of teaching experience; has selected and adapted elements of House Sense periodically in past years; first time observer has visited teacher and school.

Grade/class. 4th grade; 21 girls.

School. An independent day/boarding school, grades K-12, for girls in a large southern city; a spacious campus marked by stately Georgian structures, green commons, and extensive modern facilities; students' work decorates the hallways of the lower-school facility.

Community. Residential area of the city with large single-family houses and nearby apartments; school is adjacent to a 123-acre golf course.

Classroom setting. Bright room on ground floor overlooking school campus; instructional kits, references, materials available; students' work decorates classroom, which is also used by another teacher and other groups of students. (This science class meets twice per week in this room.)

Seating pattern. Four to five students are seated at each of five large tables.

Synopsis of Classroom Observation. [*Note*: This is a follow-up lesson about city planning based on a field-walk to a nearby golf course the prior week.]

10:30. Standing in front of the room hanging a large map that she made, the teacher welcomes the students as they enter. She explains that the map depicts the field-walk site and asks what is missing. "A stream," one child notes. Teacher adds the stream and colors the position of roads as students suggest their locations. "What did we see on the walk?" prompts rapid responses: "rocks," "a creek," "golf balls," "droppings"—"What kind?" the teacher probes. "Rabbit," several respond. Still eliciting more observations, the teacher gives each child a smaller map and suggests they add to it the pond, stream, and roads. She hangs the small map next to the large one and circulates from table to table. [Students immediately work on the maps, recalling and sharing elements of the field-walk; the hum of students at work permeates the room.]

10:40. Instructing them to refer to their field-walk observation notes, the teacher smilingly emphasizes "*Before* you plan [to develop] an area, you must know what is there. What was in the area we visited?" Hands swing up around the room. Using questions and building upon student responses, the teacher elicits a broad range of field-walk observations and writes the location of each on the large map. In one area, a student recalls "grass, trees, bushes, pine needles and cones, cone trees, and dandelions." [Teacher repeats student's answers and uses them to build the next question.] Teacher: "What is important about cone trees?" "They provide food for birds," another student responds. "Did we see birds?" teacher asks. "Yes!" the group exclaims. "Butterflies were also seen there!" a student exclaims. Responding to a follow-up query, two students add, "Butterflies pollinate" and "provide food for birds." At another area of the map, teacher elicits from students data revealing "sweet gums" "oak" and "blackberry." "What is important about those?" she inquires. "More food for animals," another student responds. "Well, what kinds of animals could live there?" Hands go up all over. "Rabbits" is a fast response. "Was there evidence of rabbits?" the teacher probes. "Holes," "Droppings," two students respond. "What other animals could live near a wooded area?" teacher asks. "Racoons," "Deer," others respond. "Did we find any human artifacts?" "Golf balls!" several exclaim. Indicating another area of the map, the teacher elicits from different students recollections of "woodpeckers," "nuts," "sassafrass," "sycamore," "milkweed," "onions," "deer," "spiders," "squirrels," and "worms." Teacher re-emphasizes, "What you need to know before you plan [to develop a site] is what is there." Highlighting directions on the board, the teacher instructs, "Now, take a few minutes to plan something for this site and include in your plans the proposed use of the land, location of buildings and facilities, lists of wildlife habitats your plans might disturb, and possible physical problems. For example, if you plan to develop housing, you will have problems with the creek or with flooding from the river." One student proclaims, "I want to keep it just as it is!" The teacher smiles and explains, "In this assignment, you are not owning or controlling, you are developing it [the land] for something else."

10:55. Students work busily in predetermined pairs and small groups at the tables. Teacher circulates, asking and answering questions. Observer overhears creative ideas and practical concerns in their conversations.

11:10. For their next lesson, teacher instructs all groups to be prepared to present their plans. For practice, she asks a volunteer to share briefly her group's plans. In listening to the plans, the teacher suggests that all consider the proposed development: What could be done differently, and what is the effect on the site? Standing in front and using the map for reference, the student proposes a hotel complex be built which includes a bridge, post office, roads, and peripheral parking lots. Through teacher and peer questioning, it becomes clear that such plans might alter grazing patterns; cause noise, air, and water pollution; develop drainage, erosion, and flooding problems; and disrupt the habitats of local animals. Group discussion stimulated by teacher's questions gives rise to such alternative plans as inclusion of a monorail or another hotel location on the site.

11:20. Teacher thanks the student for her presentation and reminds the class before they leave to come prepared to present their plans.

Enter the Hypothetical: Postobservation Analysis and Discussion

At this juncture in our journey into the curriculum development process, we take a sharp turn to embark upon a series of hypothetical "next steps." Our journey has taken us into the varied communities of three classroom teachers and has permitted us to observe lessons taught about diverse issues of housing and neighborhoods. For the remainder of our journey, we will explore how, as curriculum developers, we would work with teachers within these three school settings.

Within the curriculum development process, the first postobservation feedback conference is best transformed into a collegial session rooted in open dialogue and mutual inquiry. Unlike some traditional supervisory sessions, which focus upon a critique or an evaluation of the teaching process, the initial postobservation session offers the free-lance curriculum developer and the teacher a time to (1) offer introductory remarks and general reactions to the observation; (2) clarify roles; (3) share and analyze specific needs, interests, and resources; and (4) outline a preliminary list of supportive next steps. Such a session would provide time to explore the *seen* (the observations) within the context of the *unseen* (the philosophies and sets of assumptions). It would be a time to set a foundation of trust, respect, and honesty between the curriculum developer and the teacher, both of whom are colleagues possessing overlapping yet disparate areas of expertise and who function under diverse time constraints and daily pressures.

Offer Introductory Remarks and General Reactions to the Observation

I would arrange a meeting with the teacher as soon as possible after the initial observation. Such a meeting would serve a dual function; for the teacher it would be a time to gain reactions and insights from the consultant; for the consultant it would serve as a job interview. Clearly, such factors can cause anxiety for both the teacher and the consultant. Thus, a prompt meeting in a convenient setting would serve to reduce tension.

Without immediate or overt reference to the collected data (that would come later in the session), I would start the meeting by emphasizing the positive or most interesting elements of my general observations. In most instances, I prefer to use positive reinforcement whenever it is appropriate, honest, and not overdone. Such an approach provides an initially useful and cordial context for subsequent in-depth analysis of curricular concerns.

With each of the three teachers observed for this case study, such an initial positive approach would come easy. To many, at first, the teachers might even seem to need little or no assistance from an outside consultant. All revealed enthusiastic confidence in their subject matter, ease in their teaching style, sensitivity to the developmental level of their students, facility for questioning techniques, and natural creative flair for extending and adapting curricular materials. Yet all professionals benefit from an exchange of new ideas and opinions. Based upon my observations, I would first acknowledge the teachers' interest in housing-related issues and their adeptness in extending the House Sense program to address the needs and interests of their students, their subject areas, and their communities. I would suggest to each teacher that our goal be to work as a team to develop new curricular dimensions to the House Sense program. These dimensions would not only serve the individual teacher's instructional needs but could ultimately be shared with other teachers in similar settings.

Clarify Roles

Our curriculum would not be developed in the isolation of remote offices far removed from the school settings. On the contrary, at all stages of the curricular research and development process, teacher and administrator input would be actively encouraged. To overlook, deny, or circumvent such input or to attempt to produce "teacher-proof" curricula would be at best naive and at worst arrogant.

To clarify my own role, I would discuss with each of the teachers my intention to first ask for their help in order to gain insights into local curricular needs, interests, and resources. Then I would provide them with a curricular product designed to meet those needs. I would develop a curricular program by researching, designing, and writing instructional materials and by organizing resources that would build upon or revise curricular content; permit teachers to meet curricular requirements while simultaneously adding new issues and topics; welcome adaptations and continuous teacher-input at the classroom level; encourge teachers, through ready resources, to pursue worthwhile and emergent curricular tangents; incorporate enjoyable, productive "fun" activities; motivate cooperative involvement by all sectors within the school community; and include easy access to increased field experience and guest speakers.

In seeking the help of teachers, I would ask that they specifically employ three of the many roles inherent in the teaching process: researcher, curriculum decision maker, and evaluator. Then, using the teacher's time judiciously—thus keeping meetings to a minimum—I would request that teachers identify current curricular problems; reveal insights about students' ability levels, interests, and special needs; provide feedback on curricular materials as they evolve; field test the curriculum within their own classroom; and throughout the process share ideas, resources, and enthusiasm to generate interest and involvement among all sectors of the community.

Analyze Needs, Interests, and Resources

Throughout our initial meeting, I would encourage the teacher to ask questions, offer opinions, and make suggestions. I would realize that both the teacher and I have an agenda for the meeting. As the initial postobservational meeting evolves, I would stimulate structured discussion of curricular needs, requirements, interests, and resources by sharing openly with each teacher my broad-view observational data. I would offer copies of my notes and tapes for subsequent personal reference and analysis.

Then, as a springboard for analysis in our meeting, we would use four general curricular aims as a frame of reference. These aims reflect elements of what I look for when I analyze observational data, and although not new they are recurrent in recent literature and warrant renewed attention. The four aims and highlights of our hypothetical analysis of each observation follow.

(a) *Curricula should provide clear goals that are accepted as important and that set high, yet realistic, expectations for the learner (and for the teacher); such goals must then be reinforced through appropriate learning experiences* (Clark et al., 1980; Goodlad, 1983c; Tyler, 1981). First, the teacher and I would identify long-term, short-term, and immediate curricular goals and requirements. Within the context of yearly, unit, and lesson plans, we would analyze whether or not the observed lesson sufficiently addressed such objectives.

In Observation #1, reinforced goals include that the student appreciate diverse perspectives; develop, analyze, and evaluate strategies for conflict resolution; evaluate rights and responsibilities; and understand the basic role of the judiciary in our society. Observational data of verbal reactions reveal that in this lesson more than 94 percent of the students participated voluntarily and most participated more than once. This suggests that the students were challenged by and actively engaged in the experience.

In Observation #2, reinforced goals include that the student describe his environment noting colors, shapes, and sizes; convey thoughts through speech, writing, and drawing; and attend when others speak. Data reveal that the lesson, which was highly structured and paced to accommodate short attention spans, evoked full participation mainly through direct teacher-student dialogue.

In Observation #3, goals include that the student be aware of the benefits of environmental planning; appreciate the need for compromise; develop, analyze, and evaluate diverse land-use plans; and work cooperatively with peers. Here, data reveal widespread, fast-paced, highly enthusiastic participation. Throughout the lesson, students remained on-task without overt reminders from the teacher.

Based on the three sets of data, the quality and quantity of student on-task behavior indicate that in each classroom the level of expectations was high enough to motivate and realistic enough not to produce undue frustration. In constructing curricular resources for the teachers, I would build upon their own goals, continuing to draw from the cognitive, affective, and psychomotor domains (especially in the case of the very young special education students).

(b) *Curricula should encourage a variety of instructional strategies integrating subject areas and developing action-oriented problem-solving opportunities that not only provide for individualization but also nurture cooperation and social responsibility* (Apple, 1983; Goodlad, 1983c; Kepler and Randall, 1977; Kohler, 1981; Molnar and Lindquist, 1982). To become familiar with the teacher's repertoire of instructional strategies, I would ask the teacher which formats she uses, which ones she and her students enjoy most, and why she did or did not enjoy the observed lesson. As revealed in each observation, the topic of housing lends itself to the integration of myriad subject areas [e.g., science, law, and at the lower grade level prereading skills and basic geometry]. The teachers already recognize that the topic of housing is interdisciplinary and generates problem-solving activities that can focus upon economic, aesthetic, environmental, historical, social, or structural problems.

Housing is also a topic that the teachers realize touches home and provides an emotional and motivational engagement for students. In each observation, the data reveal students enjoying their struggle to solve local problems—wrestling with landlord-tenant conflicts; "constructing" a house; cooperatively designing land-use plans. The data imply that this productive enjoyment stemmed from many factors, including the students' personal interest in the topic and format; the teacher's own enthusiasm; the diversity of instructional strategies employed within a single lesson; the teacher's ability to listen to, acknowledge, build upon, and appreciate an individual's contribution within a cooperative endeavor; and the undergirding clarity and consistency of classroom rules and expectations.

Because of my lack of special education expertise, I would require close consultation with the teacher and other specialists before designing learning experiences for the students in Observation #2. However, to enhance problem-solving and peer dialogue, I would encourage structured and informal play, such as building houses with blocks or draped materials, dramatic play, role-playing, and doll-playing "house" (Gessell et al., 1977). With guidance from the teacher, I would design formats to involve the paraprofessionals even more directly in the lesson, thus permitting the teacher more time and flexibility to work with individuals and small groups.

To save each of the teachers time, I would include within each curriculum ready resources that encourage diverse instructional formats: games, songs, model constructions, cooking recipes, movement excercises, puzzles, art activities, readings, discussions, writing, field trips, guest speakers, and models of teaching including role-playing, synectics, concept attainment, and concept formation (Joyce and Weil, 1980). Such formats would be designed to stimulate individual, small group, whole class, club projects, peer-tutoring, and activities with parents and community members. Reflecting my constructivist philosophy, fun activities would lace the curriculum to motivate both teachers and students; enhance student engagement in learning;

and increase hard work, interest, and rigorous cognitive and affective development (Popkewitz et al., 1982, pp. 99-109).

(c) *Curricula should draw from the community environment to create resources and opportunities for students to develop knowledge and basic skills in a real-life context for use in everyday life now and in the future* (Apple, 1983; Kohler, 1981; Molnar and Lindquist, 1982; Passow, 1982; Strickland, 1982). I would engage each teacher in an informal discussion about what is meant by "the basics" and about the nature of the relationship between the classroom, the home, and the community. Based upon my observations, I would expect each teacher to view the basics much more broadly than the traditional Three Rs and to value the community as a natural extension of the classroom.

Building upon their interest in the community, I would ask the teachers if they knew of any topics relevant to housing that had not been pursued in class because of a lack of time or resources. In the 5th/6th grade inner-city setting, such a prime topic for curriculum development might be the plight of the homeless, an issue that defies simple solutions and which is both seen and felt within the school community. On the other hand, in the 4th grade science class, topics worthy of curriculum development might be the history (social, environmental, and technological) of the city's land use and predictions for future local development. To enrich the content and process of such a curricular endeavor, I would suggest that we work cooperatively with the school's history teacher.

To further broaden perspectives, I would develop a curricular exchange to promote dialogue between the northern 5th/6th graders and the southern 4th graders. This exchange would include student and teacher letter-writing, photo-essays, community interviews, and perhaps even student visits. The two settings are quite different. Yet in both settings, the students' interest in community environmental issues is unusually strong. Much could be gained by both student and teacher through such curricular sharing and dialogue.

Within the special education setting of Observation #2, I would not suggest a change in the curricular focus; rather, I would work very closely with the teacher to design more resources to study neighborhood housing. To save her time, and because it is her first year in the neighborhood, I would do much of the preliminary leg work to research the neighborhood. We would then design an instructional "Neighborhood Housing" kit that would include manipulatives, walking-tour guides, trip-books, model constructions, and maps.

In all three settings, I would work with the teachers to develop a curricular career component. It would include a network of speakers and field experiences drawn from parents, alumni, faculty, public officials, and community members.

Based upon experience, I would expect the teachers to suggest that our curricular resources include background readings, student activity sheets designed to stimulate group discussion, active involvement of local artists and residents, content-supportive photos and illustrations, the names and phone numbers of individuals participating as guest speakers or field-trip organizers, capsule suggestions for lessons rather than highly detailed, tightly sequenced plans, "sharing" assignments to be done at home by the student with family members [to get the housing information home and to encourage parent-child dialogue about a topic familiar to both], hypothetical real-life problem stories for older students, and bibliographies for the teacher and student.

(d) *Curricula should encourage teacher input, creativity, and risk-taking in the development, adoption, or adaptation of materials and programs* (Apple, 1983; Boyer, 1983b; Goodlad, 1983b; Hechinger, 1983a, 1983b). Too often, the curriculum-development process overlooks the classroom teacher as a curricular resource. In our curriculum, the teacher's special talents and experiences will play an important role, and opportunities for sharing such interests with both students and colleagues will be nurtured. To discover the teacher's needs, interests, and resources, and just to become better acquainted, I would eventually ask the teacher to reflect on: her own housing interests both as a child and adult; why she originally entered teaching, her hopes, ambitions, practical concerns; and identification of the rewards and frustrations of classroom teaching. Such personal reflection and autobiographical analysis unveils ideas and feelings important to the curriculum development process (Brubaker, 1982; Tyler, 1949, p. 22).

Because curriculum development is a creative, professional, and emotional process, such reflection serves to sensitize the free-lance consultant to teacher concerns. Based upon both experience and, to some extent, the literature (Boyer, 1983a, 1983b), I would expect that most teachers would cite such frustrations as time constraints, lesson interruptions, lack of ready resources; requirements that block exploration of valuable tangents or serendipitous learning experiences, clerical chores, lack of appropriate respect and credit from both the general public and the profession itself, curricular guidelines or required texts that discourage teacher input and creativity, limited time with some students; and feelings of isolation from other adults within the school community.

A curriculum developer must not only be a good listener but must also be able to transform information gleaned from such discussions into a curricular structure that enhances the rewards of teaching and reduces the frustrations. To accomplish this, our curriculum development project would include participation by teachers on a strictly voluntary basis; time-saving instructional resources; a flexible scope and sequence to encourage pursuit of worthwhile tangents as emergent curricula; learning experiences that encourage interaction and participation by diverse sectors and varied age levels in the school community; many channels to give credit and say thank you to teachers; avenues for teachers to share their ideas with colleagues in their school and elsewhere[3]; opportunities for multi-grade-level implementation; and special projects and events to encourage teachers, staff, and students to work cooperatively toward identifying, planning, and realizing a common curricular goal.

Such special projects and events (musicals, award ceremonies, murals, gardens, neighborhood tours, photo exhibits, restorations of nearby parks, adopt-a-house or landmark proposals, a housing-theme quilt, debates, a housing fair, etc.) should be an integral part of our curriculum. These projects are not merely curricular "add-ons." They are linked specifically to networks of learning experiences. They are designed to bring diverse groups together; enable teachers and students to share ideas, talents, and interests; exhibit students' work; give credit and recognition to both students and teachers; make a permanent contribution to the community; create momentum within the curriculum development process; revive old school traditions; encourage cooperative group work; and increase the levels of enjoyment within the curricular program.

The three observed teachers all revealed a propensity for creative adaptations of curricular materials. Despite the range of their teaching experience, each teacher drew creatively upon individual talents and diverse curricular resources to enrich the students' learning experiences. Not one of the teachers used a "prepackaged" instructional format. In each lesson, the teacher used teacher-created materials as well as House Sense resources and elements from other published curricular kits.[4] Although time consuming, this personal input permits teachers to inject their own style into the lesson and to shape the content and format to meet the particular needs of the students. All of the teachers truly "owned" the curricula they implemented.

As a curriculum developer, I have a commitment not only to welcome such teacher adaptations but also to encourage, or more accurately to re-

---

[3]Sharing would be encouraged through workshops, informal dialogue, and curricular newsletters. When appropriate, the New York City teachers would be encouraged to apply to the Impact II Program, which is administered by the Division of Curriculum and Instruction of the New York City Board of Education [the program has been replicated in other regions of the United States]. Its goal is to set up a system whereby teachers who develop exemplary programs can receive grants and join a network that enables them to disseminate their programs to other interested teachers.

[4]In addition to the House Sense Program's curricular resource collection, *Home Sick? Try House Sense!*, the teachers employed, in Observation #1, *Harry Stottlemeier's Discovery* (Upper Montclair, N.J.: The Institute for the Advancement of Philosophy for Children, Montclair State College, 1980); in Observation #2, *Ready Steps*, a pre-kindergarten kit from Houghton Mifflin, and *The House: See How It Is Made* (Cleveland: Modern Curriculum Press, 1983); and in Observatiokn #3, *Project Wild: Elementary Activity Guide* (Western Regional Environmental Education Council, 1983), and "The Planning Game" (1974) and the "Planning the Human Community Simulation" kit (1974), both produced by the Society for Visual Education, Singer Education Division.

quire, teacher input and curricular decision making. This commitment rests upon the premise that change must come from within the school and not just from outside consultants. Local educators must "own" the change process for it to be enduring and meaningful. At best, the curriculum developer serves as a resource provider and a catalyst for change.

To promote local ownership of the curriculum development process, I would write and develop curricular resource collections[5] rather than traditional, tightly sequenced curricular formats. Such resource collections draw their theoretical base from a rational-empirical curricular development process (Tyler, 1949) yet also encourage pursuit of emergent curricula. The design of the resource collection has a deliberately unfinished quality. This requires teachers to use the collection selectively and to add their own finishing touches to make the curriculum whole and appropriate to their particular instructional circumstances.

Outline Supportive Next Steps

Drawing from past experience and information gained from our discussions, I would outline with the each of the three teachers the supportive and practical steps needed to realize our curricular aims. Free-lance curriculum developers usually are working on several jobs at one time; yet visibility and availability are essential to building credibility within a school setting. The following steps enhance this credibility and promote the sharing of ideas and resources with teachers at every stage of the process.

To gain knowledge of the community, I would continue to take walking and photo tours; use local facilities; engage in informal conversations with neighborhood workers and residents; read local newspapers; study area census reports; research relevant local history; and meet with community organizations to inform them of our curricular plans and to seek their active support.

To build curricular content and to write a complete curricular resource collection, I would research the topic of housing through review of professional journals, books, magazines, newspapers, opinion polls, speeches, un-

---

[5]The resource collection format includes goals and objectives (cognitive, affective, psychomotor), evaluation components, and for every topic to be studied, teacher background readings; focus questions; understandings to be developed; supportive photographs, illustrations, and social commentary cartoons; discussion/comprehension questions; a wide array of student activity sheets (with answer keys for teachers) with sharing assignments to be completed at home with family members; supplementary pamphlets, brochures, and so forth; suggested activities; vocabulary lists; bibliographies for students and teachers; and suggestions to correlate special projects and events. The teachers may use as many sections of the collection as they want and in any sequence. Many of the materials are ungraded so that the teacher determines whether they are suitable or should be adapted for use with a particular class. There are also optional sections that outline a variety of topic sequences and suggest grade levels for each activity sheet. A list of specific guest speakers and field trips is included in the resource collection.

published reports, and federal, state, and city laws. Personal interviews would be employed to gain content information and feedback from experts in the housing field; request brochures, pamphlets, photos, etc. for inclusion in the resource collection; seek financial or material support; and develop a network of guest speakers and field experiences. If I were working with a project editor or administrator from a public agency, I would suggest visiting the school as often as possible to talk with the teachers and to gain a better understanding of the neighborhood setting.

To develop curriculum within the school, I would work closely with a core group of teachers from a variety of grade levels and subject areas; seek general plan approval from the superintendent; confer regularly with the principal; attend all faculty meetings; meet with parent associations; seek support from the school secretarial and custodial staff; meet with groups of students; write newsletters, personal notes, and fliers to all teachers to give updates, share ideas, and say thank you for teacher contributions; take part in other school activities and programs; request a mailbox and display space; place all curricular materials not only in the school library but also in the public library to increase public awareness of our efforts; attend field-trips and guest speaker engagements; photo-document progress and share the photos with the teachers and staff; and develop teacher committees for special projects and events.

These basic steps reflect an ecological perspective of the whole school community (Foshay, 1975). It is a perspective that views change as a personal, emotional process that is "accomplished by individuals not institutions" (Loucks and Pratt, 1979, p. 213); a perspective which appreciates that change in one part of the school ecosystem requires adjustment in other parts (Heckman et al., 1983); a perspective which, based upon my own experience, recognizes that such adjustments have the potential to generate a ripple-effect wave of enthusiastic participation.

As this phase of our journey into the process of curriculum development draws to a close, the process itself would continue. Too often curriculum development ends prematurely without successful or sustained implementation (Patterson and Czajkowski, 1979). To me, implementation is actually an integral part of the development phase; thus, I would assure the teachers that I would be available before, during, and after the curricular materials are developed. The implementation phase is the time when you see your curricular materials come alive in the hands of administrators, teachers, parents, and students. It is a time not to be missed!

Because of the lasting professional relationships that can grow out of an enjoyable, productive, sharing process, the school door need never close entirely behind the free-lance curriculum developer.

References

Apple, M. W. "Curriculum in the Year 2000: Tensions and Possibilities." *Phi Delta Kappan* 64 (January 1983): 321-326.

Boyer, E. L. *"High School: A Report on Secondary Education in America.* New York: Harper & Row, 1983a.

Boyer, E. L. Keynote address presented at the Impact II Fifth Anniversary Convention, New York City, November 5, 1983b.

Brubaker, D. L. *Curriculum Planning: The Dynamics of Theory and Practices.* Glenview, Ill.: Scott, Foresman and Company, 1982.

Clark, D. L., L. S. Lotto, and M. M. McCarthy. "Factors Associated with Success in Urban Elementary Schools." *Phi Delta Kappan* 61 (March 1980): 467-470.

Foshay, A. W. *Essays on Curriculum.* New York: The A. W. Foshay Fund Committee, 1975.

Gessell, A., F. Ilg, and L. B. Ames. *The Child from Five to Ten.* Rev. ed. New York: Harper and Row, 1977.

Goodlad, J. I. "Improving Schooling in the 1980s: Toward the Non-Replication of Non-Events." *Educational Leadership* 40 (April 1983a): 4-7.

Goodlad, J. I. "A Study of Schooling: Some Implications for School Improvement." *Phi Delta Kappan* 64 (April 1983b): 552-558.

Goodlad, J. I. "What Some Schools and Classrooms Teach." *Educational Leadership* 40 (April 1983c): 8-19.

Hechinger, F. "New Study Finds Lack of Creativity." *The New York Times*, March 29, 1983a, p. C-7.

Hechinger, F. "Plan to Harness Energy of Teachers and Pupils." *The New York Times*, April 5, 1983b, p. C-7.

Heckman, P. E., J. Oakes, and K. A. Sirotnik. "Expanding the Concepts of School Renewal and Change." *Educational Leadership* 40 (April 1983): 26-32.

Joyce, B., and M. Weil. *Models of Teaching.* 2nd ed. Englewood Cliffs, N.J.: Prentice-Hall, Inc., 1980.

Kepler, K. B., and J. Randall. "Individualization: The Subversion of Elementary Schooling." *The Elementary School Journal* 77 (May 1977): 358-363.

Kohler, M. C. "Developing Responsible Youth Through Youth Participation." *Phi Delta Kappan* 62 (February 1981): 426-428.

Loucks, S., and H. Pratt. "A Concerns-Based Approach to Curriculum Change." *Educational Leadership* 37 (December 1979): 212-215.

Michaelis, J. U., R. H. Grossman, and L. F. Scott. *New Dimensions in Elementary Curriculum and Instruction.* 2nd ed. New York: McGraw-Hill Book Company, 1975.

Molnar, A., and B. Lindquist. "Traveling Through Cities—Thinking About Schools." *Educational Leadership* 39 (March 1982): 405-410.

Morin, K. *Home Sick? Try House Sense!: A Comprehensive Housing Resource for New York City Neighborhoods* (Vols. I and II). New York: The New York City Department of Housing Preservation and Development, 1982.

Passow, A. H. "Urban Education for the 1980s: Trends and Issues." *Phi Delta Kappan* 63 (April 1982): 519-522.

Patterson, J. L., and T. J. Czajkowski. "Implementation: Neglected Phase in Curriculum Change." *Educational Leadership* 37 (December 1979): 204-206.

Popkewitz, T. S., B. R. Tabachnick, and G. Wehlage. *The Myth of Educational Reform: A Study of School Responses to a Program of Change.* Madison: The University of Wisconsin Press, 1982.

Story, J. C., Director, House Sense Program, New York City Departmernt of Housing Preservation and Development, Office of Program and Management Analysis, personal interview, 1984.

Strickland, D. S. "Integrating the Basic Skills Through the Content Areas." In *Basic Skills: Issues and Choices.* Washington, D.C.: National Institute of Education, 1982.

Tyler, R. W. *Basic Principles of Curriculum and Instruction.* Chicago: University of Chicago Press, 1949.

Tyler, R. W. "Curriculum Development Since 1900." *Educational Leadership* 38 (May 1981): 598-601.

12. Working Together to Improve Teaching

Karen Kepler Zumwalt

... different people need different things at different times. Sometimes what is rewarding at one time turns out to be draining at another; what one person needs experience in may have always been part of the repertoire of another (Lieberman and Miller, 1985).

UNDOUBTEDLY THE 11 CONTRIBUTORS TO THIS YEARBOOK, WITH THEIR OWN INDIVIDual conceptions of how they might work with teachers to improve teaching, will have varying appeal to different teachers—growing professionally has different meanings to different teachers at different times.

As professionals, teachers should be able to choose the kinds of experiences they believe will be most professionally rewarding and profitable in terms of improving their own teaching. This yearbook is intended to array some possible ways teachers might utilize outside expertise in teacher-initiated professional development activities. Obviously, working with outside expertise is not necessary and the 11 approaches represent only a sample of the possibilities if outside assistance is desired. The authors were selected not to define the universe but to illustrate how different orientations and expertise affect the nature of professional growth experiences and to illuminate the consequences of different teacher choices.

My intention in this chapter is to begin the process of helping teachers and others clarify and articulate the approach that best meets their own current needs and their conception of improving teaching. I do so with some hesitation as there is so much in these chapters, and they truly best speak for

Karen Kepler Zumwalt is Associate Professor of Education, Teachers College, Columbia University, New York City.

themselves. I have chosen to focus on some of the differences and similarities among the authors that seem particularly relevant to me at this point—others with their own agendas will choose to highlight other aspects as they compare their own views with those represented here. There cannot be a definitive, concluding chapter in such a book whose primary purpose is to stimulate reflection and dialogue among educators, all of whom bring their own meanings and resources to our individual and collective efforts to improve teaching.

Goals

"Working with teachers on their teaching" was the common goal stipulated in the simulation exercise. The authors interpreted this common goal differently depending on their own assumptions about good teaching, their own specialized expertise, their role, and the specific context in which they were observing. Hence, they came to their common assignment with their own agenda and conceptions of how it would "play out" over time.

Given their roles and the specific contexts in which they were observing and working, the authors might be grouped as having four primary goals in working together to improve teaching:

1. To support teachers, individually and collectively, in becoming autonomous learners in charge of their own professional development.

2. To support teachers, either individually or collectively, in developing a more effective program for their students.

3. To make the "familiar" problematic and assist teachers in becoming more reflective and analytic as they learn from their own teaching.

4. To expand ways teachers think about teaching and means to alter it by exposure to concepts and findings from research and theoretical literature in education.

One could quickly categorize the authors according to the goals they emphasize: Goal No. 1: Heath, Dillon-Peterson, Rodriguez/Johnstone; Goal No. 2: Bang-Jensen, Apelman, Morin; Goal No. 3: Griffin, Erickson; Goal No. 4: Stallings, Good/Weinstein, Corno. Although such a categorization might be helpful to some, it is also misleading because all four goals are interconnected. What holds them together is a conception of teachers as active, reflective professionals concerned about the growth of their students and themselves and who view their work as involving professional deliberation and problem solving. Without question, different authors have different priorities among the four goals, which shape their approach to improving teaching. But a further analysis indicates that most of them, despite their emphasis, explicitly or implicitly accept the other goals as important ways to improve teaching. While accepting the goals, however, their own individual interpretations of what those goals mean and how they can be accomplished provide teachers with some clear choices as to which approach best meets their present needs.

Besides tapping elements of what it means to be a professional teacher, the emergence of these four goals serves as a reminder that the recent focus on the "application of research"—in particular, teacher effectiveness research—as the means of improving teaching is strikingly narrow. Other complementary vehicles to improve teaching include supporting teacher-driven, ongoing professional development activities and teacher efforts to develop and adapt their programs to meet the needs of their students, themselves, and the larger communities they serve; and encouraging a reflective, analytic stance toward teaching. In actuality, when activities that are designed to "apply research" are undertaken in a context where the other goals are simultaneously being pursued, the nature of the goal is subtly changed from one in which research, with its authoritative trappings is "applied" to one in which it is "transformed" as professional teachers make sense of it for their own setting.

Observing

In observing classrooms, some authors chose to look very generally and some chose to look in a more focused manner—focused because of the context of the situation and their role or because of their particular research interests. Whether their intent was to look generally or specifically, what they looked for and saw was influenced by their own personal and professional beliefs, experiences, and agendas. Understanding the explicit and implicit lenses of a classroom observer is important in deciding whether that person and approach best matches an individual, school, or district's professional development needs and goals.

General Observation

Four of the authors chose to do general observations of the classrooms (Peterson, Rodriguez/Johnstone, Griffin, Apelman). But as Apelman reminds us, "I may look at the classroom without a specific plan but what I *see* is organized and analyzed according to my personal beliefs." While looking at many of the same things the other observers looked at (e.g. room arrangement, activities, class routines, task involvement, teacher-child interaction), she was particularly sensitive to three areas (emotional support, positive social interaction, intellectual stimulation), which are central to her view of good teaching. Her role as a teacher center advisor and her particularly strong commitment to a vision of education made it natural for her to become a *participant* observer, and to make judgments as she observed in relation to her belief that the "challenge of every teacher is to guide, uncover, reawaken children's inborn drive to learn." Teachers must "create an atmosphere of emotional trust and intellectual excitement and they must know how to make diverse subject matter accessible to children of widely differing backgrounds." Likewise, Griffin reminds us that not only does our conception of teaching guide our responsiveness to what we see but also how we judge what we see. As a professor of curriculum and more recently having been involved in direct instruction research, he is very explicit about what he admires in teaching: "a consequence of decisions that result in a blend of styles, a mix and match amalgram whose parts are suited to specific curriculums, student groups, and purposes of instruction." Like Apelman, Griffin's "own predilection for teaching tends toward the activity-oriented, experience-based mode," but his observations and judgments are not driven by the same commitment to the vision as Apelman's. Instead, despite his own predilection, he finds no one orientation to teaching "entirely satisfying," and hence, is looking more for the "mix and match" he feels is the hallmark of good teaching. That is his commitment and the lens he uses in his general observation of classrooms.

Context-Specific Observation

Three of the authors' observational lenses were focused by contextual factors. As a colleague, Bang-Jensen had been specifically asked to focus her attention on the writing curriculum and, as a curriculum consultant, Morin had been invited to observe the interdisciplinary curriculum concerned with housing and community improvement. And in her business context as a consultant accountable to management, Corno chose to focus her observation on the three areas (instructional activity, instructor's performance, student learning/satisfaction) in which instructors are typically evaluated and which "fit" the vision of teaching held at Compuco.

Although role and setting encouraged these authors to focus their observations, what they looked at and saw was also filtered through their own beliefs and perspectives developed through experience and professional studies. Undoubtedly Corno, who views herself as specializing in educational psychology and motivation, chose her three areas not just because they "fit" the vision of teaching held at Compuco, but because they are very compatible with her own areas of expertise and the visions of good teaching evident in the literature on instructional psychology.

In contrast, Morin and Bang-Jensen's conceptions of good teaching and what they are looking for in teaching writing and interdisciplinary studies are heavily influenced by concepts and visions of goodness found in the general curriculum literature, as well as their subject-specific literature. In the particular elements they choose to look at and what they see, both seem to have internalized a personally adapted version of the Tylerian model of curriculum and to view the teacher as a curriculum developer.

Besides a specific approach to teaching writing, Bang-Jensen speaks "of bringing to my observations a synthesis of variables and a generalized conception of the elements that go into effective teaching. Fundamental to effective teaching are: a knowledge of the subject area; an appreciation of children's social, emotional, and cognitive development; a concern for both the planned and 'hidden' curriculum; a repertoire of instructional techniques and classroom management skills, an awareness of one's own strengths, and the needs of each particular class. A coordinated approach that considers and synthesizes all these elements into an effective program to meet one's goal is, in my view, the essence of good teaching." Obviously, as a teacher, she has chosen a process approach to teaching writing because it is compatible with her views of good teaching. What she brings to her observation and work, which another advocate of the same approach might not, is a sensitivity to the necessary coordination and desired connectedness of different elements and activities that make up the curriculum.

Likewise, Morin, besides being focused by her subject matter to look for the "environmental connectedness of child, classroom, and community," is also influenced by "baggage drawn from years of personal and professional life experience." She professes "a constructionist philosophy and psychology of schooling that draws upon a tradition which views individuals as capable of constructing knowledge through experiences both in and out of the school setting and which rests upon the tenet that democratic, reflective, group problem-solving experiences are central to education and even to social progress." Yet she admittedly draws heavily upon Tyler's rational-empirical view of curriculum in the way she looks at classrooms and works with teachers. Although some might feel these are contradictory views, Morin has woven them together in a vision of good teaching that emphasizes the teacher as developer of curriculum and, to some extent, the child as a constructor of curriculum.

Research-Focused Observation

What four of the authors looked for in observing teaching was shaped by their own research interests (Heath, Stallings, Good/Weinstein, Erickson). Despite their common research-driven focus, the different substance of their research and their varying methodological approaches generated very different approaches to looking at teaching.

Heath—basing his approach on "25 years of research-based understanding of how healthy adult growth proceeds" *and* visits to hundreds of classrooms—looks to "everything that tells me what the people are like in this school." He wants to "learn very quickly just how much freedom and independence teachers feel they have . . . to understand if teachers feel they can change, dare to risk." He specifically looks for signs of the "four handicaps that can critically hurt if not bar our growth and efforts to improve our classroom and schools." Two of these handicaps to improvement might be considered curricular (i.e., not identifying priority goals and not knowing how to design systematic, sequential strategies by which to achieve goals), and two are attitudinal (i.e., not being reflective and fearing risks). His research and experience focus his "looking" on signs of these curricular and attitudinal factors as starting points for working with teachers.

In contrast, Stallings views her classrooms primarily with a formal observational system designed to generate data about each teacher's classroom to match data generated by research on effective teachers—teachers whose students have gained more on achievement tests. Using her observational tools, she focuses her observations on the type and duration of activities provided, who took part in the activities, the nature of the interactions between the teachers and students, students' on-task rate, intrusions from outside the classroom, and the classroom climate. So her focus in "looking" is based on those variables that research on effective teaching has revealed as critical.

In a similar vein, but without a formal observational system, Good and Weinstein look at areas in which prior research indicates teachers communicate differential expectations. For them, research on teaching provides a framework to think about expectations and focuses their "looking" at certain critical variables, such as grouping practices, locus of responsibility for learning, feedback and evaluation practices. The framework gives them categories of areas to focus their observations rather than categories to check off on an observational system. So their research-driven observation, in this case, has generated qualitative descriptions of teaching rather than the quantitative descriptions that Stallings was able to generate.

Coming from a different research tradition (ethnography) and with a different model of teaching (sociocognitive), Erickson's ways of looking at classrooms provide another varient of the influence of research. As he observes, he keeps running narrative fieldnotes of what is happening in the classroom, paying particular attention to the task environments that teachers and students create for each other, in particular, in two related strands of curriculum that are woven together—the structure and content of subject matter and the social relations by which the learners and teachers engage the subject matter. As Erickson writes, he notes major phases within events, clock time of the beginning of each new phase, and the action in each phase. He transcribes "as much as I can get down of the children's speech, trying to show in the notes the exact words, timing, intonation used . . . salient nonverbal actions by the teacher and students, attempting to describe them in detailed behavioral terms rather than in terms that involve inference of intent." As an ethnographer and a social constructivist, Erickson, assuming no one really knows what is going on in a classroom, envisions his task as observer is to produce a detailed objective narrative that will make the enacted curriculum visible.

Hence, we see that being research-driven in one's observations of teaching does not necessarily imply a research-derived observational schedule such as Stallings has utilized, but that research may generate other methodologies such as Erickson's narrative field notes, specific frameworks such as Good/Weinstein's teacher expectancy, specific concepts such as Erickson's teacher- and student-created task environments and Heath's four handicaps to professional growth and improvement of teaching.

And like the authors who chose to "look at" the classroom generally and with context-specific lenses, these research-oriented visions are also clearly reflective of each author's conceptions of what good teaching is all about. Not only does choice of substance and methodology reflect their values, but when they actually take their "research eyes" to classrooms, we see that while research provides a focus for their viewing, they also "see" other aspects of teaching—aspects that in most cases violate their conception of good teaching, which may or may not be part of their original research-driven way of observing. For instance, Good/Weinstein comment, "although our case studies demonstrate a number of important expectation issues, it is interesting that few of these specific instances involving the communication of low expectations are directly comparable to those in the (research-generated) list presented earlier in this chapter. We were most sensitive (in approaching our observations) to low teacher expectations that might be communicated to individuals or groups of students; however, in these classrooms the major problem was the expression of *low expectations*" to *entire classes*. They were looking for the communication of differential expectations to groups and individuals; instead, they were disturbed about the appropriateness of the reading/language arts curriculum evident in their admittedly brief observations. Their call for "classroom tasks that are more meaningful, demanding, and interesting" reflect a vision of good teaching that complements their commitment to revealing differential expectations. Someone, for instance, with a different vision of good teaching might not view the particular conception of reading/language arts curriculum as communicating low expectations.

Focused ways of observing, whether the focus is determined by context or research, do influence what "one sees." But like observers who "look" generally, what is actually seen is influenced by the personal and professional beliefs, experiences, and values of the observer. Likewise, the initial feedback one gives a teacher is influenced by what one was "looking for" and what was "seen" as well as one's views of how an outsider might work with teachers to improve teaching.

Working with Teachers

With one notable exception, the initial "feedback" to teachers after the observation seems structured to engage the observer and teacher, individually or in a group, in a dialogue about what is happening in the classroom; to establish a feeling of trust and mutual respect; and to anticipate future directions. Corno, who was observing teachers in a business setting, provides the contrast. As she explains, "in business consulting situations, it is common for such a summary (including interpretations and action recommendations) to be presented to instructors and management as a preliminary report." In striking contrast, the observers working in schools chose face-to-face feedback, tended to downplay their own interpretations and recommendations, and did not feel compelled by institutional norms or policy to share their conclusions with administrators.

Despite their different goals and approaches to observation, the authors working in the school settings all wanted to involve the observed teacher(s) in self-analysis and reflection. Generally, they obtained the teacher's impressions and further information on goals, shared their observations, and tried to engage the teachers in analysis of what happened.

How they shared their observations did differ. Some offered comments, or asked questions; some shared their descriptive field notes verbally or in writing; some provided teachers with a tape of the observations; and others provided them with data collected using particular observational instruments. And one, Erickson, had the teacher and observer both write recollections of the events to stimulate a discussion of the different views and meanings they *each* constructed from observing the "same" event.

The authors also differed in how explicitly they used this initial time together to obtain *teachers'* assessments of their own needs and to assess the views of teachers toward teaching, the students, curricular priorities, and help. When actually done explicitly here, the variation that we know exists was exposed. For instance, both Bang-Jensen and Apelman discovered that their more experienced teacher wanted to use them as a sounding board, whereas their first-year teacher wanted them to be more directive.

While none of the authors explicitly provided the teacher initially with a list of "action recommendations" as in the business setting, none could avoid expressing their judgments, either indirectly through questions or more directly through praise or specific suggestions. While suggestions seem most likely to flow from the use of observational schemes that have implicit in them some conception of "goodness," it should also be clear that suggestions may just as easily flow from the general observation of an author, such as Apelman, with a strong sense of "goodness." Authors differed in how direct they were in sharing their judgments and how specific and authoritative they were in their suggestions, when offered at all.

They also differed in how they viewed the future agenda—one had a predetermined process and content focus, for some only the process or content was clearly set out, and for others the process and content of the continued work were unknowns emerging from their work with the teachers. While Stallings' approach involved the most explicit predetermined process and content, most of the others said that the needs and interests of the teachers would determine the future directions. Some, like Heath, Dillon-Peterson, and Rodriguez/Johnstone, had a specific set of processes that would influence the assessing and addressing of needs and interests. For others, the determination of teacher needs and interests would be influenced by the expertise and interests of the authors, such as the particular subject matter foci of Morin and Bang-Jensen; Good/Weinstein's concerns about teacher beliefs, which represent a "vicious self-defeating cycle of low expectations"; or Apelman's commitment to a certain vision of education. Even the least predetermined approach of Erickson, who asserts that outwardly "no one knows where it will lead," carries with it a methodology and his own constructivist way of viewing, which will shape the themes and approaches that evolve out of the collective exchange and analysis of videotapes.

Clearly, how predetermined and explicit are the process and content of their plans is only one of the many differences in their approaches. Not unexpectedly, they sketch out 11 different strategies or visions for their continuing relationship. While they clearly offer different options, almost all of them seem to agree with Bang-Jensen that to improve teaching means "redefining teaching to include work with peers." After the initial feedback, some, like Health, want to move immediately to working with the whole faculty as a group; others, like Rodriguez/Johnstone, work on personal and school-level problem solving, decision making, and goal setting simultaneously; while others continue working with the individual teacher or a small group of teachers, later expanding their work to a larger group within the school, and, in the case of Morin, to colleagues in other schools using the developed curricular material. "Seeing and talking" across classrooms through exchange visits and shared videotaping or observation data are evident in many of the strategies. Empowering teachers through collective analysis, reflection, deliberation are common themes in many of these chapters. For example, Heath speaks of "corporate learning groups," Dillon-Peterson of "consensus building processes," Rodriguez/Johnstone of "collegial support groups," Griffin of "cohort groups," Apelman of networking, and Erickson of "deliberation through peer consultation." While all are somewhat different because they are embedded in different processes and contexts, they all assume that improvement of teaching is something that can and should happen in a group context.

In a related fashion, the authors are working to empower the groups or individual teachers to assume responsibility for their own continued growth *and* in some cases for that of their colleagues. Such professional leadership is structured in Stallings' "pyramid program" and Corno's rotating master instructors. Bang-Jensen talks of the "snowballing" effect as Kate and Linda have taken on the responsibility of working with colleagues and, more informally, Morin speaks of the "ripple effect . . . creating waves of enthusiastic participation" as teachers develop House Sense Curriculum for their class and school.

While intrinsic rewards are definitely the major propelling force of these individual and collective efforts to improve teaching, there is also some acknowledgment that legitimization and recognition by administrators are important. For instance, Corno suggests attendance at conferences, social activities, and notes on performance ratings might be appropriate recognition for progress. Erickson speaks of release time necessary for time-consuming developmental inquiry, and Griffin adds money, salary schedule, credit, and ceremonial support as evidence of district legitimization. Bang-Jensen notes the importance of the periodic spots at faculty meetings allotted to teachers working on writing. As administrators, Rodriguez/Johnstone understandably build administrative collaboration into their process. And

Morin provides teachers with recognition through participation in a national network of teachers developing House Sense Curriculum.

Perhaps another less obvious motivating factor is that many of the authors—even when they have process strategies that involve group work or strong personal educational commitments—are sensitive to different needs of the individual teachers. For a "strong teacher," Heath would work on "improving skills like analyzing and articulating her goals" while for a Mr. Schmidt, he would emphasize "character-transforming" exposures "to awaken his emotional potential." For George, Apelman wants to "help him understand what intense involvements with materials can do for a child's self-concept" and "help him differentiate between intervening to settle arguments and to further children's learning," while Sheri, being at a different stage, wants Apelman to focus on curriculum development. To help them gain control over their teaching, Griffin wants to help Carol counteract her feeling of being in an "undertow" while helping Elaine "more clearly articulate how she makes decisions to deviate from district expectations." In so many of these cases, although the authors can outline an approach, the uniqueness of each teacher's needs and interests demand individually tailored responses on the part of the authors. The emphasis on empowering teachers as a collective, so evident in many of these chapters, does not seem to be done at the expense of the individual teacher.

As the authors respond to teachers as individuals and in groups, they also take on a wide variety of roles that reflect their different goals, concerns, expertise, and personalities. Peterson speaks of her role as "manager rather than leader . . . facilitator, broker, provider, reminder, encourager, question-asker, coach, cheerleader, and celebrator." Other roles taken on by the authors include collaborator, researcher, instructor, resource, organizer, trainer, administrator, co-teacher, reactor, assistant, model, consultant, provoker, translator, analyzer, recorder, evaluator, and colleague. The particular combination of roles and relative emphases are likely to have different appeal to different teachers, as are the different approaches and the underlying assumptions of the authors.

Underlying Assumptions

Using these 11 chapters, we could tease out a multitude of assumptions the different authors make about learners, subject matter, society, teachers, learning, teaching, curriculum, evalation, and the aims of education. Some of these have already become apparent as we have viewed similarities and differences in their goals, what they looked for and saw in observing, what kind of initial feedback they gave to teachers, and the approaches they proposed in continuing their work with teachers. Teasing out other assumptions might be a useful task for readers hoping to clarify their own views about improving teaching. Space limits me to consideration of three assumptions central to my own concerns expressed in the Introduction: the relationship between effective teaching and curriculum; the relationship between research and practice; and the vision of the teacher as a professional. To me, how one views these areas will have a major impact on how we work together to improve teaching.

Relationship Between Effective Teaching and Curriculum

One of the reasons the authors differ in their approach to improving teaching is that they have different conceptions of "effective teaching," its aims and its relationship with curriculum. Some of these differences have been indicated throughout this chapter, so let me just focus on a few additional illustrations here.

Some of the authors either state or imply that the aim of teaching is to improve students' achievement scores. For instance, teachers in Stallings' groups match their own performance against observation profiles of teachers who have been judged as "effective" because their students gained more on achievement tests. In contrast, Heath believes the aim of teaching "should be to enable our students to become more mature persons capable of adapting effectively to the problems they will confront." Understandably, the principles of "effective teaching" generated by Heath and Stallings are quite different.

And because of their different views of "effective teaching," the authors have different starting points. Heath looks for signs of four handicaps, because "if they are present then I know to work with a faculty on technique or specific curricular issues is not likely to result in sustained improvement." Good/Weinstein assert that "unless basic problems of low expectations are solved, any improvement resulting from alteration in instruction is apt to be transitory." And Erickson believes if we "never subject the taken-for-granted to scrutiny we are unable to deliberate on it when we need to do so." Such underlying assumptions drive the approaches described in this book.

Another influential factor is each author's conception of the relation between curriculum and teaching. Like their predecessors, contemporary educators continue to disagree about the definition of curriculum and whether curriculum and instruction (teaching) are indeed separate domains. While the scholarly treatment of this issue continues, however, life in schools goes on and the nuances of the debate at times seem rather academic and distant. Yet our acceptance or rejection of the dualism at a very general level has a profound influence on our view of teaching and how to improve it.

Curriculum, as reflected by its use in this book, means many different things. For some, it is equivalent to the subject matter outlined for a grade/course; for others it is embodied in the textbook or commercial program; for some it is the goals and learning experiences teachers develop for their specific class; and for others, it is that which is constructed through the interaction of teacher and pupils and has different meanings for different participants.

Not only do the authors use the word differently, but they clearly vary in their approach to improving teaching, depending on whether they focus on instructional behavior or see curricular and instructional issues intertwined in the teaching process and, hence, focus on both simultaneously. For three of the university-based authors (Heath, Griffin, Erickson), the teacher (Bang-Jensen), the teacher center specialist (Apelman), and the curriculum consultant (Morin), an analysis of their goals, what they were looking for and saw in observing, and their initial feedback to the teachers indicate that to them, albeit in different degrees, improving teaching involves addressing curricular *and* instructional issues. For them, at least in practice, the dualism between teaching and curriculum is not functional. The very act of teaching does or should involve the making of curricular and instructional decisions.

In contrast, four other university-based authors (Stallings, Corno, Good/Weinstein), the staff developer (Dillon-Peterson), and the principal (Rodriguez/Johnstone) appear to focus more on instructional behavior in their observations and initial feedback. Whether or not this instructional focus is indicative of a dualistic view of curriculum and teaching cannot really be discerned from these chapters, but what is clear is that regardless of their initial focus on instructional behavior, their later work with teachers on improving teaching included, either spontaneously or according to plan, a concern with curricular issues. The centrality of curricular issues in relation to improving teaching varies greatly among these seven authors, but it does come into play.

Stallings, whose observations and goals are perhaps most driven by research on teacher behavior, does include a workshop where the group critiques each teacher's prepared unit and lesson plans. Dillon-Peterson's initial observation is guided by Madeline Hunter's system, which clearly focuses on instructional behavior. But she later describes a "consensus building process to explore our basic educational philosophies" and a "discrepancy assessment of each principle." Additionally, Dillon-Peterson illustrates the power of her model by describing a group of junior high teachers who designed a special program. Corno, who is working with instructors who see subject matter knowledge as *the* key ingredient of effective teaching, reminds them that "there is a difference between knowing the structure of a subject and knowing how that subject is efficiently learned." While focusing on instructional behaviors, she also touches upon their "naive" views of pedagogical knowlege—how a subject is transformed to make it accessible to students of varying abilities and interests. Good/Weinstein, directed by expectancy research on teacher behaviors to look for the ways teachers communicate low expectations to individuals and groups, are struck by the fact that the curriculum, as envisioned by these teachers, communicates low expectations to the entire class. And Rodriguez/Johnstone, although focusing on instructional factors in their initial observation, clearly move over to curricular concerns in their comments about the teacher who "merely progressed in sequence from topic to topic through the text." When describing ways to continue to work with teachers to improve teaching, they specifically dismiss a focus on instruction. "While there is no question that the improvement of instruction is of critical importance to increasing student achievement, it is also true that teachers who are not encouraged (nor even allowed) to participate in the school's goal setting, decision making, and planning are not going to be teachers who are motivated to perform at their highest potential." In their vision, the professional teacher needs to be involved in curricular planning at the school as well as classroom level.

While the authors certainly differ on the emphasis they give curricular issues and how intertwined they are with instructional issues, when reading these chapters as a whole, one might conclude that in practice, these distinctions are blurred. Most of the authors would seem to agree as Rodriguez and Johnstone note: "focusing solely on classroom observation and delivery of instruction is too limited an approach." Improving teaching involves consideration of curricular, instructional (and managerial) issues. By assigning curricular decisions elsewhere and relegating teachers to instructional and managerial decisions, one limits the discretionary freedom expected of most professionals and restricts the teacher's ability to create effective educational experiences for their students. As Erickson reminds us, unless one assumes that a curiculum can really be student-proof and teacher-proof, "the ability of the teacher to look at and deliberate on the enacted curriculum—its content and process—is pedagogically crucial."

Relationship Between Research and Practice

In his introduction to *Using What We Know About Teaching*, Philip Hosford states that "between the discovery of knowledge and its successful application lies a swampland of fears." Using teacher effectiveness research as a current example, he blames the "Fearful Ones" for undermining the bridgebuilders who are attempting to "link knowledge to its logical application."

The chapters in this volume remind us that there are many different kinds of bridgebuilders and bridges. There are some, like Hosford, who view the relationship between research and practice as one of application. And there are others, like Erickson, who believe that the time-on-task research is "meaning-stripping" and "deskilling teachers." While Hosford might label Erickson a "Fearful One," it would be hard to classify the intensive joint inquiry envisioned by Erickson and his teachers as nonbridgebuilding (although Erickson with his constructivist view would probably reject the metaphor itself).

Hosford's view stems from a research paradigm that lends itself to thinking of the utilization of research in terms of applying it to practice. Researchers discover the knowledge, skills, and attitudes that lead to desirable outcomes for students. The teachers are trained to exhibit more of these desirable knowledge, skills, and attitudes to improve student achievement.

One can be critical of the teacher effectiveness research in terms of its generalizability outside basic skills in reading and math at the primary grades, its restricted definition of educational goals (achievement test scores) and its focus on instructional behaviors. But I suspect that an even greater difference between Hosford's version of bridgebuilders and some of his "Fearful Ones" is a questioning of the research paradigm itself and the linear application relationship between research and practice.

Viewing teaching as bringing to bear one's experience, intuition, values, understanding of particular learners, subject matter context, and education in a fast-paced, continuous, complex problem-solving and decision-making process, these people see research as providing a resource as teachers constantly make choices about means and ends. "Research is used to help teachers develop their thinking and decision-making capacities and to help them reflect on and learn from their own experience." (Zumwalt, 1982) rather than prescribe the correct behavior. Good/Weinstein conclude after reviewing the extensive research on teacher expectancy, it is "only useful if used as a framework for thinking about classrooms rather than a general definition of how teachers should behave in the classroom. . . . Research does not yield answers but new insights and new challenges."

A related contribution of this book is to remind us that the knowledge base for teaching is much broader than the process-product variety of research on teaching and much broader than research itself. In these chapters, the most frequent sources of knowledge mentioned were, in Griffin's terms, the human and intellectual resources brought by the teacher, the teachers collectively, and the author. The authors in varying degrees seem to echo the conviction of Ann Lieberman and Lynne Miller in another recent ASCD publication:

It is our strong conviction that teachers possess the major portion of available knowledge about teaching and learning, and it is only through a recognition of that knowledge and an articulation and understanding of it that we can begin to find ways to improve schools.

The teachers and author bring knowledge and construct new knowledge as they work together. But as Griffin reminds us, "teachers, like other professionals, need to be linked to the most powerful assistance in terms of the problems they face. It is important for Carol and Elaine to discover how others have thought about their concerns, how both scholars and practitioners have dealt with their dilemmas, and how complex problems have been treated outside the boundaries of their classrooms." Thus, in envisioning how they might work with teachers to improve teaching, all of the authors utilized other knowledge bases. These included knowledge of particular fields of study such as staff development, professional development, adult development, curriculum development, subject matter knowledge, pedagogical knowledge, research on teaching, child development, educational psychology, philosophy, and understanding of specific contexts such as the children, teachers, school, community, and state. All of these sources were given particular meaning based on the author's experiences, intuition and values. Probably most importantly, a particular view of good teaching, either implicity or explicity, affected how the authors used resources and the strategies they employed to improve teaching.

In his introduction to the 1984 yearbook, Hosford notes, "Much is yet to be learned regarding the knowledge, skills, and values of the bridgebuilder." This set of papers hopefully broadens the definition of bridgebuilder to include those who may be "fearful" of Hosford's type of bridge building, but who are nonetheless deeply concerned about improving practice by building different kinds of bridges.

The Vision of Teacher as Professional

One might attempt to classify the authors' approaches to working with teachers in any number of ways. For instance, using Zeichner's (1983) categories, one might place Stallings as behavioristic, Heath as personalistic, Apelman as tradition-craft, and Griffin as inquiry-oriented. But while these types of categories may be useful to some and certainly signal different emphases, it is also clear that most of the authors, including those mentioned, cut across categories in practice. For instance, Heath's recommendation about white water canoeing, hiking in Austria, or working in an industrial lab is very consistent with his aim of "drawing out ignored potentials to become a richer, more cultured, mature human being." But while psychological maturity drives his approach, it is clear that his four handicaps and working with the school as a whole also have elements of the inquiry and tradition-craft approaches.

What seems to appeal to all of the authors is a vision of the teacher as a professional and a desire, in Griffin's words, "to push back the growing tide of paraprofessionalism that promises to reduce teaching activity to that which is easily taught to teachers, readily observed, and mechanistically remediated." There is no question that the vision of "professional" implicit in each chapter has some very different dimensions and emphases, but all the authors seem to share a commitment to self-generated professional growth; to the value of exposure to new ideas, people, and experiences; to a reflective and analytic stance toward one's teaching; and to helping teachers develop better educational experiences for their students.

Professional teachers, writes Apelman, are "intelligent, creative, sensitive individuals who will approach their task with energy and compassion and who will be committed to their own continued learning and growth." As Morin notes, many of the observed teachers "may not look like they need help, yet all professionals benefit from infusion and exchange of new ideas and opinions." As Stallings says, the aim of working with others to improve teaching is to help teachers "feel powerful and professional, not powerless . . . We want them to find the excellence inside themselves and to trust it." In addition, collaboration with others, as Dillon-Peterson says, "builds the feeling of support, ownership, competence, and commitment to professional development of self and others."

The authors have outlined different approaches, which they feel contribute to teachers' feelings of professionalism. While there is definitely a need for different approaches, two approaches described here could, *if misused*, lead to just the opposite feelings. The consultant report Corno is required to send to management and Stallings' approach, which stresses predetermined observable, teaching skills, could both be misused by other "staff developers" or administrators whose visions of improving teaching lean toward control rather than encouragement of autonomous learning.

For these authors, the emphasis on reflection and analysis as a means of improving teaching is central to their conception of professional teachers. This belief is echoed by Gail McCutcheon in the 1985 ASCD yearbook:

Each day practitioners face a host of complex, context-specific problems about which there are no easy answers. No singular "right" course of action is available, although practitioners can envision certain courses as better than others. In facing these problems, they *must* take action. Underlying these actions is a personal, guiding theory. By pausing to reflect, by reaching inward and attempting to understand that personal theory of action, teachers and administrators exercise the most professional aspect of practice (p. 48).

But many of the authors realize that changes are necessary to enable such a vision to exist. "Teachers," as Dillon-Peterson says, "are seldom encouraged by the system, which continues to be heavily bureaucratic with pressure toward centralization and conformity rather than supportive of individualization and differentiation." She places a great deal of trust in teachers knowing what's good for them but wonders whether we are ready yet to trust each other as true professionals. Erickson suggests that it is necessary to provide time for reflection each week and hold teachers accountable for the systematic study of their own practice. That, he realizes, would require "a fundamental change in the role of the school teacher as a professional. Such change will not come easily. It may well be necessary, however, if the quality of teaching is to improve generally and if teachers are to find their profession worthy of continued interest and effort. . . ."

Obviously, time for reflection is not enough. "Only when teachers are given full responsibility for their job and learn to take this responsibility will teaching become a respected profession," Apelman notes. Teachers need to be given the freedom to act like professionals in their classroom and school community. As professionals they do and should be expected to make decisions that are both curricular and instructional in providing quality educational programs for students, and to be reflective and analytic about their own teaching and professional growth.

While the 11 different approaches represented here address only a small number of the possible choices that might appeal to different people at different times, hopefully, this collection of papers will help teachers and those who work with teachers clarify and articulate how they would like to address the common goal of any professional—to improve one's own practice.

References

Hosford, Philip L., ed. *Using What We Know About Teaching.* Alexandria, Va.: Association for Supervision and Curriculum Development, 1984 yearbook.

Lieberman, Ann, and Lynne Miller. *Teachers, Their World, and Their Work: Implications for School Improvement.* Alexandria, Va.: Association for Supervision and Curriculum Development, 1984.

Molnar, Alex., ed. *Current Thought on Curriculum.* Alexandria, Va.: Association for Supervision and Curriculum Development, 1985 yearbook.

Zeichner, Ken M. "Alternative Paradigms of Teacher Education." *Journal of Teacher Education* 34 (3): 3-9.

Zumwalt, Karen K. "Research on Teaching: Policy Implications for Teacher Education." In *Policymaking in Education*, eighty-first yearbook of the Society for the Study of Education, edited by A. Lieberman and M.W. McLaughlin. Chicago: University of Chicago Press, 1982.

ASCD Board of Directors

Executive Council
1985-86

President: Carolyn Sue Hughes, Principal, Ludlow School, Shaker Heights, Ohio

President-Elect: Gerald Firth, Professor and Chairperson, Department of Curriculum and Supervision, University of Georgia, Athens, Georgia

Immediate Past President: Phil C. Robinson, Principal, Clarence B. Sabbath School, River Rouge, Michigan

Roger V. Bennett, Dean, College of Education and Human Service, University of Wisconsin, Oshkosh, Wisconsin

Donna Jean Carter, Superintendent, Independent School District 281, New Hope, Minnesota

Patricia Conran, Superintendent of Schools, Benjamin School District 25, West Chicago, Illinois

Robert C. Hanes, Deputy Superintendent of Schools, Charlotte-Mecklenburg Schools, Charlotte, North Carolina

Anna Jolivet, Director of Planning Services, Tucson Unified School District, Tucson, Arizona

Marcia Knoll, Principal, Public School 220, Queens, Forest Hills, New York

Elizabeth R. Lane, Principal, Mt. Pisgah Elementary School, Cordova, Tennessee

Jean Marani, Supervisor, Early Childhood and Elementary Education, Florida Department of Education, Tallahassee, Florida

Loren Sanchez, Assistant Superintendent, Instruction, Upland School District, Upland, California

Bob L. Sigmon, Director for Elementary Education, Richmond City Schools, Richmond, Virginia

Board Members Elected at Large

(Listed alphabetically; the year in parentheses indicates the end of the term of office.)
Richard Babb, City of Auburn Public Schools, Auburn, Maine (1986)
Doris Brown, University of Missouri, St. Louis, Missouri (1987)
Rita Foote, Southfield Public Schools, Southfield, Michigan (1989)
Geneva Gay, Purdue University, West Lafayette, Indiana (1987)
Delores Greene, Richmond Public Schools, Richmond, Virginia (1988)
Lois Harrison-Jones, Richmond City Schools, Richmond, Virginia (1986)
Jessie Kobayashi, Berryessa Unified School District, San José, California (1986)
Robert Krajewski, University of Northern Iowa, Cedar Falls, Iowa (1989)
Richard Kunkel, National Council for Accreditation of Teacher Education, Washington, D.C. (1988)

Marian Leibowitz, Teaneck Board of Education, Teaneck, New Jersey (1986)
Lillian Ramos, Catholic University, Ponce, Puerto Rico (1989)
Arthur D. Roberts, University of Connecticut, Storrs, Connecticut (1987)
Ann Converse Shelly, Bethany College, Bethany, West Virginia (1986)
Thelma Spencer, Educational Testing Service, Princeton, New Jersey (1989)
Arthur Steller, Mercer County Public Schools, Princeton, West Virginia (1987)
Lois Fair Wilson, California State University, San Bernardino, California (1988)
George Woons, Kent Intermediate School District, Grand Rapids, Michigan (1989)
Claire Yoshida, Konawaena High School, Kealakekua, Hawaii (1988)

Unit Representatives to the Board of Directors

(Each unit's President is listed first.)

Alabama: Annette Cox, Anniston City Schools, Anniston; Millie Cowles, University of
   Alabama, Birmingham; Richard Brogdon, Auburn University, Auburn
Alaska: Don McDermott, University of Alaska, Anchorage; M. Denice Clyne, Sand Lake
   School, Anchorage
Arizona: Robert Stahl, Arizona State University, Tempe; Ellie Sbragia, Arizona Bar
   Foundation, Phoenix
Arkansas: Steve Floyd, Russellville Public Schools, Russellville; Jerry Daniel, Camden
   Public Schools, Camden
California: Loren Sanchez, Upland School District, Upland; Ronald Hockwalt, Cajon
   Valley Union Elementary School District, El Cajon; Doris Prince, San José; Bob
   Guerts, Sonoma Valley Unified School District, Santa Rosa; David Phillips,
   Encinatas Union, Encinatas; Shareen Young, Management Consultant, Santa Cruz;
   Dorothy Garcia, Colton Joint Unified School District, Bloomington; Bob Garmston,
   California State University, Sacramento
Colorado: Tom Maglaras, Aurora School District 28J, Aurora; Donna Brennan, Cherry
   Creek School District 5, Englewood; Cile Chavez, Littleton School District, Littleton
Connecticut: Arthur D. Roberts, University of Connecticut, Storrs; Tom Jokubaitis,
   Wolcott Public Schools, Wolcott; Bernard Goffin, Monroe Public Schools, Monroe
Delaware: Eva Adams, Delaware State College, Dover; Frederick A. Duffy, Lincoln
District of Columbia: Phyllis Hobson, Lenox Administrative Unit, Washington, D.C.;
   Romaine Thomas, Ketcham Elementary School, Washington, D.C.
Florida: Mabel Jean Morrison, Okaloosa County Schools, Crestview; Mary Jo Sisson.
   Okaloosa County School Board, Ft. Walton Beach; Hilda Wiles, Littlewood
   Elementary School, Gainesville; Eileen Duval, Buckhorn Elementary School,
   Valrico
Georgia: Priscilla G. Doster, Monroe County Schools, Forsyth; Charles L.Shepherd.
   State Department of Education, Calhoun; Gerard F. Lentini, West Georgia College,
   Carrollton
Hawaii: Virgie Chattergy, University of Hawaii, Honolulu; Les Correa, St. Louis High
   School, Honolulu
Idaho: Linda Clark, Joplin Elementary School, Boise
Illinois: Stephanie Marshall, Batavia Public Schools #101, Batavia; Perry Sodwedel,
   Pekin Public Schools, Pekin; Al Cohen, Wilmot Junior High School, Deerfield;
   Carolyn S. Kimbell, Downers Grove School District #58, Downers Grove; John
   Fletcher, Park Ridge School District #64, Park Ridge; Richard Hanke, Thomas
   Junior High School, Arlington Heights
Indiana: Marvin Odom, Carmel Clay Schools, Carmel; Sue Pifer, Bartholomew
   Community School Corporation, Columbus; David Ebeling, Monroe County
   Community School Corporation, Bloomington

North Dakota: Richard B. Warner, Fargo South High School, Fargo; Andy Keough, North Dakota State University, Fargo

Ohio: Irma L. Griggs, Lake Local School District, Hartville; Eugene Glick, Ohio ASCD, Medina; David Kirkton, Westlake City Schools, Westlake; Larry Zimmerman, Marysville Exempted Village Schools, Marysville; Ronald Hibbard, Malone College, Canton

Oklahoma: James Roberts, Lawton Public Schools, Lawton; Charles Dodson, Sapulpa Public Schools, Sapulpa

Oregon: Tom Roberts, Cedar Park Intermediate School, Beaverton; Art Phillips, Ashland; LaVae Robertson, Oak Elementary School, Albany

Pennsylvania: Donald Wright, Montgomery County Intermediate Unit, Erdenheim; John P. Jarvie, Northwest Tri-County Intermediate Unit #5, Edinboro; John T. Lambert, Administration Center, East Stroudsburg; Therese T. Walter, General McLane School District, Edinboro; David Campbell, Rose Tree Media School District, Media

Puerto Rico: José A. Acosta-Ramos, University of Puerto Rico, Rio Piedras; Ramón Claudio Tirado, University of Puerto Rico, Rio Piedras

Rhode Island: Nora Walker, Greenwood Elementary, Warick

South Carolina: Evelyn Blackwelder, Lexington School District #5, Ballentine; Milton Kimpson, State Industrial Commission, Columbia; Karen B. Callison, Union County Schools, Union

South Dakota: Donna Gross, Vermillion School District, Vermillion; Virginia Tobin, Aberdeen Central High, Aberdeen

Tennessee: Cindi Chance, K.D. McKellar School, Milan; Robert Roney; University of Tennessee, Knoxville; Kay Awalt, Franklin Elementary School, Franklin

Texas: Charles Patterson, Killeen Independent School District, Killeen; Genevieve Mandina, Sam Houston State University, Huntsville; Margaret Montgomery, Tyler Independent School District, Tyler; Bonnie Fairall, El Paso Independent School District, El Paso; Nancy Barker, Carrollton-Farmers Branch Independent School District, Carrollton

Utah: Allan Nelson, Jordan School District, Sandy; Corrine Hill, Salt Lake City School District, Salt Lake City

Vermont: Suzanne Bryant Armstrong, Franklin Central Supervisory Union, St. Albans; George Fuller, Orleans Central School District, Orleans

Virginia: Judith Whittemore, York County Public Schools, Grafton; Evelyn Bickham, Lynchburg College, Lynchburg; Shelba Murphy, EDIT, Inc., Alexandria; Marion Hargrove, Bedford County Public Schools, Bedford

Virgin Islands: Yegin Habteyes, St. Thomas

Washington: Judy Olson, Educational Service District 101, Spokane; Bob Valiant, Kennewick School District, Kennewick; Monica Schmidt, State Board of Education, Olympia

West Virginia: Barbara Divins, Fairmont State College, Fairmont; Corey Lock, Marshall University, Huntington

Wisconsin: Neva Hodge, Elkhart Lake-Glenbeulah Elementary, Elkhart Lake; John Koehn, Oconomowoc Area School District, Oconomowoc; Arnold M. Chandler, Wisconsin Department of Public Instruction, Madison

Wyoming: Allen Buckner, Albany County District #1, Laramie; Donna Conner, University of Wyoming, Rawlins

International Units:

Canada: Clay Rutherford, Campbell River School District 72, British Columbia

Germany: Clyde Finnell, Department of Defense Dependents Schools

United Kingdom: Richard C. Strickland, Department of Defense Dependents Schools

ASCD Review Council

Chair: Barbara D. Day, University of North Carolina, Chapel Hill, North Carolina
J. Arch Phillips, Kent State University, Kent, Ohio
Pete Quinby, Joel Barlow High School, West Redding, Connecticut
Elizabeth S. Randolph (retired), Charlotte-Mecklenburg Schools, Charlotte, North
    Carolina
Dolores Silva, Temple University, Philadelphia, Pennsylvania

ASCD Headquarters Staff

Gordon Cawelti, *Executive Director*
Ronald S. Brandt, *Executive Editor*
Jean Hall, *Associate Director*
Diane Berreth , *Associate Director*
Lewis Rhodes, *Assistant Director*
Jan Adkisson, *Manager of Research and Information*
John Bralove, *Business Manager*

Samantha Anderson
Sarah Arlington
Barbara Beach
Joan Brandt
Dorothy Brown
Colette Burgess
Raiza Chernault
Sandra Claxton
Nancy Condon
Marcia D'Arcangelo
Lois Davis
Pam Dronka
Anita Fitzpatrick
Cerylle Fritts
Janet Frymoyer
Valerie Grande
Sandy Hightower
Mary Hines
Consuella Jenkins
Debbie Johnson
Jo Ann Irick Jones
Teola Jones
Michelle Kelly

Amy Lashbrook
Indu Madan
Debbie Maddox
Joey Manlapaz
Gary Maxwell
Clara Meredith
Frances Mindel
Nancy Modrak
Kelvin Parnell
Lorraine Primeau
Gayle Rockwell
Nancy Schroer
Fran Schweiger
Bob Shannon
Carolyn Shell
Charlotte Staten
Lisa Street
Dee Stump-Walek
Cindy Titus
Liz Trexler
Mary Tyrrell
Al Way
Sylvia Wisnom